Queer Constellations

Queer Constellations

Subcultural Space in the Wake of the City

Dianne Chisholm

University of Minnesota Press
Minneapolis • London

MIN
NE
SO
TA

Lines from "A Few Days" from James Schuyler, *Collected Poems* (New York: Farrar, Straus, and Giroux, 1993). Reprinted with permission of Farrar, Straus, and Giroux.

Lines from "An American Poem" and "Hot Night" from Eileen Myles, *Not Me* (New York: Semiotext(e), 1991). Reprinted with permission of The MIT Press.

An earlier version of chapter 1 was previously published as "The Traffic in Free Love and Other Crises: Space, Place, Sex, and Shock in the City of Late Modernity," *Parallax* 5, no. 3 (1999): 69–89, and as "Love at Last Sight, or Walter Benjamin's Dialectics of Seeing in the Wake of the Gay Bathhouse," *Textual Practice* 13, no. 2 (1999): 243–72; reprinted with permission of Taylor and Francis, http://www.tandf.co.uk. A slightly different version of chapter 2 appeared as "The City of Collective Memory," *GLQ: A Journal of Lesbian and Gay Studies* 7, no. 2 (2001): 195–243; copyright 2001 Duke University Press; all rights reserved; reprinted with permission of Duke University Press. A portion of chapter 3 appeared as "Paris, Mon Amour, My Catastrophe: Flâneries in Benjaminian Space," *Canadian Review of Comparative Literature/Revue Canadienne de littérature comparée* 27, no. 1 (2000): 51–93; reprinted with permission.

Copyright 2005 by the Regents of the University of Minnesota

All rights reserved. No part of this publication may be reproduced, stored in a retrieval system, or transmitted, in any form or by any means, electronic, mechanical, photocopying, recording, or otherwise, without the prior written permission of the publisher.

Published by the University of Minnesota Press
111 Third Avenue South, Suite 290
Minneapolis, MN 55401-2520
http://www.upress.umn.edu

Library of Congress Cataloging-in-Publication Data

Chisholm, Dianne, 1953–
Queer constellations : subcultural space in the wake of the city / Dianne Chisholm.
p. cm.
Includes bibliographical references and index.
ISBN 0-8166-4403-9 (hc : alk. paper) — ISBN 0-8166-4404-7
(pb : alk. paper)
1. Gays' writings—History and criticism. 2. Homosexuality in literature.
3. Cities and towns in literature. 4. Benjamin, Walter, 1892–1940. I. Title.
PN56.H57C55 2004
809'.8920664—dc22

2004015437

Printed in the United States of America on acid-free paper

The University of Minnesota is an equal-opportunity educator and employer.

12 11 10 09 08 07 06 05 10 9 8 7 6 5 4 3 2 1

In memory of Anna Pellatt,
social justice activist and cherished friend,
1954–2002

Contents

and the gay bathhouse that exemplifies the metropolitan dreamhouse in "Paris Diary." These figures constitute the "denaturalized" physiognomy of urban sexuality. A rogues' gallery of allegories, they shatter the aura of capitalist romance and bourgeois cultural reproduction into irreconcilable facets of the city's dialectical production. *Queer Constellations* foregrounds these figures in its rereading of Benjamin, before illustrating and analyzing their likeness in dialectical images of the late capitalist era. It is my intention that this queer return to Benjamin spark a productive, if perverse, wedding between these two fronts of cultural critique.

Edmonton, Alberta, 2004

Acknowledgments

The first stage of this project was facilitated by a visiting research fellowship to the Humanities Research Center (HRC) at the Australian National University in Canberra from May to September 1993. I am indebted to Liz Grosz for promoting my application to the HRC, and to that incomparable group of scholars with whom I spent an exotic winter down under exploring topical issues in the politics, history, and culture of sexuality; Henry Abelove, Cindy Patton, Gayle Rubin, Carole Vance, John D'Emilio, Lisa Duggan, Brian Massumi, Sandy Buckley, Jill Matthews, and John Ballard were the primary interlocutors of my entry into queer studies. From 1995 to 1999, a grant from the Social Science and Humanities Research Council of Canada financed my visits to the lesbian and gay archives, community centers, art exhibits and performances, and cruiserly neighborhood spaces of New York, San Francisco, Montreal, London, and Paris. It also afforded my participation in two conjoint assemblies on Walter Benjamin in Amsterdam in July 1997: the transatlantic workshop "Passagen 2000: City, Space, and Place," directed and organized by Mieke Bal for the Amsterdam School for Cultural Analysis (ASCA), and the first congress of the International Walter Benjamin Association, "Perception and Experience in Modernity/Wahrnehmung und Erfahrung in der Moderne." These assemblies, especially the ASCA workshop, galvanized interest in the use of Benjamin's *Das Passagen-Werk* (which had yet to be translated into

English) in reading current developments in mass culture, and vice versa. There, I met Susan Buck-Morss, whose poignant encouragement of my work in progress confirmed my belief that the *Passagen* could be critically brought to bear on the metropolitan production of late-twentieth-century sexuality.

On a more peripatetic note, I owe profound thanks to Jennifer Schaffner, whose nomadic career and expeditionary cruising auspiciously coincided with my own itinerant research, and who hosted me so magnanimously in her Upper West Side apartment and later in her big bay-windowed flat in San Francisco's Mission. I am also grateful to Dessy Tzatzov for inviting me to stay in her East Village flat, which I did just prior to 9/11 while writing my chapter on Sarah Schulman and walking Lower Manhattan's bourgeoning redevelopment projects. Sarah Schulman herself kindly guided me on a native's tour of the neighborhood that brought Lower East Side history concretely to life for me. Her diligent and instructive reading of an early draft of "The Lesbian Bohème" helped clarify and substantiate many of my principal contentions.

A host of others have read various parts of my book in various phases of production. My thanks to Henry Abelove, Alan Sinfield, Carolyn Dinshaw, David Halperin, and Robert Wilson for their editorial review and support of my work. Special thanks to Amelia Jones, Cindy Patton, and Katherine Binhammer for their perspicacious and incisive readings of the entire manuscript. Very special thanks to Gail Scott for her sharp commentary on drafts of chapters 2 and 3, for showing me her Montreal, and for her part in our illuminating conversations on Benjamin and everything related to writing.

My colleagues and students at the University of Alberta, who invited me to present the 2002 Edmund Kemper Broadus Lectures and who mustered critical mass for an engaging reception of my work in progress, I salute with appreciation. I am also honored by student and faculty members of the graduate program and Program for Cultural, Social, and Political Thought at the University of Victoria, who organized an international two-day colloquium in 2002 on themes related to my research. Though vastly interdisciplinary, "Transformative Space: Politics, Literature, Culture" generated an illuminating network of intersecting inquiries by talented new scholars. I learned more there than I delivered, and am particularly grateful to Tanis MacDonald and Smaro Kamboureli for their stellar hospitality and intellectual company.

The final preparations of this book were completed while I was recovering from the death of my beloved mother, Helen Chisholm, the death of my best friend, Anna Pellatt, and my own treatment for cancer. Those friends and family members, especially Earl Chisholm, Carol Bellehumeur, Carole Marshall, Daphne Read, Rosa Spricer, Athena Economides, Nathalie Kermoal, Julie Rak, Heather Zwicker, Karyn Ball, Jocelyn Brown, and Chris Fox, who so graciously and generously cheered me through this darkest period of my life, I embrace with love. To the women—Dr. Salma Murji and Dr. Kelly Dabbs—directly responsible for my medical care, and to whom I owe my health, if not my life, I express my deepest gratitude. On another existential level, I could not have survived without the concerted attentions of my partner, Kate Binhammer. With humility I receive her gift of solidarity.

Abbreviations

AP Walter Benjamin, *The Arcades Project*, translated by Howard Eiland and Kevin McLaughlin (Cambridge: Harvard University Press, 1999). Prepared on the basis of the German text *Das Passagen-Werk, Gesammelte Schriften V* (2 volumes), edited by Rolf Tiedemann (Frankfurt am Main: Suhrkamp Verlag, 1982). References to material in *The Arcades Project* are given by page number, followed by Convolute letter.

SW1 Walter Benjamin, *Selected Writings*, vol. 1, *1913–1926*, translated by Edmund Jephcott et al. and edited by Marcus Bullock and Michael W. Jennings (Cambridge: Harvard University Press, 1996).

SW2 Walter Benjamin, *Selected Writings*, vol. 2, *1927–1934*, translated by Rodney Livingstone et al and edited by Michael W. Jennings, Howard Eiland, and Gary Smith (Cambridge: Harvard University Press, 1999).

SW3 Walter Benjamin, *Selected Writings*, vol. 3, *1935–1938*, translated by Edmund Jephcott, et al. and edited by Howard Eiland and Michael W. Jennings (Cambridge: Harvard University Press, 2002).

SW4 Walter Benjamin, *Selected Writings*, vol. 4, *1938–1940*, translated by Edmund Jephcott et al. and edited by Howard Eiland and Michael W. Jennings (Cambridge: Harvard University Press, 2003).

retrospective insight and prospective doubt. Less impressed by the city's futurity than its diminishing diversity, he recalls stories and memories that archive a realm of satisfying contact and testify to the potency of old Times Square's promiscuity. Mindful of what could come to pass, he prescribes an archeological remedy to the advancing catastrophe that neocapitalism has in store for us. He witnesses the mounting of disaster since the early 1960s and he tracks the accelerating, profit-based modus operandi of cataclysmic reconstruction.[6] Yet he dwells on the *utopian* dimension of the city's unfulfilled history.

Recasting the scene of his casual sexual encounters, Delany remembers the porn cinemas and their audiences in colorful physiognomies and he theatricalizes the memory of his city outings. He returns, again and again, to *his* Times Square, countering devastation with a projection of urban possibility. Mixing myriad anecdotal recollections with speculations of what the neighborhood could be, were it to develop with regard for diversity, Delany foresees "a new, lively bohemian and entertainment neighbourhood" (168). "*My* Times Square" (89) figures as *the* city in miniature—the city in the making, on-the-make, and in the unmaking, driven by forces as utopian and emancipatory as they are exploitative and exclusionary.

To cast his urban project/ion as a viable alternative to the "Project" officially underway, Delany deploys a mode of fiction (*science* fiction?[7]). He subverts and inverts capitalism's urbanization of society that proceeds catastrophically by casting its own fictions about "redevelopment" and "safety." Timed for reading at the end of the millennium, *Times Square Red, Times Square Blue* mobilizes desire for a more adventurous city, a city of imagination and eroticism opening onto historically unrecognized terrain. By placing queers at the visible and knowable center of thriving urban intercourse where they have, at least clandestinely, always been, and by highlighting scenes of democratizing, casual contact in the theater of collective memory, Delany defies urban planning's safe and marketable staging of a city-that-never-was with nostalgic fantasy. With political angst, he retrieves the past from the city's repressed, remaindered, and real history for reimagining and saving the metropolis of today.

This outline of Delany's writing on New York at the end of the 1990s has largely been informed by Walter Benjamin's writing on Paris in the early decades of the last century. To be sure, Delany's advocacy of diversity is distinctively contemporary and American, and specifically "black gay male."[8] At the same time, Delany's city invites ready and instructive comparison with Benjamin's urban investigations. Like Benjamin's *Arcades Project* and Baudelaire essays, *Times Square Red, Times Square Blue* sketches an urban physiognomy with the sensuous attentiveness of the flâneur, the collector, the rag picker, and the poet, all rolled into one. Just as Benjamin focuses on Paris's commercial arcades as spaces of mass distraction and communion, Delany focuses on Times Square's porn cinemas, Broadway theaters, and other pleasure palaces where contact between city goers is prime. With Benjamin, Delany shares an emphasis on the erotic as the terrain and perspective from which to recast the shock of urbanization and to reveal changes most powerfully wrought upon the human sensorium.

If, for Benjamin, the female prostitute of the arcades is the supreme allegorization of capitalism's commodity-captivated, interiorized street life, for Delany it is the cruising gay man of Times Square's porn cinemas who figures as the hero of late capitalism—who absorbs the aura of urban sensuality and uses commercial space for public sex.[9] Yet, like Benjamin's prostitute, whose exhibition and exchange value varied with that of the building wherein she displayed her wares, so Delany's cruising gay man is degraded along with the aura of Times Square as redevelopment forces the old neighborhood to depreciate economically, socially, and aesthetically. Cruising side by side with sex-hustlers and drug-traffickers, who threaten to displace him in space rezoned strictly for business, Delany's gay, pleasure-seeking street-walker signals the city's paradoxical cultivation of connection and corruption. Moreover, just as Benjamin regards the age of the Paris arcades as a rising-falling constellation of metropolitan capitalism, so does Delany regard the era of Times Square theatergoing and movie-house cruising. Benjamin cites/sights Paris's epochal "metrocosm" in images of extreme contradiction. Likewise, Delany views the space of the city and the space of city history in montage. If Benjamin images the city of *high* capitalism, queer constellations image the city of *late* capitalism, where paradoxes of development are intensified.[13] This is the city of enhanced consumer seduction, where commodity spectacle and advertising technology saturate and dominate space. A postindustrial city (like New York), it clears inner-city factories and working-class quarters for office high-rises and designer storefronts. And/or a postmodern city (like New York, San Francisco, Montreal, or Paris), it recuperates older, immigrant districts and inner-city decay and generates capital redevelopment through inflated real estate speculation, gentrification, and high-tech industry. This is the city where the city itself is a commodity fetish-on-display, exhibiting and marketing its "historic" sectors, and selling (selling-out) its "alternative" neighborhoods and "bohemian" lifestyles.

Dialectical images view history as the space of an era (monad) that clashes or compares with the cultural inventions of other eras. They shock the viewer into recognizing not evolutionary differences so much as the eternal return of the same. They also constellate the "star" productions of that era in montage not to showcase cultural treasures but to subject the commodity phantasmagoria wherein sublime objects of desire are circulated and suspended to a "profane illumination." Dialectical imaging entails collecting and re/collecting sites and citations not yet incorporated into official history or lost in the fragmentation of perception that characterizes urban experience. Above all, it entails juxtaposing city images in montage assemblies so as to foreground contradictions that capitalism's panoramas of expanse and narratives of progress obscure. Seen through the eyes of cruising gays and lesbians, who, in "shock," behold themselves as fetishes-on-display, queer constellations heighten the reader's exposure to urban antitheses.

Queer City

The making, and unmaking, of queer society and culture shares the same space as that of the modern metropolis: the process unfolds in the modernizing capitals of capitalism, where the stage was first set (and is repeatedly reset) for lesbian and gay outings in the public sphere. Michael Sibalis notes that "urbanization is a precondition to [the] emergence of a significant gay culture."[14] Moreover, as Dennis Altman reflects, urban homosexuals "pioneered the values and behaviour that have become the norm in modern consumer society," despite their continuing subjection to homophobic social violence.[15] Urban history has still to recognize the queer character of urban reality. Yet it cannot deny the now well-documented perception that urbanization mobilizes society's "homosexualization."

Gay urban histories trace the emergence of a gay scene to bustling nineteenth-century European and American capitals, where public and commercial architectures afforded city goers attractive meeting places. Aaron Betsky hazards an even earlier date, tracing the etymological and material origins of a new spatial practice called "cruising":

> One of the places where modern queer space first appears is in the Netherlands, and in the annals of its courts in the seventeenth century we can find the record of its emergence. . . . The word "cruising" derives from a Dutch word, and designates the areas where men would find each other in the bourgeoning cities of the Lowlands . . . often right in the heart of the central institutions of the Dutch state, including the courthouse, the meeting places of the councils, and the stock exchange.[16]

Queers entered center stage of a "bourgeoning" metropolitan capitalism, or as Betsky speculates: "It is as if queer men were tracing the very contours of the emerging middle-class society."[17] Cruising insinuated homosexual exchange into urban commerce and vice versa. It is not commercial sex that urban traffic solicited but free love, or sexual free trade—casual contact without financial tariff, conjugal responsibility, or bourgeois propriety. The historic city had always harbored brothels for paid sex, as well as parks and quays for clandestine embraces outdoors. But the modern, capitalist city provides exquisite "cruising grounds": boulevards and arcades, cafés, brasseries, and public baths for loitering, congregating, and communing with the crowd. Cruising and hustling on Parisian homosexuals, particularly lesbians, in the naturalism of the 1880s and 1890s and highlights their "public presence" in Zola's novels and notebooks that sketch his visits to a table d'hôte on rue des Martyrs and to one of several, notorious "bathing stations."[36] She underscores the entry of "the new society lesbian" into the popular novel of the mid-1880s, "cruising in public places and crashing the gates of the lesbian *demi-monde*" to "pick up women in the theater, the Rat-Mort, arcade boutiques, the flower market, even the church of the Madeleine."[37] Above all, she emphasizes the cross-class character of this cruising—"the frightening convergence of high and low, long a cliché in representing gays, had nonetheless become a staple of discourses on lesbians."[38]

Late-nineteenth-century realism, naturalism, and documentary literature of all kinds evidence the public presence of gay men throughout Paris—on the Champs-Élysées and its environs, in the arcades (notably the Passage des Panoramas and Passage de l'Opéra), the public toilets around Les Halles (the city's primary food market), and public baths, including those on rue de Penthièvre, which "were in the news in 1891, following a bust involving eighteen men who represented . . . 'an amazing confusion of races and social classes.'" This literature further attests to the interpenetration of lesbian and gay urban subcultures. "Gay men congregated around Saint-Augustin, lesbians in Asnières, for example. Yet they also shared many neighborhoods and institutions, from Montmartre and the boulevard to the brothel (gay or otherwise), the theater, the masked ball, the *brasserie*, and the dance hall." The first realist novel devoted to "Sodom" (1883) features a "compendium of information on the Parisian subculture," including the original and sensational description of a high-class male brothel; Henri d'Argis's *Sodom* stirred massive appeal with city readers, "going through no fewer than six editions within the year."[39]

Paris is not the only city to entertain reclamation by queer historiography. Amsterdam, London, San Francisco, Rio de Janeiro, Lisbon, Moscow, and other global cities offer rich historical records of queer urban life. If Paris stands out as the queer capital of the nineteenth century, it is because it is here that capitalism mobilized queer outings, in deed and in writing, with a revolutionary industrialism and urban exhibitionism that, at the same time, mobilized a voyeuristic reading public ready to consume sensational (queer) representations of the city. Similarly, New York stands out as the queer capital of the twentieth century, and not just as site of the Stonewall riots in the latter half-century but as the setting of heightened phantasmagoria—"delirious Manhattan"—as Rem Koolhaas describes the engineering follies of skyscrapers, cosmic amusement parks, and ziggurat health clubs that mesmerized the early half-century.[40] Chauncey's *Gay New York: Gender, Urban Culture, and the Making of the Gay Male World, 1890–1940* (1994) features gay cruising sites that foreground gay visibility, particularly the arcade-like spectacle of the gay bathhouse with its luxury body parlors, gas-lit cooling rooms and steam rooms, and phantasmagoric inducement of mass sex.[41] Charles Kaiser's *Gay Metropolis: The Landmark History of Gay Life in America since World War II* (1997) showcases gay celebrities on the glamorous world stage of New York high society. The queer city is written into urban history as a capital spectacle. Delany's polemical memoir of Times Square poses an exception. Though Delany locates his queer city in New York's most spectacular and spectacularly represented neighborhood, he reveals the catastrophe at the heart of urban fantasy. Setting his queer sites, dialectically, on the neocapital of capitalism, he perceives a mounting of monumental disaster. Yet the dialectics of seeing is not, generally, a device of queer urban historiography.

Literary modernism represents queer city sites with many and varied devices, on both sides of the Atlantic. Colette, Gide, and Genet follow Proust in raising Paris's lesbian and gay underworlds into the sphere of high art. Yet it is only after World War II that the city's gay community publishes self-representational writing. Paris's first long-lived gay periodical, *Arcadie*, alluding, like the arcades, to classical utopia, appeared from 1954 to 1982.[42] But as Edmund White decries, even the most modern French writers have been reluctant to come out in the world of letters, tending to see themselves as republicans first and as gays only secondarily. The debate over the politics of identity among Parisian lesbians and gays affords Parisian literati critical distance on the evolving gay scene. A notable deployment of the pun on "*gai*/gay Paris" by Parisian writer Benoît Duteurtre, in his novel *Gaieté Parisienne* (1996), cynically compares contemporary queer Paris to the grandiose, apolitical self-absorption of the *Belle Époque*.

Alternatively, queer outings on the scene of American modernism appear early and outwardly with Whitman in the mid-nineteenth century, though they were not acclaimed as such until the rediscovery of "the homosexual tradition in American poetry" in the late twentieth century.[43] Whitman's "City of Orgies" salutes the spectacle of Manhattan's bourgeoning capitalism with republican *gaiety*:

> City of orgies, walks and joys,
> City whom that I have lived and sung in your midst will
> one day make you illustrious,
> Not the pageants of you, not your shifting tableaus, your
> spectacles, repay me,
> Not the interminable rows of your houses, nor the ships at
> the wharves,
> Nor the processions in the streets, nor the bright windows
> with goods in them,
> Nor to converse with learn'd persons, or bear my share
> in the soiree or feast;
> Not those, but as I pass O Manhattan, your frequent and
> swift flash of eyes offering me love,
> Offering response to my own—these repay me,
> Lovers, continual lovers, only repay me.[44]

Whitman's city poet derives joy from the abundance with which passers-by reflect ("repay") his investment of desire. He interpellates the "frequent and / swift flash of eyes offering me love" of bustling pedestrian city traffic with a gay gaze. The look of prospective fulfillment in the eyes of city goers reflects the express eroticism of consumer delights that "pageants," "shifting tableaus," "spectacles," and "bright windows" advertise. It is a look of homosocial/homosexual exchange between city lovers—

a "robust love" between fellow Manhattanese.[45] Such a look could not contrast more sharply than with the compromised gaze that, contemporaneously, animates the streets of Paris's first city poet. The passer-by of Baudelaire's sonnet "À une passante" strikes the poet with a look that is so simultaneously seductive and mortifying it leaves him quaking with "sexual shock."[46] This, according to Benjamin, is the distracted and distracting, disembodied gaze of the strolling commodity that every fashion-conscious, streetwalking citizen has become. It is worn by the prostitute who is "dressed to kill" with insatiable consumer desire, or to inspire what Benjamin paradoxically describes as "love—not at first sight, but at last sight."[47]

After Whitman, the American avant-garde literati becomes ever preoccupied with representing queer city sites, though never again with the same republican idealism. Joseph Boone reads "Harlem," "The Left Bank," and "Greenwich Village" as exemplary "queer sites in modernism," and he shows how the lesbian and gay appropriation of space coincides with that of literary bohemianism and experimentalism.[48] In the cold war years that were to follow the Second World War, city poets represent queer city life with increasing flamboyance and/or dissidence. Writing the queer city is a dynamic, if ambiguous, device of the San Francisco Renaissance (notably in the poetry of Robert Duncan and Jack Spicer), the New York School (Frank O'Hara and James Schuyler), and the Beats. Allen Ginsberg's "Howl" (1956) replaces Whitman's "Manhattan" with "Moloch," a fallen, sterile city that only hipster, homosexual "angels" can redeem with uninhibited and sacrificial passion. Sexual and racial outsiders, James Baldwin and John Rechy subvert American cold war puritanism by exploring the heart of darkness evoked respectively by the queer "Paris" of *Giovanni's Room* (1956) and the hustling arenas of innumerable American inner cities that constellate *City of Night* (1963). With lesbian and gay liberation, queer city writing combines literary with sexual avant-gardism, as seen in Rechy's *Sexual Outlaw: A Documentary* (1977).

If not the capital of the twentieth century, San Francisco is another prime scene of queer city writing with its own (distinctive sense of) gay urban history.[49] Popularly regarded as gay mecca of the west coast, "the San Francisco of legend, myth and nostalgic remembrance has been far better documented than the day-to-day realities of most of its historical developments."[50] To writers like Jack Fritscher, who lived through the "golden age of liberation" that was San Francisco from "1970 to 1982," gay mecca commands remembering. Given the paramount dreamworld that gay men made and enjoyed of the Castro during these years, this remembering can only take the form of a "docudramedy story" or "historical novel"—a fiction of history that on reflection acquires the character of a "fable":

> This all began, once upon a time, back in the madcap days before real estate boomed in San Francisco, in the days when the first Irish and Italian merchants in the Castro sold out to Tommy's Plants and the Castro Café, in the days when gays bought dumps and everybody on Castro was a carpenter, in the days when gays were more hippies than clones, long before New York faggots arrived to Manhattanize the Castro, long before fisting and coprophagy, when crystal was still something collectible on the sideboard, long before murders, assassination, disease, and Death, when sex three times a day was still the great adventure. It dissolved. It changed. What first seemed like Mecca shifted on the faultline to someplace east of Eden. They were innocents. For all they did right, for all they did wrong, for all their pursuit of sexual adventure, what they searched for in the bars and baths and cruised on the streets was, heart and soul, for them all, no more and no less than human love.[51]

"Death" prompts Fritscher to romanticize the dreamworld that the Castro once was. It has an opposite effect on Gary Indiana. Indiana's gruesome novel *Rent Boy* (1994) images the queer city in its most fallen state. His eponymous antihero reluctantly hustles the streets of early-1990s Manhattan in what remains of the downtown gay scene after it has been wasted by deregulated rents and unregulated traffic in sex, drugs, and body parts. Indiana's Manhattan is Moloch minus the redemption of homosexual angels and overcome by the ruins of queer heaven. Indiana's maligned city is capitalism's totalized space, where even cruising succumbs to the commodity's rough trade. An era of queer city writing that began with Whitman's gay urban pastoral ends with Baudelairean spleen.

In the wake of the (queer) city, Indiana's fiction is a resounding wake-up call and not just for the city's queers but for anyone who has known and enjoyed its layers and labyrinths of history and diversity, its real and potential emancipation. *Rent Boy* shares the same stage with municipal activism, raised to militant heights against unchecked redevelopment in the late 1980s and early 1990s. This is the time that artist Martha Rosler mobilized other artists, activists, and theorists to collaborate on a project to raise local consciousness about apocalyptic homelessness in gentrifying lower Manhattan, published as *If You Lived Here: The City in Art, Theory, and Social Activism* (1991). It is also when leftist urban sociologist Robert Fitch published his damning *Assassination of New York* (1993), following Louis Chevalier's iconoclastic *L'Assassinat de Paris* (1977, translated 1994). Robert Siegle places Indiana at the scene of "downtown writing" that, in the seventies, began waging a "guerilla campaign against the imminent transformation of American consciousness into a shopping mall."[52] Alarmed by the suburban ethos that was terrorizing and colonizing urban art and life, downtown writers forge a synthesis of gritty urban realism and experimental postmodernism that gives an "edge to the real postmodernist writing" and delivers literary avant-gardism "from liberationist illusions about free space and unmediated time." Indiana forms a front with Kathy Acker, David Wojnarowicz, Lynne Tillman, and others, whose writing "seeks not liberation but liberty, real rather than full sensation" and "opens space—mentally, psychologically, semiotically—where simulation, repression, and convention have converged to predetermine our Being." Edgily *queer*, downtown writing "shakes up reified relations—roles, genders, social structures—so that at least momentary experiences of various sorts of Other might take place before the great culture machine swallows it up again."[53]

Overlapping downtown writing are multiple small press publishing projects and literary circles or movements that share this return to the real. For example, *The Portable Lower East Side* (1984–94) was a locally produced chapbook that featured adventures in "slumming realism" by multiethnic writers and low-renters in underrepresented occupations. These adventures were collected in sporadic special issues such as *Latin Americans in NYC* (1988), *New Asia* (1990), *New Africa* (1993), and *Queer City* (1991).[54] Concurrently, Amy Scholder and Ira Silverberg edited two *High Risk* anthologies of "forbidden writings" (1991) and "sex, death, and subversion" (1994), highlighting illicit urban eroticism—primarily homosexual promiscuity and sadomasochism—in protest against the city's crackdown on "unsafe" sex in its panicked response to AIDS. These are closely followed by Semiotext(e)'s publication of *The New Fuck You: Adventures in Lesbian Reading* (1995). Edited by Eileen Myles and Liz Kotz, *The New Fuck You* is a dyke-reincarnation of *Fuck You, a magazine of the arts* (1962–65), Ed Sanders's mimeograph project that helped wage sexual liberation in the East Village. Like *High Risk*, *The Portable Lower East Side*, and downtown writing in general, *The New Fuck You* presents shocking, in-your-face, rough-edged fragments of the urban real, stressing lesbian exposure to contemporary urban calamity. New York predominates as the locus and focus of this small press production, but there are also queer initiatives coming out of San Francisco, like "Small Press Traffic" and "New Narrative," that illuminate the real in other urban contexts. It is from these circles and productions that I draw my primary texts—fictions that constellate urban reality in the cataclysmic wake of the city. (I shall return to this at the end of the "Introduction.")

Given the abundant representation of the queer city in literature, what of the queer city in literary criticism? Inasmuch as literary criticism considers the city in literature, it omits investigation of its queer character. Richard Lehan's *The City in Literature: An Intellectual and Cultural History* (1998) surveys the field of urban poetics according to periodicity (Enlightenment, Modernism/Urbanism, American) as demarcated before and after T. S. Eliot's *The Waste Land.* En route he overlooks queers and queer city writing, along with city women and women's city writing. Classical studies like Burton Pike's *The Image of the City* (1981), Marshall Berman's *All That Is Solid Melts into Air: The Experience of Modernity* (1982), and Marc Blanchard's *In Search of the City: Engels, Baudelaire, Rimbaud*

(1985) also focus on the modernist city, and they engage the theory and practice of Walter Benjamin; yet they neglect questions of gender and sexuality, including those raised by Benjamin himself. Deborah Parsons's *Streetwalking the Metropolis: Women, the City, and Modernity* (2000) begins to correct this omission with a feminist revaluation of the modernist city, as does the anthology *The Sex of Architecture* (1996), while omitting the queer city of modernity. Joseph Boone's (Benjamin-inflected) analysis of "Queer Sites in Modernism" in his book *Libidinal Currents: Sexuality and the Shaping of Modernity* (1998) is a bold exception, though it stops short of investigating queer sites in postmodernism.

Inasmuch as literary criticism investigates queer literature (or que-[e]ries literary representation), it tends to rely on queer theory/post-structuralism. Broadly speaking, queer theory views and deploys queer signifiers as a general deconstructive strategy and not as a (dialectical) representational technique. Queer theory's queer tropes are content-less metaphors for deconstructing such pervasive, discursive binaries as homo/hetero, sex/gender, universal/marginal, inside/out that naturalize and normalize essentialist myths of sexual identity. Unlike downtown writing that gives post-structuralism a queer, urban edge, queer theory–inflected literary criticism remains indifferent to urban realism. Queer theory–inflected criticism ignores the city in literature, just as dialectical approaches neglect the city's queer character. An outstanding exception is Ross Chambers's *Loiterature* (1999) that reads the dilatory wanderings or "loiterliness" of fictional flâneurs and cruising subjects as deconstructive figures *on location*—that is, as figures of a counterdisciplinary, antidiscursive practice whose wayward and wanton flâneries permeate, traverse, and transgress the boundaries and grids of urban architex/cture.

Queer Space

The idea and analysis of "queer space" appear in academic writing in the 1990s and have been advancing primarily in urban geography, urban sociology and anthropology, and urban architecture. The most provocative conceptualizations of queer space derive from Henri Lefebvre's theorization of *the production and practice of space*, and from Michel Foucault's genealogy of the *carceral* subject in *disciplinary space*, as well as the latter's notion of "other spaces" or "heterotopias." Foucault's thinking on sexuality, and particularly on the spatialization of (the history) of sexuality, has been much discussed and adapted by queer scholarship. As early as 1984, Gayle Rubin outlined the importance of Foucault to the "new scholarship on sex," applying his analysis of how new sexualities are produced and contained in space *to* specific spaces in late-twentieth-century urban America (notably San Francisco).[55] Since Rubin, it has become de rigueur for queer scholars to refer to Foucault's *Discipline and Punish* and *History of Sexuality* when mapping homophobic zoning and policing of public sex and, alternatively, homosexual outing in panoptic space. Furthermore, proponents of queer space are apt to invoke Foucault's notion of heterotopia to rethink the gay bathhouse and gay village as "countersites, a kind of effectively enacted utopia in which the real sites, all the other real sites that can be found within the culture, are simultaneously represented, contested, and inverted."[56] Delany, for instance, conceives of the sex cinemas of old Times Square in terms of Foucault's heterotopias—real, utopian countersites within the heart of New York City. Aaron Betsky's *Queer Space: Architecture and Same-Sex Desire* (1997) invokes the notion as archetype of past and future queer design.[57]

Lefebvre's *Production of Space* (1974, translated 1991) offers another basis for the elaboration of queer space. For Lefebvre, space is not an empty container but a material production. Space fills urban reality with signs by which city goers conduct their lives. *Urban* space is semiotically dense and conducive to the regulation of social relations. Yet city goers are able to occupy and appropriate the city with spatial practices ranging from the everyday to the revolutionary. City builders, planners and developers, municipal administrators are not the only producers of space. Home owners, streetwalkers, and commune militants at their barricades also produce space, or effectively alter production. Ultimately, however, urban space is dominated space—space abstracted into grids and regimented by the collaborative, corporate powers of government and capitalism for profitable exploitation and social control. History itself is a production of space that, with the advent of capitalism, explodes into decentered, total space:

> Capitalism and neocapitalism have produced abstract space, which includes the "world of commodities," it's "logic" and its worldwide strategies, as well as the power of money and that of the political state. This space is founded on the vast networks of banks, business centres and major productive entities, as on motorways, airports and information lattices. Within this space the town—once forcing-house of accumulation, fountainhead of wealth and centre of historical space—has disintegrated.[58]

Lefebvre fears the abstraction of the historic city—of *historicity*—and especially the destruction and renovation of old gathering spaces, like Les Halles's central market, where all classes of people once met.

The making of livable space entails constant struggle by city dwellers to appropriate and reappropriate city space for purposes other than means-end productivity and official traffic and trade. For Lefebvre, this means, above all, the appropriation and reappropriation of the city for the body, since the abstraction of the body, like that of the city, has been violent and pervasive: "Confined by the abstraction of a space broken down into specialized locations, the body itself is pulverized. The body as represented by the images of advertising (where the legs stand for the stockings, the breasts for the bra, the face for the make-up, etc.) serves to fragment desire and doom it to anxious frustration, to the non-satisfaction of local needs."[59] Lefebvre directs coming revolutions to take back the city for nonreproductive (homo?)sexuality:

> Dominated by overpowering forces, including a variety of brutal techniques and an extreme emphasis on visualization, the body fragments, abdicates responsibility for itself—in a word, disappropriates itself. . . . Any revolutionary "project" today, whether utopian or realistic, must . . . make the reappropriation of the body, in association with the reappropriation of space, into a non-negotiable part of its agenda. . . . As for sex and sexuality, things here are more complicated. . . . Any true appropriation of sex demands that a separation be made between the reproductive function and sexual pleasure. . . . The true space of pleasure, which would be an appropriated space par excellence, does not yet exist. Even if a few instances in

> the past suggest that this goal is in principle attainable, the results to date fall far short of human desires.[60]

Writing from Paris in the aftermath of the worker/student riots of 1968, as well as the dissolution of the Situationist International in 1972, Lefebvre calls for a revolutionary project that has yet to make space for sex and sexuality. In retrospect, he seems to have been answered by the sexual revolution that appropriated space for the gay meccas of Manhattan's Village and San Francisco's Castro.

Twenty years later in the wake of gay mecca, the editors and contributors of *Queers in Space: Communities, Public Spaces, Sites of Resistance* (1996) elaborate strategies for an ever more fluid and expansive reappropriation of queer space.[61] They outline a radical appropriation of space that traverses and neutralizes structures of power with passive and excessive queer eroticism. As Jean-Ulrick Désert asserts:

> Queer space crosses, engages, and transgresses social, spiritual, and aesthetic locations, all of which is articulated in the realm of the public/private, the built/unbuilt environments. . . . A queer space is an activated zone made proprietary by the occupant or *flâneur*, the wanderer. It is at once private and public. . . . Our cities and landscapes double as queer spaces. . . . The squares, the streets, the civic centers, the malls, the highways are the place of fortuitous encounters and juxtapositions. It is the place in which our sensibilities are tested, it is the place of "show." The public space is the space of romance, seen as landscape, alleys, and cafés. The public space is the space of power in the form of corporations or factories. It is the (blue, white, or pink collar) ghetto of the everyday. This fluid and wholly unstructured space allows, in its publicity, a variety of readings, re-readings, and misreadings, given the observer's individual propensities toward power, mystery, and how these desires fold into the passive space of Eros. . . . a space where desire intertwines with visceral sensibility, in the space of the everyday.[62]

Deploying the prepositional phrase "queers *in* space," these new geographers map a flexible occupation of everyday space by queer nomads.

They revive the nineteenth-century flâneur as appropriative strategist and accredit the substantial role played by the projection of spatial imagination—"Queer space is in large part the function of wishful thinking or desires that become solidified: a seduction of the reading of space where queerness, at a few brief points and for some fleeting moments, dominates the (heterocentric) norm, the dominant social narrative of the landscape."[63]

Queers in Space breaks out of the empirical frame of urban geography, including that which maps the (differential) spatial organization of lesbian and gay communities, lesbian perceptions and experiences of everyday space, and gay contribution to "the urban renaissance."[64] It also expands Lefebvre's concept of appropriation beyond the targets of a revolutionary collective to include the everywhere of capitalism's dominated space. However, in becoming strategically "lost in space," the proponents of *Queers in Space* lose sight of history while acting out "fleeting moments" of queer desire. As such, queer appropriations of space read as exclamation points in capitalism's narrative of progress.

Queer constellations of (queer) space do not read this way. Instead of punctuating the narrative of progress they blast it apart, reassembling fragments of collective history into dialectical images of an era. This is the era of the modern city that, as queer historiography has abundantly demonstrated, is a queer era, even if that historiography, like the theory of queer space, views it as boundlessly expansive and progressive. The writing of space that grips me returns to the historic (queer) city that capitalism colonizes but not with the aim of recuperating queer landmarks or tracing ever more fluid (de)territorializations. Smashing dominant narrative and dominated space into montage, it reveals with shock the devastation and suspension of the city's revolutionary past.

Queer Constellations

Queer constellations are fictions of space. "Fictions" not because they are false or fantastical but because they reinvent avant-garde techniques of representing real, historical catastrophe that is otherwise veiled in urban spectacle. Like Delany's *Times Square*, they reflect critically on narratives

Mimesis reflects the arcade's collection of objects on commodity display. Montage re/collects these objects (as historical referents) by pulling them out of market circulation or salvaging them from obsolescence and reassembling them in colliding juxtapositions of meaning—or what Susan Buck-Morss identifies as incommensurable categories of "wish-image," "ruin," "fetish," and "fossil." Monadology recognizes that "historical objects are first constituted by being 'blasted' out of the historical continuum," where otherwise they recede into the past as forgotten products of progress.[70] Representing a whole era, these objects have and are seen to have a "'monadological structure,' into which 'all the forces and interests of history enter on a reduced scale'" as "'dialectics at a standstill.'"[71] In other words, Benjamin's arcade is a monadological "'force-field, in which the conflict between its fore- and after-history plays itself out.'"[72]

Benjamin's constellation is, above all, a "constellation of awakening" (AP 458 [N1, 9]). Its montage/monad targets precise objects, namely those spellbinding dream houses and fairy scenes of nineteenth-century technological machination. These objects were the arcades and other newly engineered structures—winter gardens, panoramas, wax museums, railway stations, public spas—that captivated mass assemblies and transformed them into spellbound consumer crowds. Dialectical images destroy the commodity aura of these structures instead of reproducing it on an aggrandized scale like the constructions of contemporary capitalism. They represent the deteriorated potentiality of nineteenth-century urban industrialism in shocking constellation with the bedazzling present, displacing capitalism's ever-engrossing fantasy with historical materialism's "dialectical fairy" (*dialektische Feen*).[73]

Each Convolute of Benjamin's *Arcades Project* comprises a constellation of historical objects, including a constellation of arcades (Convolute "A").[74] *The Arcades Project* as a whole may be thought of as one giant constellation, although arguably the 1935 exposé (and its 1939 revision), entitled "Paris, the Capital of the Nineteenth Century," best demonstrates the constellatory method. The essays on Baudelaire that Benjamin abstracted from *The Arcades Project* and intended for a book consist of constellations of "The *Bohème*" and "The Flâneur."[75] Benjamin's memoir of Berlin may also be viewed as a constellation, or as a chronicle starred with constellations. Positioned at the crossroads of Benjamin's earlier physiognomies ("Naples," "Marseilles," *Moscow Diary*) and his Paris archeology, "A Berlin Chronicle" conducts a flânerie into city memory with jarring stops: these are caesurae of shock where forgotten passages of youthful socialism are contrasted with present scenes of capitalist and fascist development in dialectical disruptions of historical narrative.

Queer constellations represent (or, more precisely, re-represent) late-twentieth-century fairylands, notably those of gay mecca, in whose constellation the gay bathhouse stars as an exemplary historical object for dialectical imaging. The historical referents for these constellations include referents from queer history (e.g., histories of the gay bathhouse). But the main source of reference is literature—my primary texts. If queer histories of the city find sources in realist and naturalist fiction, queer constellations find historiographical materials in the "realism" of queer postmodernism. Poignant, first-hand, fictionalized accounts of visits to the gay bathhouse by Gary Indiana, Alan Hollinghurst, Robert Glück, and Samuel Delany comprise the archive for a queer constellation of the gay bathhouse era. Sarah Schulman's New York trilogy suggests (material for) a constellation of the lesbian bohème. Gail Scott and Edmund White produce ready-made constellations of the flâneur in millennial Paris. Neil Bartlett, Gail Scott, and Eileen Myles narrate projected wanderings in late-twentieth-century London, Montreal, and Manhattan respectively; their retrospective cruising of queer haunts supplies the material for a constellation of collective memory. These constellations comprise the chapters of this book.

Sexuality is a guiding star in Benjamin's constellation of nineteenth-century dreamworlds and catastrophes. It is nonetheless missing from Graeme Gilloch's *Myth and Metropolis: Walter Benjamin and the City* (1996), a scholarly exegesis of Benjamin's city and a thorough analysis of the urban motifs that evolve over the course of his oeuvre. Gilloch uses Benjamin's paradoxical phrase "love at last sight" at various points in his study to highlight the sensation of loss that generally accompanies the experience of urban modernity.[76] He glosses over Benjamin's intense, if ambivalent, curiosity concerning Baudelaire's erotology and the "queer" desire that is solicited by the commodity and induced by commodity space. Conversely, *Queer Constellations* orients its reading of late urban reality, and its rereading of Benjamin, to precisely the sexuality it finds there.[77]

Urban eroticism posed to Benjamin one of the greatest enigmas of big-city life. Questions of sexuality spur his investigation of the "new nature" of urban technology and society and are as evident in his early work (e.g., "On Love and Related Matters," 1920) as they are in his last sketches for future study (e.g., "Central Park," 1938–39).[78] Typically, these questions disclose the erotic perversity that characterizes social-sexual relations in commodity exchange and circulation. The theme of commodity fetishism explodes in *The Arcades Project* into myriad motifs of critical inquiry. Benjamin's constellation of these motifs shows how love, like art, in the age of mechanical reproduction, loses its "aura." In place of traditional romance between the sexes, there arises the penetrating allure of commodity-spectacle. In place of love at first sight, there is the empty and passing gaze of fetish-bodies-on-display. Contesting conjugal, heterosexual reproduction are erotic fashions and recyclable lifestyles whose model is the chic and sterile mannequin. As Benjamin represents it, city space is a galvanizing force of social-sexual transformation and the consumer crowd is an agent of "revolutionary" desire.

Contemporary queer writing displays a similar (but different) interest in urban configurations of sexuality. *Queer Constellations* identifies these similarities, returning to Benjamin's critical juxtapositions to highlight the practice of dialectical imaging in contemporary montage. My study draws upon a number of Benjamin's constellations of motifs and, in particular, the following.

Dream Houses and Fairy Grottos

As *The Arcades Project* represents them, mass architectures of industrial capitalism display a revolutionary technological capability that provided material foundations for a classless society, yet remained trapped in the aura of instrumental rationality. The Paris arcade was a prototype of such transformative architecture. With its glass roof and iron beams, it afforded pedestrian traffic luxurious interior space for strolling, communing, and shopping. Here, the crowd was protected from inclement weather and muddy, carriage-choked streets *and*, at the same time, it was exposed to the worldly display of merchandise, produced by adjacent factories and expropriated through colonial trade. Though the technology and materials of construction were wholly new, design ventured no further than to reproduce the luxury of bourgeois interiors and adapt the elegance of aristocratic establishments to public commerce. Eventually the proletariat and indigent were barred entrance to the arcade, where the products of labor were exhibited for fashionable promenaders. The alienation between consumers and producers, and between strangers who knew each other only as buyers and sellers, was cloaked in an aura of cozy familiarity and intoxicating desirability. With their rich phantasmagoria, the arcades became the exemplary "fairy grottos" (*Feengrotten*) of industrial capitalism.[79] Paradoxically, they amassed new congregations in their interiors only to disperse revolutionary energies in collective dreams.

The entrepreneurial gay bathhouse is a late manifestation of this "fairy grotto." Benjamin records a visit to such an establishment in his "Paris Diary" (1930), observing how "the atmosphere" emanated "a pervasive family mood" and how a "landscape of cobblestones and peace" together with the "frosted-glass panes of the reception room" screened "adjoining rooms, where offensive scenes might be taking place."[80] Though the proprietor stands behind "the till—a contrivance consisting of washcloths, perfumes, *pochettes surprise*, tickets to the baths, and tarty dolls," the entire commodity display is enveloped in phantasmagoria that "secretly reminded [the visitor] of boarding school."[81] Benjamin's description of this encounter may strike us today as naive but it teaches us to see the "contrivance" that veils the scene of public sex with familial sociability or "rebellious" schoolboy gaiety.

The Arcades Project illuminates the many and various dream houses of industrial capitalism. Winter gardens, crystal palaces, railway stations, and world exhibitions exhibited a mesmerizing splendor that grandiose reproductions of the future would magnify. In these spaces new commodity species were put on display, including new sexual species. From his Berlin youth, Benjamin recalls an especially memorable dream house. "The Ice Palace . . . on Lutherstrasse in the West End" was a business enterprise of his father's and a new venture in commercial entertainment that housed "not only the first skating rink in Berlin, but also a thriving nightclub."[82] But what Benjamin remembers is not what his father had taken him there to see: "So it happened that my attention was held far less by the convolutions in the arena than by the apparitions in the bar, which I was able to survey at my ease from a box in the circle. Among these was a prostitute in a very tight-fitting white sailor's suit who, though I was unable to exchange a word with her, determined my erotic fantasies for years to come."[83] The scene of the Paris bathhouse is revisited, though perversion and prostitution are screened there by an aura of family recreation, whereas here they are brought to the fore. Benjamin testifies to the spellbinding eroticism of this "apparition" whose exoticism draws on the surrounding phantasmagoria and its vertiginous "convolutions." He also shows how the enterprising license and licentiousness of commodity space may subvert patriarchal economics even as it obtains patriarchal investment.

Sexual Revolution, or Fashion Prostitution

The will to pleasure may spearhead sexual revolt but technology destroys the aura of love by acting as a catalyst of "lascivious commerce."[84] In the new Paris arcade, technology had its heyday. A microcosm of the capitalist metropolis, the arcade made space for spectacular sexuality wherein relations between the sexes and the very nature of human eroticism were radically and irrevocably changed. The arcade interpellated female citizens as female consumers and transformed female consumers into fashion fetishes-on-display. Women who strolled the arcades' interior streets of store fronts were urged to see themselves among the wares where women's fashions were prominently exhibited. The fashions on exhibition and the women exhibiting these fashions fused into the same promenading commodity. Fashion aimed to advertise women's sexuality and sexual accessibility to men, whose consumer disposition was the primary subject of solicitation (AP 80 [B10, 1]). By turning her into a spectacle of desire and parading her in apparel designed to attract rapacious interest, fashion transformed every well-dressed woman into a prostitute for the industry. Professional prostitutes were licensed to set up shop in the arcades where they promenaded the latest styles and found a niche for self-marketing. But once fashion made a commodity of respectable women, the professionals were banished from the arcades as if to conceal the traffic in female eroticism (AP 43 [A4, 3; A4, 4]).

Benjamin reveals how sexual revolution is embodied in fashion's dialectics. Fashion distracts love from its "natural" course of marriage and sexual reproduction and offers eroticism a radical, alternative expression in the seduction and consumption of sexual commodities. In postrevolutionary Paris, women seeking liberation from the ancien régime of patriarchal family life are seduced by fashion whose designs promote their optimal mobility (AP 74 [B5a, 3]) only to signal their sexual appeal and men's predatory attentions.[85] In the era of high capitalism the devaluation and depreciation of women as spiritual beings and the embodiment of love accompanies their sexual emancipation.

Dilemmas raised by homosexual revolution in the era of late capitalism are heir to this dialectic. Sarah Schulman's reporting on "the marketing of gay America" discloses some of the more pernicious ways that advertising sells-out the gay body politic to commercial fashion.[86] Her fiction reflects complex interactions between agents of sexual liberation and market capitulation. Robert Glück allegorizes gay romance as a pornographic affair of gay capital and mass media whose emancipatory eroticism is a prime product of commodity fetishism. As Glück sees it, there is no transcending this condition since the market (and market aura) is ubiquitous and gay pornography is an effective medium for mobilizing queer desire against repressive homophobia. The protagonists of queer constellations are all strolling commodities and/or streetwalking souls who empathize with the commodity and its abject exhibitionism. Scott's autonomous, streetwalking lesbian constantly checks her reflection in Paris storefronts, watching with delight and horror her becoming-likeness to fashion mannequins.

Love at Last Sight

For Benjamin, love in the big city is inextricably bound to commodity traffic, where everyone is dressed to attract a buyer (employer, client, customer, john). The subject not yet inured to this scene exposes herself or himself to the crowd's allure and becomes vulnerable to the spectacle. It is "love—not at first sight, but at last sight" that enthralls his gaze, for no sooner has an apparition in the crowd solicited his attention than it passes on by, destined for mass circulation and repeated exchange. Though love has been stirred it is never reciprocated and is intended for but fleeting consummation. This is "the gaze . . . of the object of a love which only a city dweller experiences."[87]

Queer constellations feature cruising lesbian and gay subjects with a similar look, one that is not open to trade but easily tempted by commodity seduction. It is the gay gaze invested with desire for free exchange, and it is always underscored by the gaze of the other: capitalism's look for the body of greatest purchase. We see this look, and its internalized dialectic of frustration, in Indiana's rent boy who confuses hustling with loving. It is also reflected in the gaze of Glück's bathhouse patrons who appraise each other's erotic capital while accumulating orgasms. It is also this look that Scott's "bride," queerly wedded to the Main, defies; she turns the commodity's gaze into surreal focus on unmarketable and delinquent objects.

The Lesbian: Heroine of Modernity

Lesbianism, prostitution, and male-to-female transsexuality figure throughout *The Arcades Project* and most conspicuously in "Central Park," where Benjamin outlines "Baudelaire's erotology."[88] For Benjamin, prostitution is the supreme allegory of commodity society, where everything and everyone is other than what they appear to be, disguised in the dress of desirability and on display for market speculation. In Baudelaire, the prostitute allegorizes the decline of *amour*. But she also signifies the return of eros in a different guise since "love for the prostitute is the apotheosis of empathy with the commodity" (AP 511 [O11a, 4]) and "prostitution opens the possibility of a mythical communion with the masses."[89]

Baudelaire's ecstatic immersion in the crowd reflects "the possibility of enduring a life in which the most immediate objects of our use have turned more and more into mass commodities," and it also implies an uncanny empathy with the mass-produced article that "in big-city prostitution, the woman herself becomes."[90]

"The lesbian" of *The Arcades Project* and the Baudelaire essays is a constellation of motifs: she is, at once, a figure of historical idealism (Sapphic classicism); of avant-garde aestheticism (sublime "pure love" as opposed to "natural" sexuality and utilitarian reproductive technology); and of moral outlawry, if not ecclesiastical blasphemy (for which *Les Fleurs du mal* was tried for obscenity). These are motifs that comprise Baudelaire's iconographic and iconoclastic "heroine of *la modernité*."[91] As a strategy to market his poetry, Baudelaire magnifies lesbianism's erotic character to the exclusion of other aspects. Noting how poorly acquainted Baudelaire was with actual lesbians, Benjamin traces his metaphor to extraliterary sources. He unearths the political lesbianism of the Saint-Simonian circle of utopian socialists and of the Vésuviennes who participated in the February Revolution, and thus amplifies the "constellation of modernity."[92] Baudelaire's constellation combines the *fetish-fantasy* of lesbianism's damnable and beautiful "pure love" together with the *ruin-allegory* of the prostituted decline of love and the ascendant sterility of erotic perversity. To this, Benjamin adds the *wish-image* of (lesbian) utopian socialism and the *prototype* of industrial female labor whose altered "feminine habitus" could transform ("masculinize") the female body and emancipate women from domestic servitude and sexual slavery.[93]

Queer constellations are populated by queer types that are more allegorical than psychological, and more conflicting than cloned. They represent actual personalities less than the multiple and contradictory character of urban sexuality itself. Lesbians and lesbianism, including lesbian bohemianism, figure largely as constellations of the most extreme antitheses of big-city life—more extreme than their gay counterparts, given the disproportionate poverty, marginality, unmarketability, and delinquency of lesbian culture, together with the disproportionate susceptibility of lesbians to women's geography of fear and visibility of "lesbianism" in mainstream pornography. The streetwise "brides" of *Main Brides* form a constellation of tropes that reflect all of these extremes in context of the city's, in this case Montreal's, culture of antifeminist violence. Likewise, the manifold "girls" of *Chelsea Girls* form a constellation of lesbian images conjured from traumatic memory. Reflecting the rebel wishes and severe abuses of metropolitan girlhood, these images illuminate a counterhistory of America's "free love" era. The sundry dyke-types that populate Schulman's fictional East Village are the stars of her constellation of bohemian "Lesbiana." Not all of these stars are true bohemians. False bohemians (like the mercurial "Muriel Kay Starr," who becomes a best-selling, sell-out artist) can be detected alongside the true, while true bohemians are seen to be *falsely* represented, at best, for mainstream consumption. Schulman's constellation reveals the extreme contradictions of lesbian cultural production in the latest incarnation of bohemian New York.

Some Motifs in Queer Constellations

The constellation of late-twentieth-century urban reality entails, like Benjamin's constellation of the nineteenth century, the deployment of various motifs or literary devices. Primary, or macro, devices are mimesis, montage, and monad, a combination of which constitutes the art and apparatus of the dialectical image. The specific rendering of these devices in queer constellations takes on a queer (and) postmodernist character—one that amplifies the queer (and) modernist character of Benjamin's constellation. Benjamin adapts the montage of avant-garde modernism, notably that of surrealism; queer constellations readapt modernist (surrealist) montage with parodic reflexivity. Like surrealism's authors, the authors of queer constellations enter their fictions as experimental writers where they test and lay bare revolutionary techniques of representing the technologically revolutionized metropolis. Like Benjamin, they refunction surrealism's montage and/or other devices. More critically, they refunction *Benjamin's* adaptation of surrealism. For example, the narrator of Gail Scott's *My Paris* stands in self-consciously for the author as she assumes the role of writer and inscribes Benjamin's "montage-method" in a diary she keeps of her daily flâneries. She is made alert to the Paris of revolutionary surrealism by regular excursions through *Paris, capitale du XIXe siècle*. The task of the critic of queer constellations is to disclose the neo-avant-garde's queer refunctioning of Benjamin, in light of, and as compared to, Benjamin's refunctioning of the historic avant-garde.[94]

In addition to mimesis, monad, and montage, queer constellations adapt and deploy a number of tropes and techniques that derive from Benjamin or are illuminated by reference to Benjamin (his adaptation of avant-garde modernism). These are, unlike the macro devices used to frame the general space of urban modernity, specific figures of space that apply differently to different cities—or specific(c)ities.

Porosity

The city of queer constellations is, queerly, a "village" enveloped in the phantasmagoria of global capitalism. It is the gay village in the world city, a local, bohemian production that occupies the historic and/or inner city as space for waging and enjoying sexual revolution. Real and imaginary space, this village-within-the-city solicits the gay gaze with its urban look as much as it reflects the projection of gay desires. An enclave of intimacy in a cosmos of strangers, it is the paradoxical center of commodity space. The barriers it raises to bourgeois enterprise and commerce are *porous*. Queer constellations image this porosity as a flow of exchange across layers or zones of revolutionary history, inner-city community, and urban development, as well as boundaries dividing public and private life. Here the borders of ghettoization and gentrification are always shifting, and the agents of insurgency and complicity are easily confused. For the cruising gay flâneur, the gay village poses a labyrinth of speculation in the mainstream of progress.

Porosity figures prominently in Benjamin's early city portraits. It signifies the fluid boundaries of space that he experienced on strolls in southern Mediterranean cities—precapitalist cities on the verge of industrialization. "Naples" highlights the confluence of business affairs and family life, or commerce and romance, in the outdoor theater of its lived-in streets and windows wide open onto indoor scenes. To the eyes of a northern urban dweller accustomed to zones and grids, the border between private, interior space and public, exterior space seems shockingly permeable and uncannily in-between. "Marseilles on Hashish" foregrounds the physiognomy of a city that is simultaneously archaic (archetypal) and foreign. The faces of strangers appear surreally familiar in the flâneur's drug-enhanced vision of city types. Using surrealism's trick of juxtaposing images (together with taking hallucinogens), Benjamin perceives the modern metropolis in constellation with capitalist prehistory. "Porosity" is the name he gives this constellation before seeing in terms of dialectical optics.

The porosity of the city of queer constellations enables us to see the confluence of history even as it is engulfed in the capital(ism) of postmodernity. The "gay village" is exceptionally porous. Here gay life is lived out on streets that are conduits to intimate and communal contact *and* prime arteries of commodity traffic. The gay bathhouse interiorizes the passages and meeting places of the external city and, magnifying the city's cruising capacity, returns bathhouse patrons to the streets transformed. Delany's fictional memoir, *The Motion of Light in Water*, recounts the author's first trip to the St. Marks Baths in the early 1960s from New York in the late 1980s. The memory of mass sex in the Baths invokes the space of sexual revolution *before* the advent of gay militancy. Shades of revolutionary prehistory bleed into the postrevolutionary present, after AIDS has decimated the Village. The effect of this bleeding is to shock the author into perceiving revolutionary potential that has been lost, but could be recovered, in the current crises. The borders of Schulman's East Village bleed into, and with, the revolutionary history of the Lower East Side. The space of bohemia is permeated by anarchic, lesbian socialism, at the same time as it is invaded by gentrifying forces. For the lesbian flâneur who cruises the Main in Scott's *Main Brides*, the faces of streetwalking women conjure forth unfulfilled fantasies and traumatic memories. Cued by their location on the colorful boulevard, these are less the projections of individual desire than the collective fantasies and memories of a Montreal not yet known to history. The cruising subject is herself porous; the "Main bride" of *Main Brides* dissolves into the street, where the scene unfolds well beyond her limited narrative point of view. The same could be said of Bartlett's narrator who, as he cruises the West End scene of the early 1980s with its nineteenth-century facades, shifts in and out of Wilde's London of the 1890s. The effect of this shifting is to trouble the immediacy of the present that closets the history of gay emergence and its contradictory legacies from view.

Flânerie

Flânerie is a primary documentary technique for queer interrogations of urban space. A narrative technique, flânerie plots the city-on-the-move in fleeting physiognomies of city spaces and types. Queer constellations cross flânerie with cruising to produce streetwalking narratives that linger and falter at the crossroads of urban development. Instead of reiterating the dominant narrative of progress, the cruising narratives of queer constellations record collisions between urban gentrification and sexual emancipation, between embourgeoisement and bohemianism. Cruising flâneries prompt queer narrative performances that collapse into incoherence before sites/sights of unbearable historical contradiction.

Like the classical flâneur of nineteenth-century realism (Balzac's man-about-town, for example), the cruising flâneur of queer constellations strolls city passages with leisurely fascination at a loiterly, anti-industrious, pace. And like the classical flâneur, the cruising flâneur is piqued with desire—desire that the city itself has induced with its intoxicating promenade of commodities. Unlike the classical flâneur, famed for his aloof observations, the cruising flâneur loses composure (or decomposes) with exposure to the city's erotic spectacles. The former confidently documents his travels with empirical positivism, whereas the latter documents his—or hers (since the cruising flâneur is frequently a lesbian)—with emotional, if not abject, acuity. Unlike the classical flâneur, for whom there is no object, the cruising flâneur is on the outlook for love, where the gay gaze is misrecognized for the look of the commodity. A city lover, as much as a lover of his or her own sex, the cruising flâneur gravitates to the city's erotic hot spots in search of a companion. En route, she or he encounters the other in commodity drag, and vice versa, the commodity dressed in gay masquerade. In either case, the deception is as devastating as it is exhilarating.

The flâneur first appeared on site of the Paris arcades, where the urban spectacle was optimally enjoyed by luxuriously accommodated strolling. By the time of Baudelaire, the arcades had been replaced by Haussmann's heavily trafficked boulevards. Benjamin regarded Baudelaire's efforts to flan against the crowd as heroic. Embodying the return of the flâneur, Benjamin strolled the Paris of the 1930s where the arcades lay in ruins and bore but faint traces of their former elegance. From his perspective Paris presented a ready-made montage in whose architectural and archeological facades one could perceive the passage(s) of early industrialism and utopian socialism (arcades and *phalansteries*) in shattering juxtaposition with those of capitalist imperialism and failed communism (boulevards and barricades). Benjamin extended his flâneries to the Bibliothèque Nationale, losing himself in the labyrinth of city archives while undertaking his massive re/collection of the nineteenth century. Though his findings are cited with few markers identifying his own time and place, and with minimal theoretical and/or narrative speculation, the documentation of *The Arcades Project* is not simply objective. His disjointed notes of flâneries through historic space suggest less the self-composed aloofness of Balzac's hero than surrealism's revolutionary nihilism. They are calculated, at least covertly, to crystallize the contradictions of the era and to destroy the complacency with which future generations regard progress.

The cruising flâneur of queer constellations is an even later imitation of the nineteenth-century flâneur and, in some cases, a direct imitation of Benjamin's flâneur. Edmund White's *The Flâneur* loosely reiterates Benjamin's "Return of the *Flâneur*" in reflections and reminiscences on Paris through the ages.[95] White's flâneur adapts Benjamin's flânerie to include memories of cruising the Tuileries Gardens and Île St. Louis. At the same time, his *Stroll through the Paradoxes of Paris* highlights the dialectical character of city history, including the contradictory position taken by gay Parisian literati on coming out as minority revolutionaries. In *Who Was That Man?* Bartlett models its cruising flâneur on the narrator of "A Berlin Chronicle." This is the flâneur who actively loses his way in the city in order to rediscover what he had not witnessed before.[96] Bartlett's flâneur also takes to strolling the city archives, in this case the holdings of the British Museum. Finding these holdings unforthcoming on *gay* London, he loses himself in the archives in order to sight/cite the recalcitrant object. He cruises the labyrinth of sources like he cruises the streets. But with dialectical hindsight, he uncovers paradoxes in history that cruising (in) the present overlooks.

The narrator of Scott's *My Paris* fancies herself a "flâneur of interior" Paris—that is, the Paris of embourgeoisified space, now hyper-embellished in the era of capitalist postmodernity. This includes the luxurious writer's studio wherein she discovers a copy of Benjamin's *Paris, capitale du XIX*[e] *siècle* and the Convolute on "L'Interieur." Scott accentuates Benjamin's attention to interiors in proportion to how today's city seeks escape from its accelerated traffic and amplified congestion. Flanning through his *Paris,* she forges a writer's retreat from congested boulevard Raspail just outside her window. At the same time, she acquires, from Benjamin, a dialectics of seeing with which she reads actual metropolitan spaces. She revisits the dilapidated or renovated arcades. But her focus scatters across storefronts, billboards, and television screens of enhanced urban spectacle.

The most radical adaptation of Benjamin's flâneur is Scott's transgendering of his constellation. Like Benjamin's flâneur, Scott's flâneur is seduced by the sensual voluptuousness of commodity display; but, as a woman, she figures differently in the scope of the city's specularization. Interpellated as *la Parisienne* by passers-by, she is subject to intense fashion expectations, including her own ambivalent introjection of commodity fetishism. She is as apprehensive of being misrecognized as a Paris streetwalker as she is of passing inconspicuously as an adequate dresser. Yet her desire for other women places her gaze, and her look, outside the commercial circulation of femininity. She sets her sights on the *other* Paris, highlighting the lesbianism of *The Arcades Project* and with *lesbian* desire. Looking for a city of women, she stumbles across traces of not-yet-actualized revolutionary potential to generate a women's culture. Yet

Scott's flâneur is anything but heroic. In search of *la Parisienne lesbienne,* she is eternally disappointed. With self-conscious literary affectation, she parodies the flâneur's anachronism. Moreover, her vision is as divided as it is dialectical. Unable to resist the city's overt solicitations of the senses, she is also unable to affect indifference before the city's covert abuse of its others, including racially marked immigrants from French ex-colonies.

The space exposed by the cruising flâneur of queer constellations differs dramatically according to gender. Cruising *gay* flâneurs may circumscribe such (gay-)revitalized neighborhoods as the Castro and West End London, as well as the hustling grounds of the Tenderloin and Times Square and rough wastelands like the warehouse district South of Market and the waterfront on the Hudson. Cruising *lesbian* flâneurs stroll through space that is less propertied and proprietary, yet more diffuse. Bartlett situates his flâneries in the pleasure domes of expensive West End nightclubs, whereas Myles locates hers near the cheap, few, dyke bars scattered around the Village. Glück figures the gay bathhouse as the ultimate site for perceiving the dialectics of gay capital, whereas Schulman focuses her dialectical optics on the lesbian, low-rent era of East Village bohemia. Different prospects pose different perspectives, though in every case, the city is viewed through a montage of disjunctive images.

Allegory

The fictions that comprise queer constellations are allegorical, not fantastical, although fantasy figures in these fictions as a prime character of urban preoccupation. Allegorical, de-romanticizing tales of the city, they re-represent late modern, metropolitan space as, above all else, a space of commodity phantasmagoria. This is a constructed, intoxicated, and theatricalized space that is at once, as the narrative of seduction reveals, destructive, toxic, and de-composed. Allegory attacks the veneer of postmodern capital in its most insidious, erotic forms. It plots the double-edged, technologically-enhanced romance of making-it (making-out) in the city amidst showcases of fulfillment and voluptuous, uninhibited traffic.

What the city advertises as gross abundance, magnified and multiplied in disorienting simulations of consummate happiness, allegory re-cites as over-determined signs of volatile and violent marketability. Fantasy conceals the shocking human cost of its inflated expectations, just as, conversely, it absorbs revolutionary action in grandiose dreams. Allegory exposes that concealment and absorption in fictions of revolutionary nihilism, converting what remains of the city's revolutionary possibility into retrospective utopia.

The allegorical character of queer constellations is underlined in the titles of its fictions. *Rent Boy* allegorizes the prostituted body of sex in a city where everything is for rent, and vice versa, the city of deregulated rent where every city dweller must prostitute himself in order to make a living. *Rat Bohemia* allegorizes the infestation and devastation of low-rent, bohemian neighborhoods by the city's haplessly, if not criminally, administered plot to kill off poor populations and make way for gentrification. *Main Brides* allegorizes the city's seduction of women into becoming the main objects of the Main's commercial traffic that, like the displayable and disposable bodies of commodities, are made for consuming and trashing. By stressing the allegorical over the fantastical, and by allegorizing the commodity as allegory (exposing the commodity's over-determined fantasy), these fictions render visible the real of phantasmagorical city space. In doing so, they amplify Walter Benjamin's literary strategy for reading and deconstructing the city's commodity-saturated semiotics. Benjamin's "One Way Street" reads as allegorical everything and anything that the city puts on display; beyond their quotidian currency in capitalism's enveloping universe, such objects as "Underground Works," "Travel Souvenirs," and "Construction Sites" render unimagined and/or repressed metaphorical (and metaphysical) significance. Similarly, every character who walks the street of queer constellations—the rent boys of *Rent Boy*, the Main's brides of *Main Brides*, the rat bohemians of *Rat Bohemia*—represent the city allegorically. If they fall easily for the city's seductions, they are not simply duped into taking for real what is presented as reality. Moreover, they are themselves allegories—allegorical *types* of urban dwellers—that specify the queer paradoxes of negotiating late-twentieth-century urban reality in their respective cities of Manhattan and Montreal.

Allegory is also a principle mode of narration, as in Glück's *Jack the Modernist.* "Greetings from late capitalism where meaning and image have come apart," heralds "Bob," the novel's autobiographical narrator, who sees himself de-compose into manifold fetishistic constructions and projections of heavily mediated desire.[97] Bob critiques modernism's illusions about the capacity of art to bring into meaningful unity and coherence that world which commodity capital sunders apart in allegorical meaninglessness. He looks at his lover's, Jack's, precious collection and preservation of images of all the love affairs he has to date accumulated and sees, in life as in art, the vain attempt of the modernist to *shore these fragments against his ruin.* Bob rejects such aestheticism as the ultimate fetish of, and consummate capitulation to, capitalism, echoing Benjamin whose essays on Baudelaire outline the capitalist devaluation of eros: "'The man who goes the length of the path of passion of male sexuality, comes through his sacred value to be a poet. The poet to whom no social mission can be imparted, makes the market of the commodity his objects.'"[98]

Subverting the compulsion to fetishize/aestheticize, Bob re/collects the story of his love affair with Jack as a romance that is allegorically riddled with a collage of images from gay porn magazines and incisive "dialogue" between Bob and Jack together with "Lechery," "Lust," and "Pride."

Allegory functions in queer constellations as a critical rent in the (gay) gaze. It is the destructive factor of the dialectics of seeing that views urban phantasmagoria from the perspective of its disintegration. In an essay on "Allegory," Glück cites a passage from Benjamin's *Origin of German Tragic Drama*:

> Everything about history that, from the beginning, had been untimely, sorrowful, unsuccessful, is expressed in a face—rather, in a death's head. And although such a thing lacks all "symbolic" freedom of expression, all classical proportion, all humanity—nevertheless, this is the form in which

> man's subjection to nature is most obvious and it significantly gives rise to not only the enigmatic question of the nature of human existence, as such, but also of the biographical historicity of the individual. This is the heart of the allegorical way of seeing.[99]

For Benjamin, the death's head is allegorical par excellence. It lays bare the corruptibility of human nature, and the fallibility of humanity. The death's head is history's true face, not the icons we freely raise against existential reality. Facing the real of history, we find no symbol of salvation. Nothing is so sacred or so personal as to escape allegory's profane illumination. In postmodernity, the individual subject dons the death's head in the (readily deconstructed) form of mass-mediated identity and lifestyle. As Glück frankly puts it: "An allegorical frame of mind can read crumbling medieval walls as the crumbling monarchy. If personality in late capitalism is also a ruin, how would we allegorize it?"[100]

Jack the Modernist pictures this death's head in a full-page reproduction of G. Allen Gilbert's *Vanity*, a trompe l'oeil painting whose subject, depending on your perspective, appears now as a woman before a mirror and then as a skull. It bears the caption: "I relinquished the firm barrier that separated us—no, that separated me from nothing."[101] The caption is excerpted from Bob's story about paying a visit to the gay baths for an orgiastic quick fix that he hopes, in vain, will dispel the loneliness he feels with Jack. It is reinserted in the text out of context where it signals the dissolution of artful narrative and urban romance. The disillusionment Bob suffers in the baths prompts him to see not just Jack but the world with a broken heart. Through a tear in the veil of the Castro's gaiety, he glimpses catastrophe on every scale:

> Rainbows surrounded us. A crystal that hung by a string in the bay window—part of the room's new age paraphernalia—caught all the sun and released it in hundreds of slowly revolving arcs. Their colors were extremely pure and pleasurable. . . . But we had duly absorbed the horror; it became part of our bodies like the shock of a slammed door. . . . "Nuclear catastrophe, destitution, famine, additives, melanomas, losing

> face, U.S. involvement in El Salvador and Nicaragua, Puerto Rico, South Korea, Chile, Lebanon and Argentina, war in the middle East, genocide of Guatemalan Indians and extermination of the native peoples of Brazil, Philippines, Australia, answering the telephone, resurgence of the Nazis, the KKK, auctioning of the U.S. wilderness, toxic waste, snipers, wrinkles, cult murderers, my car, Jack's safety, queer bashers, South Africa, being unloved, considered second rate, considered stupid, collapse of our cities."[102]

The allegorical gaze destroys the gay gaze and the look of commodity fetishism. It initiates the critical function of negation in the dialectics of seeing. That is not all. Where it perceives things in their ruin, it also fathoms their redemption. Benjamin stressed allegory's dual capability, as Gilloch explains:

> The allegorical gaze is that of the physiognomist, and has both a destructive and a constructive moment. In emptying out meaning, allegory brings the ruination, the "mortification" of things. . . . Allegory also contains a positive, redemptive moment. . . . The world is reduced to ruins so that the rubble and fragments that result can be gathered up and reused. Benjamin notes that objects viewed through the optic of allegory "are broken apart and conserved simultaneously. Allegory holds tightly to the debris." The *promesse du bonheur* contained in the phantasmagoria of the modern is thus redeemed. . . . Ruination and redemption—these are the Janus-faces of the allegory. The allegorical vision as the overcoming of myth and the moment of historical redemption contains within it the qualities of the dialectical image, and hence becomes the fundamental basis of Benjamin's critical historiography.[103]

Jack the Modernist foresees redemption in storytelling that knits community together in the face of ruin, once the facade of gay romance is ripped off. But not all the fictions of queer constellations place equal emphasis on each side of allegory's split vision. *Rent Boy* foresees only ruination; allegory functions solely as negation in this text and resembles the nihilism of Benjamin's late writings on Baudelairean allegory. Like the prostitute of Baudelaire's "Allégorie," Indiana's rent boy personifies the commodity by giving it a human face. Therein is reflected the commodity character of the city's most intimate consumers. The look on that face turns into horror when it beholds the mirror image of another rent boy, whose body has been rent asunder by organ thieves in an execution of extremely rough trade for the city's power brokers. Conversely, *Main Brides* foregrounds the redemption it foresees in ruination. Oscillating between fantasies evoked by the Main's faces and facades and the terror evoked at the sight of a woman's corpse abandoned by her murderer in an inner-city park, allegorical vision remains split. If the narrator is distracted by her cruising fantasies of passing street-women, she is soberly recalled to the de-composing present by the haunting real of urban violence. Yet between fantasy and sobriety a revelation of history appears. A utopian dream lifts the brides from street level to the rooftops of the Main, where they dance with spears in hand. Projecting an image of the future on the city's revolutionary horizon, they unearth a layer of archaeology that has been violently obliterated by capitalism's enduring fetishism.

Narratives of the Real

The allegorical gaze foresees the city in ruins, disinterring what Benjamin identifies as the "refuse of history" (AP 460 [N1a, 8]). Comprising this "refuse" are victims of cultural conquest. These include not only the maligned and marginalized working poor but also the revolutionary dead, including dead sexual revolutionaries, whose struggle remains buried and suspended in the annals of capitalist progress. Like Benjamin's critical historiography, queer constellations excavate the ruins of the recent metropolitan past, aiming to recover and redeem history's trash in startling, revelatory assemblages. Unlike the author of *The Arcades Project*, however, they endorse narrative (and theory) as well as citation. Narrative functions in these fictions as a site of de-composition and decomposure, where the phenomenological subject of history cracks up, breaks down, falls apart in shock at sight of history's simultaneous potential and betrayal.

Close to the Knives demonstrates this cut-up technique, underlining the installation of mimesis and collage to subvert mass media's dominated space. Using material from national headlines and corporate television, together with remnants of queer existence excised from public view, it illustrates how identity is constructed inside the commodity as a *transformative* production—a production that uses the contradictory strategies of what Glück means by "autobiography": "the self as collaboration, the self as disintegration."

However disintegrated, the world that Wojnarowicz perceives is real and it refers primarily to New York City. *Close to the Knives* recasts scenes of living memory indelibly traced by cruising. The section "In the Shadow of the American Dream: Soon All This Will Be Picturesque Ruins" tracks memories of cruising in a de-composing montage, set against picture postcard America, illuminating the city's industrial wasteland of dilapidated factories, warehouses, and harbor fronts—scenes that read like derelict versions of Whitman's Manhattan. Wojnarowicz's city has even struck the attention of Rebecca Solnit who, in her popular history of walking, notes how *Close to the Knives* incorporates past strategies of flânerie and "reads like a summary of all the urban experience that came before him."[119] What especially impresses Solnit is how cruising the city functions as referential anchor in the maelstrom of Wojnarowicz's revelations: "He writes in a collage of memories, encounters, dreams, fantasies, and outbursts studded with startling metaphors and painful images, and in his writings walking appears like a refrain, a beat: he always returns to the image of himself walking alone down a New York street or a corridor."[120]

The city's refuse enter Wojnarowicz's collage as agents of insurgency. This is the maligned queer populace, who are either doomed or dead, victims of epidemiological conspiracy—the trash of recent American history. It is their collective memory that Wojnarowicz writes into remembrance. Among those he commemorates in his "Personal Acknowledgements" are the "42nd Street Movie Houses" and "the drag queens along the Hudson River and their truly revolutionary states." The call to arms that ends his memoir is wholly and abjectly arousing: "Meat. Blood. Memory. War. We rise to greet the State, to confront the State."[121]

Fictions of queer constellations, including New Narrative fiction, represent the queer space of urban reality by combining narrative *and* montage, activist *and* negative critique. They reassemble and reactivate the destructive *and* constructive components of historical materialism that (or akin to that which) Benjamin substituted for traditional historical narrative. That these techniques are antithetical is appropriate to the aim of rendering antithetical experience perceptible. As Glück reflects: "I wanted to write with a total continuity and total disjunction since I experienced the world (and myself) as a continuity and infinity divided."[122]

Queer constellations are *revolutionary* in the sense given by Benjamin—meaning absolutely *not* a "liberal-moral-humanistic-ideal of freedom."[123] Skeptical of liberations that, waged in the name of progress, capitulate to capitalism, he championed that tendency in the European literary avant-garde to treat reality with "pessimism."[124] Queer literary history shares a similar skepticism regarding gay liberation. In his study of queer literary production in the twentieth century preceding Stonewall, for example, Christopher Nealon denounces "a purely progressive or liberationist idea of queer politics" and proceeds to trace this production in the commodity domain. Seeing no other realistic plot for queer (literary) intervention, Nealon opts for a narrative of history that ends in globalization.[125]

But Benjamin, for whom the globalization of capitalist culture was no less impending, insisted on charging literature with a revolutionary task. This was the task of eliminating moral metaphors, particularly those of liberty and prosperity, from political thought, or contrasting them with images of material actuality in juxtapositions so shocking as to jolt audiences into a revolutionary presence of mind.[126] He thus urged art to destroy the aura of political optimism (exuded by social democrats) by casting a revolting "image space":

> the space, in a word, in which political materialism and physical creatureliness share the inner man, the psyche, the individual, or whatever else we wish to throw to them, with dialectical justice, so that no limb remains

interpellating big-city citizenry with intimacy, liberty, and fraternity. The gay bathhouse may be the product of historical imagination, but strangely it confounds historical interpretation.

Now that the era of the bathhouse has ended—a fact to which histories of the gay bathhouse attest, though gay bathhouses continue to exist outside the gay meccas of San Francisco and New York City[3]—gay historiography must write against the forgetfulness of mainstream culture. It does so with nostalgia in an attempt to rally collective memory. But nostalgia is haunted by phantasmagoria of the urban marketplace. Even that history that explicitly protests the closure of gay bathhouses inventories social interest with a list of commercial credits. The contrary images of erotic radicalism and economic progressivism are two sides of the same idealistic coin of gay liberalism, duplicitous face of the homoeroticization of capital.

When cast from a liberal, idealizing, perspective, the hypothesis of love in a bathhouse loses sight of real, salient, material contradictions. Instead of drawing out these contradictions and constructing an object of revolutionary cognition, histories of the gay bathhouse overlook them, in favor of a myth of lost utopia.

The purpose of this chapter is to reconsider historiography of the gay bathhouse, critique its idealist assumptions, and disclose unacknowledged antitheses that could serve as starting point for rethinking the volatility of (gay) urban space. Drawing on the technique and theories of Walter Benjamin and on contemporary gay writing of the city, I will present a *dialectical image* of the gay bathhouse as a radical alternative to the picture proposed by the historians.

Historiography of the Gay Bathhouse

Historiography of the gay bathhouse has a decidedly political beginning in Allan Bérubé's "History of Gay Bathhouses." Drafted as a "declaration" of gay rights and submitted to the California Superior Court on behalf of bathhouse patrons, this "History" campaigned against public misconceptions concerning AIDS, including the scapegoating of gay bathhouses as the alleged source of decadence and disease.[4] "As a community-based historian," Bérubé determined "to intervene in the public and legal debate over closing all the bathhouses, sex clubs, and adult theaters in San Francisco" and "to construct an alternative defense of gay baths that was based on their long history as sexual institutions, and on the right of gay citizens to use them for associational purposes that were sexual as well as social and political" (187).

The strategy of Bérubé's history is to testify to the existence of a "gay community" with well-established, community-based "institutions" of its own, institutions that, unlike those of the moral majority, were based explicitly on "physical intimacy" (187). In other words, gay community has a right to be and be *there*, like any other established community in America, guardian of democracy and home to all enterprising minorities. Above all, gay people have a right to maintain and enjoy their own social institutions, including bathhouses, which forged community in hostile territory and were "an integral part of gay political history":

> Before there were any openly gay or lesbian leaders, political clubs, books, films, newspapers, businesses, neighborhoods, churches, or legally recognized gay rights, several generations of pioneers spontaneously created gay bathhouses and lesbian and gay bars. These men and women risked arrest, jail sentences, loss of families, loss of jobs, beatings, murders, and the humiliation that could lead to suicide in order to transform public bars and bathhouses into safety zones where it was safe to be gay. In a nation which has for generations mobilized its institutions towards making gay people invisible, illegal, isolated, ignorant, and silent, gay baths and bars became the first stages of a civil rights movement for gay people in the United States. (188)

"Us[ing] terms and concepts . . . that were prevalent in the early 1980s among white gay male activists," Bérubé creates a "language" of gay community (187). Gay bathhouses figure in this language as "safety zones" for cultivating "democracy and camaraderie" (191): "for the gay community, gay bathhouses represent a major success in a century-long struggle to overcome isolation and develop a sense of community and

> refurbished by Bruce Mailman in 1979, the baths were redesigned for gay sexual expression in all its variety. . . . "At its peak, the St. Marks Baths was the hotbed of revolution in public sex that crystallized for many homosexual men the essence of what it meant to be gay in America in the late 1970s and early 1980s." (399)[17]

Yet historiography of the gay bathhouse compromises its socialist discourse with a narrative of growth and development, whereby production implies reproduction and consumption, appropriation implies commercialization and renovation, and social space is confused with the phantasmagoria of the capitalist marketplace. In a conflation of rhetoric, the gay bathhouse figures now as a commune, then as an arcade. When global capitalism threatens to incorporate the gay village, does the bathhouse strike a last stand against homogenizing forces of dominated space or accelerate mass tourism and community dispersal?

Chauncey argues that gay bathhouses deserve historical "scrutiny" since "they reveal much about the evolution of gay commercial institutions in general," as well as "patterns of gay sociability" ("The Social World of the Baths," 207). "Evolution" implies the "transition" from "mixed (straight and gay) to exclusively gay bathhouses [that] foreshadowed the arrival of other exclusively gay establishments" (207). Accordingly, by the end of the nineteenth century, gay men began to cruise and patronize the three kinds of baths that existed at that time: ritual Russian, Turkish, and Jewish baths; public baths; entrepreneurial electric and Turkish baths. Since entrepreneurial baths were the most accommodating, the transition from mixed to gay baths proceeded with a consolidation of middle-class interests (208–09). The delight Chauncey takes in describing the luxurious interiors of these baths dominates his discussion of their potential to transcend or subvert class differences.[18]

Bérubé's activist historiography also appeals to entrepreneurial progressivism, thereby undermining its political radicalism. Covering a century of development from the 1890s to the 1980s, "The History of Gay Bathhouses" is divided into "stages." Earlier stages (of "ordinary bathhouses," "favorite spots," and "early gay bathhouses") set the scene for the final stage ("modern gay bathhouses") that, from the late 1950s to early 1980s, showcases spectacular popularity and prosperity. Dramatic expansion follows "gay liberation."[19] A barrage of newly opened gay bathhouses evidences gay men's appropriation of inner-city space:

> In the early 1970s, the Everard Baths refurbished the premises after a fire and became an openly gay bathhouse, ending decades of clandestine activity. The East Side Sauna, Man's Country, Beacon Baths, Odyssey Baths, Apollo Sauna, Broadway Baths, Wall Street Sauna, Sauna Bath and Health Club, and The Barracks all opened as gay baths in Manhattan in the 1970s. (200)

But here "appropriation" implies property acquisition and refurbishing as much as appropriative social and spatial practices. Sexual enfranchisement implies commercial franchise. "The Club Baths—a newly-formed, national chain of gay bathhouses opened a bathhouse on First Avenue . . . at the site of an old Russian baths [and] . . . was Manhattan's first openly gay-owned bathhouse" (200). Gay propriety is said to make room for *total* gaiety: a hypereroticized interiorization of big-city entertainment, where baths and saunas are embellished by bars, cafés, discos, cinemas, cabarets, Hollywood movies, Bette Midler, and Barry Manilow (202–03). "The Continental Baths opened on West 74th Street, offering a disco dance floor, a Saturday Night cabaret, a pool, and clean, spacious facilities that could serve 1,000 men . . . 'a unique, total gay environment'" (200). Gay bathhouses opened their doors to the culture industry and the culture industry entered gay bathhouses, reproducing gay society for mainstream consumption.[20] And while some bathhouses exhibited local art to encourage sexual community,[21] others deployed high-tech videos to afford optimal autoerotic distraction.[22]

Bérubé interprets the recreational simulation of urban danger zones in bathhouse choreography as an overcoming of homophobia through technology and aesthetics. But in applauding the installation of "fantasy environments," he abandons his protest against social violence to hail the society of the spectacle:

> to the surface. First there is a sense of intimacy in the very centre of a public place, a powerful contrast that remains effective for anyone who has once experienced it; secondly, there is this taste for confusion which is a characteristic of the senses, and which leads them to divert every object from its accepted usage, to pervert it as the saying goes.[30]

Mystifying the "confusion" between "public place" and erotic intimacy, Aragon "senses" a cultic aura, which he imagines as "dangerous" to social order and capable of "perverting" use value into erotic value.[31] Aragon's "Baths" are the remnant of what once were the *plus célèbres* "Gymnasium Baths," whose name suggests a wistful condensation of Greek *gymnasium* and Roman *baths*.[32] Their mystery derives from a nineteenth-century fantasy of classical antiquity, whose twentieth-century ruins inspire Aragon's vision of erotic prehistory. Against enlightenment's inhibiting proprieties, the baths evoke an experience of "love at first sight." Supposing that love, especially "love in a bathhouse," harbors "an outlaw principle, an irrepressible sense of delinquency, contempt for prohibitions, and taste for havoc," Aragon "dream[s] of a people" who will occupy the baths as a temple of insurrection.[33] He implies gay patrons, since the only people "who take advantage these days, of the baths' equivocal nature" are "the pederasts, still a bit dazed by the tolerance they are beginning to encounter and used to guile and tyranny as part of life's routine."[34] Patronizing this people's struggle, he dreams of sexual revolution where forces of oppression are dissolved in steamy oblivion.

Bathhouse historians succumb, like Aragon, to bathhouse mystique. Aaron Betsky epitomizes the loss of perspective to bathhouse enchantment. Betsky views the gay bathhouse as a "precedent" of "extreme space" where coordinates of location are diffused, and where steam and water, shadow and light, are the agents of diffusion (*Queer Space*, 162). The ultimate evolution of this archetype is the sex club, whose total abstraction he applauds:

> Parodies and abstractions of social space became so stylized as to lose all connection with the outside world, so that the sex club becomes a container

> of "homoerotic spaces without their homophobic other." . . . This is an important moment in queer space, as it allows queers to create "fortresses" of self-definition against the straight world. (167)

If the sex club obscures all reference to the outside world with its unlit backroom, the gay disco does the same with its strobe lights.[35] "The Saint" in New York, for example, "was both a dance floor and a planetarium, a globe that summed up an abstracted world where everything, including straight walls, disappeared in a mosaic of continually changing rhythms of light and sound" (161).[36]

A rhetoric of globalization obscures the sight/site of resistance. Whatever tensions between body politic and urban capitalism were mobilized in gay bathhouses dissolve in this description of homogeneous spatiality. Rhetoric precludes analysis but entertains myth, such as the argument that the "extreme space" of gay bathhouses, sex clubs, and discos served as grand central station for HIV, that its hermetic enclosure meant optimal circulation for viral contagion, thereby decimating gay populations and creating "the void—the queerest space of all" (182).[37] The insularity of Betsky's vision is, in effect, *virulently antigay.*

The myth of "the void" inspires a countermyth of heterotopia to fill the gap left by gay baths. To help us imagine this heterotopia, Betsky concludes *Queer Space* with an imprint of Ingre's *Le Bain Turc* (1862), famed for its orientalist representation of the harem. The caption reads: "cruising through the city or cyberspace, the queer privateers move from their operatic colonies to dirty delights of sex clubs, opening up the tightly packed, floating communal oval of a ship, a queer ark always looking for a port. I hope it always remains afloat."[38] Commune is confused with colony, homoerotic projection with colonial gaze.

Bathhouse historiography may deploy a discourse of space, but analysis of "phantasmagoria" is conspicuously missing. Without it, the narrative of the making of gay urban life confuses the production of social space with the reproduction of capitalist dream space. Marx coined the term to signify and critique the "deceptive appearances of commodities as 'fetishes' in the marketplace" and "how exchange value obfuscates the source of value of commodities in productive labour." But for Walter Benjamin,

> whose point of departure was a philosophy of historical experience rather than an economic analysis of capital, the key to the new urban phantasmagoria was not so much the commodity-in-the-market as the commodity-on-display, where exchange value no less than use value lost practical meaning, and purely representational value came to the fore. Everything desirable, from sex to social status, could be transformed into commodities as fetishes-on-display that held the crowd enthralled even when personal possession was far beyond their reach.[39]

The historical perception of modernity is bound up in the phantasmagoria of capitalism where collective consciousness is mobilized *and* distracted. Benjamin's critique and emancipation of historical perception entails a *dialectical praxis of seeing*, a praxis we might extend to the historiography of gay bathhouses.

The Dialectics of Seeing

In notes for a "theory of progress" assembled in Convolute "N" of *The Arcades Project*, Benjamin considers the

> Delimitation of the tendency of this project with respect to Aragon: whereas Aragon persists within the realm of dream, here the concern is to find the constellation of awakening. While in Aragon there remains an impressionistic element, namely the "mythology" (and this impressionism must be held responsible for the many vague philosophemes in his book [*Paris Peasant*]), here it is a question of the dissolution of "mythology" into the space of history. (AP 458 [N1, 9])

Skeptical of Aragon's "impressionism," as it only embellishes the aura of capitalism's dreamworld, Benjamin seeks the "dissolution of 'mythology' into the space of history." His "constellation of awakening" alludes to the concept and practice of *dialectical image* on which he labored throughout his writing.[40] If finding a constellation of awakening is the question, then Convolute "N" and "On the Concept of History" propose an answer, as well as a critique of the "vague philosophemes" that compromise the logic of Aragon's bathhouse vision. Benjamin proposes that history be perceived as a *monad*, not a spatiotemporal continuum of progress and expansion. The monad crystallizes into being where the flow of history—or when progressivist thinking about history—comes to a stop in an image of extreme contradiction. A "constellation saturated with tensions," it splits capitalism's homogeneous universe into volatile antitheses.[41]

The technique of seeing history in a dialectical image adapts the technique of montage. It is, at once, destructive and constructive.[42] Destructive since it must be "blasted" from the historical continuum. "Historical materialism must renounce the epic element in history. It blasts the epoch out of the reified 'continuity of history.' But it also blasts open the homogeneity of the epoch."[43] The destructive component is "the critical momentum" of the dialectical image; it sheds historicist "empathy" with objective nihilism:

> The destructive or critical momentum of materialist historiography is registered in that blasting of historical continuity with which the historical object first constitutes itself. In fact, an object of history cannot be targeted at all within the continuous elapse of history. And so, from time immemorial, historical narration has simply picked out an object from this continuous succession. But it has done so without foundation, as an expedient; and its first thought was then always to reinsert the object into the continuum, which it would create anew through empathy. Materialist historiography does not choose its objects arbitrarily. It does not fasten on them but rather springs them loose from the order of succession. (AP 475 [N10a, 1])

Construction entails collecting verbal images of the historical object—for instance, guidebook descriptions, engineering designs, travelogue memoirs, exhibition catalogues, city archives, poetic tableaux of the Paris arcades (*Passagen*)—and arranging them in a "literary montage" where contradictory perceptions are juxtaposed in the extreme.[44] The construction of a dialectical image of history, of the historical object, is not a matter of arbitrary speculation or subjective interpretation. The nineteenth-century Paris arcades are exemplary material embodiments of the contradictory forces of history and, therefore, objects of explosive recognition. Their potential to incite political awareness is ontologically immanent but not epistemologically transparent, since obscured by commodity phantasmagoria. The *technique* of imaging contradiction and raising cognition is one of "heightened graphicness (*Anschaulichkeit*)" (AP 461 [N2, 6]) that entails a form of *citation*. "To write history thus means to *cite* history" (AP 476 [N11, 3]), that is, to cite history not as a recitation of what capitalism inventories as success but as a montage of juxtaposed antitheses collected from materials that traditional historicism overlooks as "rags and refuse."[45]

Dialectical images are not ready-made, though certain urban productions signal themselves as exemplary assemblages for historiographical de/construction. Susan Buck-Morss analyzes Benjamin's praxis of seeing as a radical pedagogy that instructs the reader how to think in flashes of politically charged insight through a strategic rhetoric of representation. Buck-Morss argues that the dialectical image, as practiced in *The Arcades Project*, might best be read as a sighting/citing of objects of commodity culture as metaphysical tropes—tropes that she categorizes as *fossil*, *fetish*, *wish-image*, and *ruin*. The entire field of objects/tropes is seen through a conceptual optics, or scope, the coordinates of which are demarcated by intersecting epistemological and ontological axes. Objects/tropes are sighted in opposing quadrants drawn by the intersecting axes of "consciousness" ("dreaming/waking") and "reality" ("petrified nature/transitory nature"). The focal point of antitheses is the commodity (Figure 1).[46] Superimposing these metaphysical axes on the massive collection of citations that comprise *The Arcades Project*, Buck-Morss throws Benjamin's dialectical image of nineteenth-century Paris into relief. Viewed conceptually through the scope of antitheses, the constellation of capitalism's contradictory volatility becomes strikingly perceptible. Buck-Morss scopes Benjamin's graphic optics in methodological detail. To construct a dialectical image of the gay bathhouses, it is useful to review the key figures of her analyses.

Fossil

Benjamin cites the industrial production of nineteenth-century Paris in terms of *natural history*, specifically paleontology. The Paris arcades, which were first erected in the early nineteenth century, appear, to Benjamin in the early twentieth century, as prehistoric caves of Parisian consumerism.[47] In less than a century their epoch had risen and fallen, their replacement by new consumer species accelerated by commodity obsolescence.[48] Only their fossils remain, indicating an earlier strata of social history when dreams of utopian socialism were first inspired by newly discovered technological capability. But the potential for using this capability to redistribute public wealth, transform social relations, and produce collective culture were unactualized. Traces of the arcades can be found in subsequent constructions, in the *grands magasins* and world expositions of the *Belle Époque*. But without proletarian revolution urban development reverts to social barbarism. The arcades figure as the ur-form of capitalist history in which the potential for social change remains trapped in a fetish evolution of spectacular consumption and bourgeois imperialism.

Fetish

Benjamin cites the new objects of industrial capitalism as fetishes. Like the fossils of obsolescent technological innovation, fetishes appear within

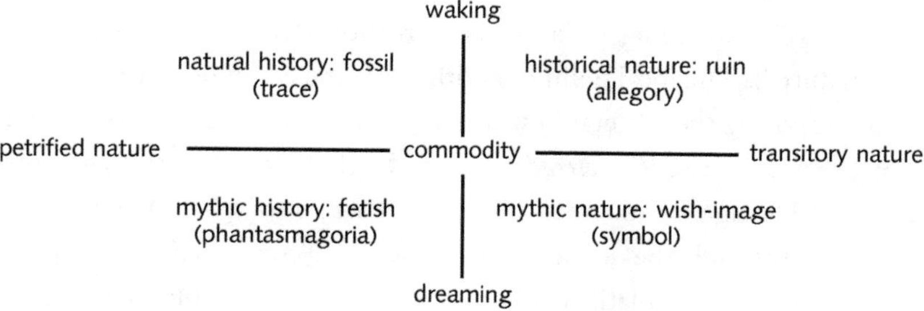

Figure 1

the field of petrified nature. But where fossils signify natural history as ur-history, fetishes signify *mythic history*. The primary fetish is novelty. The new nature of industrial technology produces new materials for construction and fabrication, new merchandise, new urban architectures, new urban masses that congregate and promenade in the milieu of these architectures, new fashions, even new sexualities. But for all its innovation, modern technology fails to emancipate the industrial proletariat from poverty, exploitation, and abjection. Novelty and fashionability are revered for themselves without revolutionary social transformation. Behind the illusion of progressive originality is the recycling of mass-marketing trends: an interminable repetition of the same.

Of all the dream houses of nineteenth-century European capitalism, the Paris arcades best exemplify the phantasmagoria of commodity space. Interiorizing the "City of Lights" and "City of Mirrors" in miniature, they traffic in spectacle. Their passages were the first "streets" to be lit by gas and, later, electrical lighting. Glowing with new merchandise, storefront windows reflected window-shopping masses as consumers "rather than producers, keeping the class relations of production virtually invisible on the looking glass' other side."[49] Strolling through this space, people wear the aura of the commodity. Every free laborer must package his product and/or himself to attract a prospective buyer. In the arcades, appearances are premium. Intoxicated by the abundance of mass-produced things, mesmerized by their reflection in window displays, miming, unconsciously, the appearances and gestures of fashion mannequins, urban crowds began to revel in the visuals of self-commodification. Where they might have congregated in the arcades in the spirit of public interest, they amassed instead as individual consumers, seduced by commercial orgies of voyeurism and exhibitionism yet separated from their fellow citizens by unrealizable dreams of private possession.

Wish-image

Benjamin regarded "'the arcades as dream- and wish-image of the collective'"[50] and the body politic of industrial Paris as a dreaming collectivity. Paris arcades were "dream houses" or "*fairy grottos*,"[51] as were all collective architectures of the nineteenth century: winter gardens, panoramas, factories, wax-figure cabinets, casinos, railroad stations, museums, apartment interiors, department stores, and *public spas.* New technology inspired dreams of building a city of heaven on earth. But instead of forging new designs, builders modeled their modern city on archaic forms. Capital's brave new world became obsessed with the past, aspiring only to reproduce the monumentality of classical, medieval, and renaissance antiquity, and thus inventing new, *mythic nature.*

Utopian wish-images cannot alone transform society; but technological capability cannot transform society without utopian vision. The dialectical image sights the transitory nature of industrial architecture that is masked behind transhistoric facades. It cites the dream of constructing heavenly cities that empire building obscures. The recovery of the dream is as important as the shattering of the myth. As Buck-Morss explains: "the wish symbols, signposts in a period of transition, can inspire the refunctioning of the new nature so that it satisfies material needs and desires that are the source of the dream in the first place. Wish images do not liberate humanity directly. But they are vital to the process."[52]

Ruin

In the footsteps of the surrealists, Benjamin walks the streets of 1920s and 1930s Paris, fascinated by the ruins of just a century ago. Unlike the surrealists, he focuses on the *historical nature* of commodity space, its built-in obsolescence and accelerated decay, its devastating construction, innovation, and expansion. For Benjamin, the dilapidation, or demolition and grandiose renovation, of the arcades signifies the betrayal of industrial utopia. Where Aragon beholds a surreal city of primordial loves that the sight of modern ruins restores to dream consciousness, Benjamin sees the wreckage of social space by Haussmann's commercial boulevards that were raised in place of utopian socialism's *phalansteries.*[53]

Benjamin uses Baudelaire's allegory as antidote to Aragon's intoxicating impressionism and modernist mythology. The dissolution of mythology into the space of history entails a radical epistemology. Allegory is its primary weapon. Allegory destroys the facade of totality, homogeneity,

room. It is the elder who pursues the younger in search of an author to chronicle the chaotic, and closeted, memoirs of his colonial exploits in Africa. Though two generations apart, Beckwith and Nantwich are kindred souls; they unconsciously haunt the Corinthian baths with the same bourgeois will-to-power with which the Club was originally built. Like Nantwich, Beckwith cruises dominated space as though all men are enfranchised with a gaiety afforded only by wealth and privilege. Traces of class suffering bleed through the cracks of imperial edifice when Beckwith visits Nantwich in the latter's home and where he feels, for the first time, what it is like to be subjected to the follies of bourgeois establishment. Looking at the frieze of the Roman bath, Beckwith sees the pain of the other, still traceable on the faces of slave boys as they are brutally sodomized by their Roman masters (80–81). He fails, however, to recognize his own exploitation of black and/or working-class young men.

The blindness with which Beckwith cruises is, in part, architected by the Corinthian Club baths. Though heralding universal brotherhood, the Club institutionalizes racism through the interpellative effects of its interior design. Composing the Club's nineteenth-century facade is "the broken-pedimented doorway surmounted by two finely developed figures—one pensively Negroid, the other inspiredly Caucasian," who together bear a banner that reads "'Men of all Nations'" (9). But from Beckwith's vantage as architecture diva we glimpse the Aryan blueprint of twentieth-century renovation:

> The lighting of this dingy, dignified underground bath is not in keeping with its decor. Originally, old photographs show, branched neo-classical lampadaries spread a broad glare over the water, whilst at the corners shell-shaped cups threw an orangey glow upwards on to the grandiose moldings on the ceiling. Until lately you could buy in the foyer upstairs a postcard, dating from not long after the war, showing white young men . . . about to jump in. . . . In the recent past, however, coinciding with the outlay on a few tins of brown gloss paint, and the filling in of some of the cracks which continuous small subsidence and shifting of the ground brought about, the pool lighting had been redesigned. Away with the wholesome

> brightness of Sir Frank's original conception, and in with a suggestive gloom, blond pools of light contrasting with surrounding shadow. Small, weak spots let into the ceiling now give vestigial illumination, like that in cinemas, over the surrounding walkway, and throw the figures loitering or recovering at either end into silhouette making them look black. Blacks themselves become almost invisible in the bath. . . . The luminous whiteness of the traditional swimming-pool is perversely avoided here. (11–12)

In the age of industrial enlightenment, even London's subterranean baths were illuminated with an aura of brotherly commonwealth. Progressive renovation darkens this fake idealism. The perversity of the place is not its clandestine homosexuality but its resurgent racism, dimly disguised as wholesome homosociality. Political recognition eludes Beckwith, however, who, submerged in white, upper-class privilege, remains captivated by the baths' fetish spatiality. Traceable in late-twentieth-century gay urban fantasy is last century's design of global fraternity, petrified in the strata of bourgeois imperialism and erased in the gaze of fascist aestheticism.

Fetish

Narrating the stages of a failed love affair, Glück's *Jack the Modernist* ponders the nature of erotic experience that constitutes the basis for negotiating gay life in early-1980s San Francisco. One episode recasts the scene of an orgy in a gay bathhouse—the city's Club Baths. The scene is reported by "Bob," the novel's fictive autobiographer and community storyteller. Bob enters the baths desiring the "community" of "ecstatic sexuality."[61] He wants hot, collective action in retreat from his self-absorbed lover, "Jack," an incorrigible "modernist" who copes with urban alienation by fashioning oases of aesthetic insularity. An advocate for the future of community that, he believes, can be salvaged through collective storytelling, Bob visits the baths for moral, as well as sexual, reassurance.

Bob experiences his movement through the baths as a passage through corporeal space. Enjoying "fluent passage from corridor to corridor with orgasm as the only stop" (59), he navigates the baths' interior as if through organs and orifices. As Benjamin observes, the experience of outer topography in images of the inner body is a capital feature of phantasmagoria: "'the dreaming collective becomes. . . engrossed in the arcades and passageways as in *the inside of its own body*.'"[62] At the same time, Bob orients his progress to a convoluted choreography of chambers, a compelling labyrinth of corridors, halls, and rooms. He senses the intoxicating paradoxicality wherein an aura of communality is cast: a communicative code of "no words" (53), dress code of nakedness (54), dark lighting (55), "music beating . . . against the silence" (55), group spectacle of solitary pleasure ("we watch the pleasure rather than the men, feeling the potential interchangeability. . . . Although they masturbated themselves to obtain immediate knowledge of my excitement, it was as spectators that they solemnly shared in what my pleasure revealed" [54]), loiterly fast pace ("naked men move swiftly even when we're standing still" [59]), mass space ("so many men: patterns of stress, dark and absorptive, hardly differentiated from the surroundings" [59]), instantaneous "passage of time" ("so little time: actually no time, opaque instants where being alive is form and content" [59]), and the alertness of distraction ("we set up high distracting turbulence and push into it, squinting eyes and parting lips" [59]).

From this crowded fantasia appears the man of his dreams. Bob is love-struck not by the man, who is a generic abstraction, but by direct solicitation of his senses: "A man grazes my right nipple; he hears my gasp and returns interested. . . . Do I describe his face?—two dots and a line. He's giving me an erection—that interests him. . . . I fondle his hair and ears, I love him so much I would do anything he asked me to, my arms are weak" (58). Love strikes but the lover moves on, a consummate passer-by. The body has its limits and when orgasm is no longer attainable or desirable, veils are lifted. The scene opens with a dream of paradise:

> One man eased his cock into my ass. My asshole went from opaque to transparent as he lifted me off the floor and fucked me slowly with authority while another blew me and occasionally took my balls in his mouth while still another tongued my nipples and kissed me and many others touched my body lightly as though they were sensual Greek breezes. (53)

But it closes with a vision of Hell:

> Finally in a big dark room on the second floor someone grabbed my cock and got it hard. I took hold of his cock and recoiled—it had warts. He abruptly swung around and shoved my cock in his ass, then turned us both around so he could balance himself on the edge of a platform that held a mattress. His ass was lubricated with the sperm of untold others—I don't know more about him—he was shorter and he had a waist. I scooted him onto the mattress and fucked him; I figured his ass was a crock pot for every disease known to man. His body spun like a pinwheel on a stick. When I finished he didn't bother turning around to his past to reminisce, he just went forward looking for his next cock. (60)

The last image is as shocking as the first is enchanting. In the wake of mythic satisfaction follows an allegory of commodification. Losing their cult aura, orgy participants now seem like automatons on an assembly line geared for surplus production. Fairyland reveals a fantasy factory where historical possibility is abolished in an eternal repetition of the same, collective memory is effaced by the drive to accumulate, and care of the self is lost to an amassing of social indifference.

En route to anticlimax, Bob is shocked by the mechanical reproduction and exhibition of seduction. "A wail of protest goes up" at the thought of the "interior life that intimacy is based on," the body's "secrets," being so publicly exposed and assessed: "what happens to these secrets once I have shared them with so many . . . that I am a machine whose quirks and eccentricities are appraised in a cheerfully businesslike way? If I'm so dispersed, what happens to the possibility of intimacy for me?" (59). Shock produces crisis, a start to critical awakening. The arcadia of "Greek sea breezes" fades before his eyes into a sex arcade where the traffic in bodies drives eros toward massive depreciation: "I haunted the halls and dark places of the Club Baths feeling less and less physically present. . . . My stock was plummeting" (60).

Bob's recognition that the baths fail to produce satisfying communal experience is ambivalent. Like pornography, bathhouse orgies detach sex from passion and "lack the actual touching that diffuses the shock of sex" (121), yet stir gay longing for positive, abundant, and variable images of minority sexuality: "it's a turn-on, it's thrilling, images of men—myself—reflecting each other into infinity, responding to desire and producing it. . . . To me these public images are photos from a dream" (121–22). Bob lingers in the passage *between* wish and ruin, in the phantasmagoria of the sex arcade. Here he can embrace gay self-love, though he looks on distantly, distracted and enchanted, as if tracking the frames of a surreal movie:

> : a waist arching calls attention to the nipples and sends the smooth ass backward giving access—someone slowly kneels
> *Two mouths, four nipples, four hands, two cocks, two*
> : the shifting of buttocks
> *scrotums, two assholes, two hundred and sixteen possi*
> : one excited man excites others to a circle of masturbation—hands and cocks group and regroup like a sudden wind shifting in a garden, or like a story: when a cock comes it withdraws from the plot
> *bilities and then another man joins you—an orgy in the*
> : someone is fucking a face he can't see, slow rhythmical ass that opens up and then clenches, its dreamtime logic has a unity that can't be dismissed or broken into parts. (56)

Wish-Image

Samuel R. Delany's memoir of coming out as a gay black writer in New York's East Village in the 1960s is punctuated by a recollection of the author's first trip to a bathhouse: St. Marks Baths in the East Village. He pauses to explain his excitement at the sight of mass sex:

> In the gym-sized room were sixteen rows of beds, four to a rank, or sixty-four altogether. I couldn't see any of the beds themselves, though, because there were three times that many people (maybe a hundred twenty-five) in the room. Perhaps a dozen of them were standing. The rest were an undulating mass of naked male bodies, spread wall to wall.
>
> My first response was a kind of heart-thudding astonishment, very close to fear.[63]

The sight is so alarming that it bypasses the register of consciousness, or *Erlebnis*, Benjamin's term for the distracted, dissociated, and fleeting form of experience through which big-city dwellers are anaesthetized to the shocks of urban life.[64] It penetrates his unconscious instead and is lost to memory until recovered, over twenty years later, by a technique of remembering Delany uses to write his book.

Delany remembers for the present, excavating political potential from the past that now calls for recognition. He stresses that while he had experienced the "libidinal saturation" of space before, this time it frightened because saturation was "not only kinesthetic but visible" (268). The sight of so many men having sex in one place "flew in the face of that whole fifties' image" of miserably isolated homosexuals: "it was the contradiction with what we 'knew' that was fearful" (268). His excitement was then, as he sees now, precipitated by the shocking apprehension of a new, and mobilizable, body politic: "whether male, female, working or middle class, the first direct sense of political power comes from the apprehension of massed bodies" (268). What was locked in private reserve is salvaged as collective memory and shared historical objective, amounting, in Benjamin's terms, to *Erfahrung*, or critically reflective experience:

> The myth said we, as isolated perverts, were only beings of desire, manifestations of the subject (yes, gone awry, turned from its true object, but for all that, even more purely subjective).
>
> But what *this* experience said was that there was a population—not of individual homosexuals, some of whom now and then encountered, or that those encounters could be human and fulfilling in their way—not of hundreds, not of thousands, but rather of millions of gay men, and that history had, actively and already, created for us whole galleries of institutions, good and bad, to accommodate our sex. (268–69)

The isolated, experiential "I" of Delany's memoirs becomes the collective "we" of gay history the moment straight urban mythology is revised by politicized memory.

The spontaneous transformation of a traumatic encounter with mass sex in the bathhouse into an *experience of gay masses* ("not of hundreds . . . but rather of millions of gay men") is a retrospective fantasy. It is framed by an anticipatory wish that "history had, actively and already, created for us" the amassing of gay front lines. What is fantastical about this fantasy is the implication that gay masses arose sui generis from bathhouse orgies, or that history is a beneficent external power that creates institutions "for us," "to accommodate our sex." What it overlooks is how the current AIDS crisis and urgent need for gay resistance sets the scene for historical recollection. "Articulating the past historically," Benjamin writes, "does not mean recognizing it 'the way it really was.' It means appropriating a memory as it flashes up in a moment of danger."[65] Awareness of catastrophe in the present "era of AIDS" (269) compels Delany to remember the past with political foresight and to elaborate a wish-image of the future:

> If I may indulge in my one piece of science fiction for this memoir, it is my firm suspicion, my conviction, and my hope that once the AIDS crisis is brought under control, the West will see a sexual revolution to make a laughing stock of any social movement that till now has borne the name. . . . Now that a significant range of people have begun to get a clearer idea of what has been possible among the varieties of human pleasure in the recent past, heterosexuals and homosexuals, females and males will insist on exploring them even further. (269–70)

Ruin

If Delany's memory of St. Marks Baths in the 1960s sparks a vision of sexual revolution in the 1980s, Indiana's allegory of gay space in the 1990s obliterates all trace of emancipatory practices. The gay bathhouse appears in *Rent Boy*'s startling climax where the eponymous hero, who goes by "Danny," narrates a trip to the Harlem Baths:

> Tell you what I did, I went up to the baths in Harlem. If you've never been to the baths in Harlem, J., I advise you to keep it that way. Once when I

> told you something that sounded like stupidly cocky and self-assured you said, Well, wait till you've had a few decades of disappointment and see how you feel about it then. It's the last thing I thought of before I passed out in one of the cubicles, which have roaches and shit and smell like bad feet and ammonia mixed with resin from crack pipes. If you've never had sex in the baths in Harlem with a guy you're not only not attracted to but find repulsive in every respect, had sex with that guy not because you want sex but because you want to finally prove to yourself that you don't exist, you don't know what disappointment is.[66]

If the gay bathhouse once choreographed a love of citizen for citizen and citizen for city, it now stages total urban devastation. "The baths in Harlem" allude to the Mount Morris Baths that, as Ira Tattelman notes, opened in the 1920s and became New York's first gathering space for gay black men and for mixing between races. In Indiana's novel, they allegorize the wreckage of every cruising space that (gay) capital has inspired.[67]

Like Baudelaire's poet, Indiana's narrator experiences big-city shock with poetic spleen. But the trauma of postindustrial New York is more jolting than that of nineteenth-century Paris, calling for a more abrasive literary form. The text is an epistolary narrative written in confessional mode by a rent boy to "J.," trick/lover in what ultimately amounts to a "Dear John" letter. A student by day, waiter by night, and rent boy after midnight, Danny is less free than the poet who prostitutes his trade on the boulevard. Though charmed by queer urban space, he is the antithesis of the baths' cruising flâneur. Hustling and cruising enjoy an intimate proximity but are hardly the same activity. Danny hustles to finance his dream of escape to the country, explaining his detour of the baths on his rounds of bars and clubs.[68] So, dependent on/addicted to the traffic, Danny abandons society outside "trade" and entertains a dangerous liaison with another rent boy.

Rent Boy allegorizes the physiognomy of a city whose urban reality is threatened above all by a radical deregulation of rents. Danny's New York is crassly, if not criminally, commercial; gaiety amounts solely to

CHAPTER 2

The City of Collective Memory

How does the city figure in narratives of memory and history forthcoming from erotic subjects whose social existence is a product of the city itself? If lesbians, gays, and queers of all sorts owe their emergence to the industrial metropolis, where they were hailed as a new "city type" in police reports and newspaper stories and, no less scandalously, in the first urban poetry (Baudelaire's *Les Fleurs du mal,* Whitman's *Leaves of Grass*), then how do they figure the city in genealogies of their own telling? How do they see themselves arising and enduring *within* urban culture but *without* the traditional means of social reproduction afforded by family, ethnicity, nationality, and religion? If the city is the space of coming out of vaguely constellated desires into a community of love that *dare not speak its name*, is this community not then susceptible to the shocks of urban development and devastation? Can social belonging be established by something as volatile as the capitalist metropolis?

Memory is possible because it is collective. An individual knows herself or himself as a being of enduring, if growing, character because she or he shares memory with others and participates in memory's collective making. Thus Maurice Halbwachs contended in *La mémoire collective*, published in Paris in the wake of World War II when memory—traumatic memory, and memory's very survival—was an urgent concern among social psychologists. Though schooled in Bergson, Halbwachs departed from the idea that memory is a matter of *durée*, the persistent recognition of images, dually facilitated by the neurophysiology and phenomenology of brain/mind. Halbwachs argued that memory is much more material than that, that it is a matter not just of consciously lived time but of socially lived space and the collective representation of that space. Older districts of foreign cities, cities we have never traveled, are able to recall us to ourselves: "indeed, the scene seems by itself to evoke [familiar impressions]—because they trigger other remembrances and the remembrances of other people."[1]

The city, for Halbwachs, is a paradigmatic image of collective memory. Relationships between individuals, and between individuals and groups, are established in relation to the things and designs of the city as part of the process of habitation.[2] The durable, inorganic materials of urban habitations generally outlive their inhabitants. The most enduring image that city dwellers possess is that of "the stones of the city" itself. When a neighborhood suffers demolition or decay, the individual inhabitant "feels that a whole part of himself is dying," whereas the group resists that assault "with all the force of its traditions" and "endeavours to hold firm or reshape itself in a district or on a street that is no longer ready-made for it but was once its own."[3] Backed by tradition, collective memory arrests progress and preserves the past through urban restoration. What tradition could this be, save one of wealth and class privilege, that Halbwachs respectfully identifies as "long time old aristocratic families and longstanding urban patriarchs"?[4]

How, then, might the city function as an image of collective memory for socially disenfranchised groups, including sexual minorities? For queers whose relationship to the world is distinctly urban, whose habitation is primarily the inner city of big cities, where wreckage and renewal are most intense, is the city not a central image and yet a most compromised one?[5] How can queer collective memory fix an image of the city when the city is stormed by redevelopment and queers cannot afford the resistance of aristocratic families and urban patriarchs?[6] How can queer city space serve collective memory where it is threatened by legal and social violence, as it is with the invading and vandalizing and endemic poverty and marginality of women-only spaces, or the raiding, razing, and closing of venues for gay men, as with New York's gay bathhouses? Finally, how does the city function as a vision of collective memory when official history and mass media dominate the universe of image production in ways that erase or deface the representation of gay city life or reconfigure that image for commercial profit?

Halbwachs's "city of collective memory" is a useful critical concept for reading experimental first-person and/or fictional narratives of queer memory, especially those narratives that struggle to articulate "Who am I?" in lieu of traditional community.[7] Histories document queer urban life with little reference to the function of the city as a motif for activating memories of an existence that is likely to be forgotten, neglected, or distorted by dominant culture. Charles Kaiser's *Gay Metropolis: The Landmark History of Gay Life in America since World War II*, for instance, documents late-twentieth-century history of gay celebrity outings in New York without investigating how city memories serve as that history's locus and focus. On the other hand, Samuel Delany's memoir, *The Motion of Light in Water: Sex and Science Fiction Writing in the East Village: 1960–1965*, represents the author's first encounters with urban homosexuality as primal scenes for which he had neither the knowledge nor language of sexual politics to comprehend what was happening. Memories of "the East Village" help recall the emergence of gay collectivity *before* the consolidation of gay community. They reinforce Delany's struggle against abandoning his past to history's dominant idea of gay life in the early 1960s as one of pathological isolation.[8]

But the usefulness of the concept is limited by its ties to establishment and tradition. Delany's city of collective memory is not Halbwachs's preserve of aristocracy and patriarchy but a terrain of defamiliarizing shocks. The St. Marks Baths, for instance, recall Delany's fearful, "heart thudding" exposure to gay mass sex.[9] Memories of cruising Central Park and the rough alleys of the meat-packing district recall the trauma of opening oneself to the embraces of strangers. Having no tradition with which to comprehend this other, *coming*, queer city, Delany suffers a nervous breakdown that only later he recognizes as a crisis of social change. Halbwachs takes our reading of this narrative only so far. We see how, by relying on memories of city spaces, Delany recovers and redeems that part of his past that is most susceptible to distortion by repression and abjection. But Halbwachs does not advance our understanding of how narrative figures the city to produce *critical countermemory.*

I have in mind three experimental narratives in which the city figures prominently, if variably, as an instigative motif of queer memory. They are Neil Bartlett's *Who Was That Man? A Present for Mr. Oscar Wilde* (1988), Eileen Myles's *Chelsea Girls* (1994), and Gail Scott's *Main Brides* (1993). Like *The Motion of Light on Water,* these narratives contest historical misrepresentations of the erotic diversity of living memory. In these texts, city memories enable their narrators to tell stories of other remembrances and remembrances of other people that challenge official history, as well as the narrators' own obscurely formed ideas of their pasts.[10] Unlike Delany, however, Bartlett, Myles, and Scott abandon the autobiographical pretense of moment-by-moment self-recall. If Delany dwells momentarily on places of past experience, he retains a chronology that locates his narrator in time (so that subjective "self-development" appears to coincide with objective "historical progress"). In contrast, Bartlett's, Myles's, and Scott's narrators strategically lose themselves in space—the space of city memory—so as to be recalled less by an (historical) idea of self than by associations between self and other(s) that city images evoke.

In Halbwachs I seek a theoretical precedent for understanding the critical function of the city in experimental narratives of queer memory. Halbwachs was first to posit that memory, though strikingly individual, is enduringly collective. He argued convincingly for the primacy of spatial images—images of group habitation, particularly city images—in narratives of collective memory. On the city as an image of *counter*memory and *other* history, however, his theorizing is preceded and surpassed by that of Walter Benjamin. In "A Berlin Chronicle" (1932), Benjamin searched the city of living memory as a site of emancipation from capitalist self-deception that, even today, has us catastrophically spellbound. He showed how memory of city objects and spaces, especially childhood memory, subverts reified reason by conjuring remembrances otherwise lost to bourgeois history. City memory displaces time-conscious autobiography by evoking discontinuous moments in space:

> Reminiscences, even extensive ones, do not always amount to an autobiography. . . . For autobiography has to do with time, with sequence and what makes up the continuous flow of life. Here, I am talking of a space, of moments and discontinuities. For even if months and years appear here, it is in the form they have at the moment of commemoration. This strange form . . . is shown not so much by the role that my own life plays here, as by that of the people closest to me in Berlin—whoever and whenever they may have been. The atmosphere of the city that is here evoked allots them only a brief, shadowy existence. They steal along its walls like beggars, appear wraithlike at windows, to vanish again, sniff at thresholds like a *genius loci.*[11]

Benjamin elaborated, if not a theory of collective memory, then a concept and practice of imaging the city for critical remembrance. This practice extends beyond "A Berlin Chronicle" to the final phase of *The Arcades Project* (1933–40) with a battery of mnemonic techniques to supplement the primary stratagem of free association. *The Arcades Project*, whose object is nineteenth-century Paris, invents a praxis of remembering that surpasses living memory, is bound up with things of the past still traceable in the present, and aims at demystifying, while conjuring, the phantasmagoria of metropolitan dream-space. I interpret these explorations of city memory as groundwork for "critical historiography."[12] My purpose is to identify techniques of figuring the city in "A Berlin Chronicle," which Benjamin highlighted for speculation, in order to foreground similar techniques in the experimental narratives of Bartlett, Myles, and Scott. From there I venture paradigmatic readings of each narrative's "city of collective memory," based on related Benjaminian concepts and practices of storytelling, collecting, and re/collecting, the calling of history to remembrance.

"A Berlin Chronicle": Memory's Queer Topography

What makes "A Berlin Chronicle" a "strange form" of autobiography is its narrative "of space, of moments and discontinuities" in place of time, chronology, and continuity. But the strange privileging of space in a "chronicle" of past experience is supplemented by other queer departures to which Benjamin drew explicit attention. For one, the faces of *the city*, not of friends or family, are remembered.[13] For another, it is the city of *childhood* memory as seen by the adult who only now begins to perceive what the child could not: the political contexts of those primal scenes of Berlin "around 1900."[14] For still another, the city of memory is a *dead* city,[15] a necropolis, haunted by specters of the German Youth Movement, including those who took their lives in despair at the outbreak of war in 1914, the Great War that would destroy a whole epoch of bourgeoning friendships and acquaintances.[16] Among lives lost was Benjamin's own youthful self, whose revolutionary and erotic stirrings were "discontinued" by the inexplicable traumas of suicide and mass slaughter.[17]

City memory recalls him to thresholds of the familiar, to the mysterious household occupation of his father's business dealings ("BC," 617–20), to the farmers' market with creatures from a premodern world.[18] He finds himself at the edge of the city he has never known—the city of the poor[19]—and experiences the shock of transgression by "crossing" the void over which the uncanny figure of the prostitute presides:

> The feeling of crossing for the first time the threshold of one's class had a part in the almost unequaled fascination of publicly accosting a whore on the street. At the beginning, however, this was a crossing of frontiers not only social but topographic, in the sense that whole networks of streets were opened up under the auspices of prostitution. . . . In great cities, there are countless places where one stands on the edge of the void; and the whores in the doorways of tenement blocks and on the less sonorous asphalt of railway platforms are like the household goddesses of the cult of nothingness. So on these erring paths the stations became my special habitat, each with its outskirts like a city: the Silesian, Stettin, Görlitz stations, and Friedrichstrasse. ("BC," 600)

His guides to this memorial city are, in the first place, domestic guardians—his mother, his nurse, his grandmother, the "household goddesses" of childhood fantasy. Later, he is guided by the errant desire of youth that the city itself seems to solicit. The Berlin of his adolescence maps a territory of sexual discoveries, which are always tentative and fleeting and *out* in public space. Against traditional, conjugal confines the urbane adventurer steals moments of love on park benches, hotel rooms, bohemian cafés. One moment recalls the erotic exhilaration with which he is spontaneously overcome when he detours aimlessly into the streets away from his obligatory attendance at a family bar mitzvah.[20] But the most arousing memory of wayward desire is recalled by the Ice Palace, where many thresholds are crossed at once. A business venture of his father's, the Ice Palace was "not only the first skating rink in Berlin, but also a thriving nightclub." Taken to see the arena, it is there before "the apparitions at the bar" that he first entertains an image of queer Berlin: "*a prostitute in a very tight-fitting white sailor's suit, who, though I was unable to exchange a word with her, determined my erotic fantasies for years to come*" ("BC," 620; my emphasis).

The city of memory harbors erotic fantasies at the thresholds of life and death, antiquity and modernity, propriety and delinquency, and transgression and prostitution. These are fantasies that possess a lonely man, the isolated, individual city dweller liberated and removed from traditions of family, religion, and race. The writing of the "Chronicle" was occasioned, moreover, by the author's state of exile. Having drafted the first notes in Berlin in January and February 1932, Benjamin composed the rest on the island of Ibiza later that year before retreating to Paris in 1933.[21] Against the specter of a Nazi-occupied homeland, he began a project of personal reclamation. But the city on which he modeled his recollection is Paris, not Berlin. It is Paris that teaches him how, as foreign alien, to relate to a "world of things" and to enter the epochal dream that reveals the "true face" of desire: "I tell myself it had to be in Paris, where the walls and quays, the asphalt surfaces, the collections and the rubbish, the railings and the squares, the arcades and the kiosks, teach a language so singular that our relations to people attain, in the solitude encompassing us in our immersion in that world of things, the depths of a sleep in which the dream image waits to show the people their true faces" ("BC," 614). If Paris, foreign capital of capitalism, arouses a desire for things that is most native to his urban character, it also allows him to see "what kind of regimen cities keep over imagination, and why the city—where people make the most ruthless demands on one another, where appointments and telephone calls, sessions and visits, flirtations and the struggle for existence grant the individual not a single moment of contemplation—indemnifies itself in memory, and why the veil it has covertly woven out of our lives shows images of people less often than those of the sites of our encounters with others or ourselves" ("BC," 614). Removed sufficiently from the all too familiar hometown, Benjamin perceives the "veil" of social relations that the city "has woven out of our lives." Further, he sees how individual fantasy is immersed in the landscape (language) of a dreaming collectivity.

Benjamin returns to memories of Berlin, not as a native but as a stranger. Estranged from the city that it has become—the anti-Semitic capital of National Socialism—and from people and places lost to traumatic processes that he has never stopped to contemplate, Benjamin cruises his haunts of old, raising the dead and traversing the ground of their and his ongoing expropriation. Fantasy and memory collaborate to produce a topography for critical, historical speculation. The motive to remember is a compulsion to see *now* what was happening, and has been happening since *then*, and to redeem a haunting sense of loss with politically awakened recognition.

"A Berlin Chronicle" is starred by a constellation of topographical topoi for imaging the city of collective memory and (in)citing countermemory. It is useful to identify these topoi for investigating the topography of queer memory.

"To Lose Oneself in a City"

To discover the city of the past one must enact "the art of straying." Benjamin personifies the art of straying as the city's most perceptive "guide." To lose oneself in a city must be differentiated from not finding one's the use of the *I* solicits a subjective mode of speculation, subverting the objectivity of formal, philosophical inquiry ("BC," 603–04). On the other hand, the sovereign subject of autobiography is subverted; the *I* of Benjamin's chronicle signifies not a conscious will to remember but a projection of unconscious memory, memory involuntarily solicited by the association of things that are proximal in space and/or linguistically related to names of places and streets. In any case, the *I* of narrative memory is as much subject *to* as subject *of* the haunts of the city.

City memory is haunted by uncanny intersections of love and death. Benjamin figures this uncanny intersection in a space that is literally called "the Meeting House." The most "harrowing experience" of his past takes place here, where he stumbles across the double suicide of his friend and comrade, the young poet Fritz Heinle, and Heinle's fiancée, fellow revolutionary Rika Seligson. No other scene in the chronicle is recollected in such detail, as if by constructing a physiognomy of the space, Benjamin might give face to unbearable and inexplicable loss. Of the dead who haunt Benjamin's living memory, it is Heinle's ghost that will not be put to rest despite Benjamin's efforts to master melancholia through prosopopoeia.[31] Yet precisely by dwelling on the haunts of the Meeting House, Benjamin is prompted to revise his memory of history.[32]

Like "A Berlin Chronicle," *Who Was That Man?* is driven by the question "Who am I?" which is really "Whom do I haunt?" On moving to London from a small provincial town, Bartlett experiences his "coming out" as a sense of forging a "*connection*" with other gay men and their gay city. He senses, uncannily, that this connection has been prepared for him in advance, not by his contemporaries but by the first generation of "gay" men to come out in the era of Oscar Wilde.[33] Thus the man who comes out and into his own in the city of the 1980s is not original. He becomes who he is by making himself over in the character of a species of urban dweller that came into existence in the late 1800s. He owes his existential becoming to a historic production. To know himself fully implies knowing the story of his urban ancestry, and of evolving his sense of connection: "*to understand that I am connected with other men's lives, men living in London with me.* ***Or with other dead Londoners. That's the story***" (xx;

emphasis in original). Finding an image of his origins calls for prosopopoeia, in this case the art of giving face to an unknown progenitor. The face that most readily suggests itself is that of Wilde himself, much photographed by the scandal press.[34] But the *true* face of the community of nineteenth-century London has been obscured by the mass media that catered to the moral outrage of the bourgeoisie. Defaced by social and legal violence, the Wilde of official history cannot fairly represent the complexity of the character or community he cultivated. So the question "Who *was* that man?" haunts Bartlett into returning to the scene, to unofficial sources, to collect contrary "evidence" and construct from the scraps of history a physiognomy of "gay" society. His inquiry leads him to the haunts of the dead as cited in the most disparate literatures of the age.

Chelsea Girls is another narrative quest for the answer to "Who am I?" more precisely and perversely articulated as "Which sex am I?" in disturbing scenes from past lives. The primary space of recollection is Eileen's apartment, the dwelling of the present and the site of narrative production. The specters of memory that haunt that space are primal acquaintances of girlhood: the dead father (to whom the collection is dedicated), but *collectively* more important, the dead and/or lost girlfriends and lovers from other places and periods with whom she explored her sexuality. At the same time, the memory of each girl's as-yet-untold story is recalled "on location" in various haunts of girlhood and young adulthood, before and after Eileen moved to the city. Since no one knew what they were doing then, though everyone who is remembered is a participant, the memory of still-troubling events and the story of their happening relies heavily on the details of setting. Thus, like Benjamin, Eileen must lose herself in the haunts of the past, where memory serves as theater of reenactment and delayed recognition.

The narrator of *Main Brides* retreats to her favorite haunt on the Main, where she is beset by flashbacks to the gruesome scene that she stumbled across at dawn and associated scenes of the city's past where women were murdered or massacred. The women of these scenes are real, but except for the "Montreal Massacre," they are unmarked by public memorial.[35] In an effort to escape haunting memories, she drinks and out. The story of "Nanette" begins with her "remembering" a woman who, "on the street where she grew up," was known to "her Greek and Portuguese neighbours" as "The Flyer" after her "habit of dangling dangerously from cornices, or upper apertures" (11). Building on these fragments and from details of the appearance of the woman in the bar, Lydia fabricates the story of a woman's flight from an abusive and restrictive home to the streets where she flirts dangerously with a pimp and a drug habit. The other stories—"Main Bride Remembers Halifax," "Dis-May," "Canadian Girls," "Z, Who Lives Over the Sign Shop," "Donkey Riding," and "Night Music"—also start with remembering, taking signs from the bar and street as cues for further fabrication. They form a collection of fictionalized memories of women who stand out against metropolitan history as survivors and high flyers of the streets.

"Our Deepest Self in Shock"

While memory attaches itself to things of everyday experience, it is "to the immolation of our deepest self in shock that our memory owes its most indelible images" ("BC," 633). Not every fragment of memory that constitutes "A Berlin Chronicle" is shocking, but every scene of trauma is remembered with "sudden illumination" where self appears dissociated from self.[42] The immolated, shocked self is projected into space, dreamily intact. Cued by details of architecture, memory engages fantasy to stage scenes of past trauma. Waking, everyday consciousness does not entail the kind of experience that arouses flashbacks of delayed recognition. Flashbacks are generated by shock experience. Memory "transfixes" images of space where shock experiences occurred and dissociated selves "are always standing at the center" (633).

The shock experiences of "A Berlin Chronicle" are related to traumatic encounters with love, sex, and death—primal scenes of childhood and adolescence. But they also relate to urban trauma. The shock of "publicly accosting a whore on the street" (600), mixed with fascination and dread, compares with Delany's "heart thudding" exposure to public sex in a bathhouse. The bourgeois appropriation of bohemian cafés where Benjamin had communed with colleagues and cocottes is figured as a devastating conquest of history (608). Though no one scene captures this shock, Benjamin's "physiology of coffeehouses" traces the destruction of an "aura" (606–09). In "On Some Motifs in Baudelaire," Benjamin elaborates his image of urban trauma into a theory concerning the critical, historiographical function of poetic representation. "One wonders," he writes, "how lyric poetry can be grounded in experience [*Erfahrung*] for which exposure to shock [*Chockerlebnis*] has become the norm?"[43] The figures that haunt *Spleen de Paris* and *Tableaux Parisiens*, including the poet, who looks aghast on such specters of devastated humanity as "Les Sept Vieillards" and "Les Petites Vieilles," express the inarticulate shock to the human sensorium of foundational changes wrought by modernization.

If shock experience is the standard experience of the big-city dweller, then cognition is limited to a highly defensive adaptation of consciousness, which focuses on the moment with routine application of perception and intellection (*Erlebnis*). Psychic mechanisms are deployed to deflect shock; hence we have little sense of the shock of urbanization, except as obsessive symptoms of trauma. Benjamin finds motifs in Baudelaire that evidence the shock felt by the destruction of old neighborhoods and mass eviction of the poor, the accentuation of class division and social disintegration, the commodification and profanation of life's most sacrosanct ideals, the automatism of human industry, and the daily barrage of commercial traffic. Baudelaire articulates a memory of shock experience for collective, critical reflection (*Erfahrung*). Poetic representation functions like a dream, where consciousness, distracted from a defensive routine, is receptive to shock and can express it in figures of the crowd, the prostitute and derelict little old men and women.

The "Evidence" collected in *Who Was That Man?* disinters a fragment of nineteenth-century London that catches the author unprepared and disturbs the image he is constructing of historic gay community. "One of the strangest police reports," the fragment describes a scene of deplorable squalor, overcrowding, and sexual exposure among the poor. Taken out of judicial context, which interprets the "overcrowding among the poor only as a sign of their indiscriminate and criminal indecency" (97) and placed in his constellation of gay London, this "extract" figures for Bartlett as *counter*evidence to the more frequently reported incidents of sex between men that occur in bourgeois interiors. Realizing how "the overcrowded bedrooms of central London were the site of frequent and casual homosexual contact," he finds that his "history of gay London is altered" (97).

"This odd detail" shocks Bartlett into seeing that "we know little of ordinary lives in this period, lives lived in stinking and overcrowded rather than public or fashionably furnished rooms" (97). The effect it has on collective memory is one that "makes us think again" (97). Though the scene of squalor does not emerge from his own experience, Bartlett regards it "as evidence of something that has to do with his own life" (97) and proceeds to rethink the present city scene. What he sees is just as disturbing: that for all the laws that have been broken "since 1885," gay men's coming out has not changed the world (215–16). Winning the right to certain designated, night town pleasures, "we regularly watch ourselves turn into the most improbable of creatures, transform back again, then set off to the office or the dole office just like everybody else" (216). Perceiving the shallowness of his community, he throws his "deepest self in shock."

Bartlett concludes his research into history only to arrive at the question "Why do we have such a short memory of our own culture?" The question raises the specter of the current AIDS "disaster" (220). This disaster, which he remembers only now, is precisely what prompts his turn to history in the first place, seeking images for an enduring collective memory against a fear of extinction. He also desires to save face against the shock of discovering that, like Wilde and his milieu, the contemporary gay community appears to lack political integrity. The shattered photograph of Wilde that closes the last chapter of "History" bears ironic testament to the unsettling task of recollecting the present.

For *Chelsea Girls*, shock experience is the norm. Every chapter of girlhood and young adulthood is starred with trauma—the everyday trauma of big-city life and the trauma of growing up female in late-twentieth-century America—which life in Manhattan streets never allows Myles to forget. In reporting scenes still resonant with shock, where the author appears at the center, *Chelsea Girls* resembles "A Berlin Chronicle." The most "indelible images" are those that throw into "sudden illumination" the site of her immolated self. "Popponesset," for instance, reenacts the scene of her gang rape, simulating with terrible poignancy the layout of the room, the mocking gestures, the assaulting body parts, and her self-loathing (189). Eileen remembers in the context of everyone else's forgetting or denying, including her girlfriend Louise who "explained that she thought she liked it" (190) and tried to reassure her that the perpetrator "doesn't even remember" (191). The whole scene is put before her, revealing in a flash the shocking complicity of an age. For *Chelsea Girls* shock experience is collective. Eileen shares the trauma of persons she remembers, including the self-immolation of her aunt and uncle—the "white trash" side of her family that the other side trashes in high-handed disgust—and the anguish of her girlfriend whose father, though a Holocaust survivor, denies her existence as a lesbian and refuses her patrimony.

Myles does not simply mount shock upon shock but remembers experiences of increasing traumatic intensity. The opening story recalls an encounter with the law, where, in a pathetic attempt to save her drunken girlfriend from police harassment, Eileen leaps on a cop with a gun and almost ends up in jail. There follows the recollection of a number of dangerous scenes with "Chris," including one in which Chris throws herself in the Hudson and nearly drags Eileen after her. Eileen tells this last story twice, first in "Epilogue," in conversation with a reliable interlocutor, and then in "Jealousy," where she recounts the details directly. In the wake of shock, Eileen is able to discern destructive from delinquent behavior and deliver herself from an addiction to confusing the two.

Main Brides deploys poetry and fantasy to create a cast of mind most receptive to shock. In this respect Scott's portraits of Montreal resemble Baudelaire's motifs of Paris. Into the space of her daydream, she projects faces of seven women and traces their spectral appearances around town. Yet, unlike "Les Sept Vieillards," whose wretched physiognomies allow us to see the shocking human cost of modernization, the Main's brides present visions of women who make of modernity what they can—despite what the metropolis hurls at them. Shock experience in *Main Brides* is mainly *women's* experience of violence. Lydia's stories are full of images of harassment, abuse, and assault—experiences that women endure as part of daily life. But when murder threatens to become a standard experience, Lydia recoils in panic. Against the memory of the murdered girl she stumbled upon that morning, she retreats into dream. The portraits, however, gather boldness in proportion to her drinking. This gives her sufficient fortitude to recall the murder scene intermittently, until she can visualize it in detail with critical regard, noting all the things that conspire to hurt women: the girl's physical fragility, the subtle cover-up by police who would protect the public from alarm, the irresponsibility of the press who aim simply to report another statistic, and the mother who feigns care in her only opportunity to partake in a drama of public significance (200). Except for May of "Dis-May," the portraits present defiant, daredevil women who elude fear and hazard the streets. Together they form an image of countershock.

"A New and Disturbing Articulation"

Dwelling in the present as he chronicles the past, the writer, Benjamin observes, "cuts another section through the sequence of his experiences" wherein he "detects . . . a new and disturbing articulation" ("BC," 599). It is not simply that the naïveté of childhood collides with adult hindsight in a corrective revision of the past. In recalling the landscape of the past into view of the city now before him, he excavates the present and "cuts into the sequence." Today's dilapidated West End, haunted by ghosts of war and specters of poverty and prostitution, is seen in constellation with the sheltered bourgeois landscape of childhood and youth. Memory of the corpses of comrades cohabits the Meeting House with that of their living selves, organizing insurrection in a once prosperous, now derelict neighborhood. Experienced *in sequence* history appears progressive making us blind to the catastrophe of political economy evidenced by human and urban devastation. What is remembered *in sequence* reassures our desire for continuity in a changing world. But memories of different epochs remembered simultaneously *in opposition* generate a sense of "disturbing" discontinuity. Like "clashing islands" ("BC," 606), opposing images come together in a moment of latent recognition—the illumination that crowns his memory of the Meeting House, demystifying the liberal optimism of his revolutionary youth:

> Today this point in space where we happened to open our Meeting House is for me the consummate pictorial expression of the point in history occupied by the last true elite of bourgeois Berlin. It was as close to the abyss of the Great War as the Meeting House was to the steep slope of the Landwehr Canal; it was as sharply divided from proletarian youth as the houses of this *rentiers'* district were from those of Moabit; and the houses were the last of their line, just as the occupants of those apartments were the last who could appease the clamorous shades of the dispossessed with philanthropic ceremonies. In spite—or because—of this, there is no doubt that the city of Berlin was never again to impinge so forcefully on my existence as it did in that epoch when we believed we could leave it untouched, only improving its schools, only breaking the inhumanity of their inmates' parents, only making a place in it for the words of Hölderlin or George. It was a final heroic attempt to change the attitudes of people without changing their circumstances. ("BC," 605)

Excavating moments of experience and collecting them in imaginary assemblages where scenes from one's remote and recent pasts collide in highly charged emotional and political antitheses, Benjamin produces for history its countermemory. "History," he conjectures, "is not simply a science, but also and not least a form of remembrance. What science has 'determined,' remembrance can modify" (AP 471 [N8, 1]). He develops this technique into a method of dialectical imaging, which structures the nonnarrative montage of *The Arcades Project*.[44] But at this earlier stage of writing, poised between looking back at Berlin and going forward into exile, Benjamin retains some crucial elements of narrative. Chief among them is the narrative subject who strolls the city of memory, excavates and collects fragments of past life, and remembers shock experience with latent, political recognition. Benjamin's chronicler raises images of collective countermemory, which, failing to plot a chronology of progress, reconstellate the space of history.

The experimental narratives of Bartlett, Myles, and Scott combine chronicle and constellation. Each narrative articulates this combination differently, but all three construct a subject who cruises the space of memory, collects the trash of history, and with latent, political awareness recollects her present place in metropolitan history. It follows that a paradigmatic reading of these narratives is not only possible but also critical to understanding the historiographical intervention made by the city of queer collective memory. Moreover, the disclosure of narrative paradigms enables comparative readings of queer memory. What different strategies of cruising, collecting, and recollecting are deployed depending on the gender, class, and nation, that is, the overdetermined location, of narrative subject? What situational differences affect the story of calling history to remembrance?

The Wilde Side of London

Bartlett sets himself the task of telling the story of his coming out in the context of the larger story of history, which begins in late-nineteenth-century London with the first public appearances of homosexual men and climaxes with the notorious "outing" of Oscar Wilde. The existence of gay subculture or a network of gay relations is evidenced by Wilde and the entourage of witnesses and accomplices put in the spotlight by his trial. But the history of *that man* and the discretionary disappearance of homosexuality from public life is told from the perspective of the enemy, the victors and proprietors of culture. Wilde's case exemplifies Benjamin's famous thesis that "There is no document of culture which is not at the same time a document of barbarism."[45] To tell the story of collective coming out, the storyteller must write history against the grain.

For Bartlett, the punitive outing of Wilde as a spectacle of "gross indecency" diminishes, obscures, and defaces the complex urban network of homosexual communing that preceded Wilde and that Wilde helped to cultivate.[46] Since he has none of the traditional storyteller's resources—

either experiences of his own (of the nineteenth century) or remembrances of others to pass down—he resorts to finding sources still extant in print, including those of the scandal press. Adapting the storyteller's ancient art to the modern age of information, he devises techniques of collecting and recollecting. His route is less disciplined than dilatory, guided by a "counter-disciplinary" desire to establish a "belonging" that "extends into the past."[47]

Cruising

To tell history's story Bartlett begins by acquainting himself with the erotic terrain of late-nineteenth-century London. He extends his practice of cruising today's city to cruising city archives, forging continuity between living in the present and researching the past:

> *So I began to try and learn my own history, and did it in exactly the same way as I learnt my way around contemporary London. You hear a man talking about a pub, or you read an address in a paper, or sometimes you simply follow someone you fancy and discover a whole new part of town. You know your knowledge is quite arbitrary. Your knowledge of the city is shaped by the way ex-lovers introduce you to their friends, by the way you hear someone's story simply because he happened to be in the same place as you at the same time. And eventually you build up a network of places and people. . . . Gradually I began to learn the geography and language of 1895 or 1881, to redraw my map of the city, to recognize certain signs, certain words. I began to see this other London as the beginning of my own story.* (xxi; emphasis in original)

Cruising overcomes the disciplinary distance and existential gap that separate city dwellers from historic community. Getting to know "this other London" in the way he came to know contemporary London, he perceives history as collective memory. Just as Benjamin allowed himself to be guided around historic Berlin by "the art of straying," Bartlett yields to an impulsive desire for "*arbitrary*" knowledge. Possessed by a city of which he has no living memory, his aim is more perverse than Benjamin's but less estranged than that of *The Arcades Project*, which images

the pleasures of consumption" (186). Morning thus dawns without (gay) awakening and *that,* Benjamin would contend, is precisely the catastrophe of (gay) history.

The Haunts of Chelsea Girls

In the early 1980s, around the time that Bartlett moved to London, Eileen moved to Manhattan. Like him, she experiences an intense, sensual, connection with the city. A passage from the last chapter of *Chelsea Girls* (titled "Chelsea Girls") evokes West Village atmosphere: "Streets were so dark that year and it was really the hottest summer. I should have been drinking vodka all night, but I was drinking beer. The smell of bread from the bakery on Carmine Street spilled over to Bleecker as we were walking by. The sidewalks looked like it had momentarily rained. Proprietors trying to cool their sidewalks off and oil in the gutters that made those teeny rainbows. Urban nothing—I liked it so much. Pizza shops, all those dangerous boys roaming the streets who were always trying to break into women's bars. . . . The summer of three dyke bars in the West Village. We were rich" (264–65).[53]

The "urban nothing" of the West Village is nothing like the gaiety of London's West End. The richness of three precariously situated dyke bars cannot compare to the wealth of gay attractions on The Strand. Strolling the gutters, alert to men's ever-threatening violence, Eileen enjoys the delights of a pauper. She savors the rainbows and aromas free of charge. By contrast, Bartlett's cruising grounds demarcate male-only territory where pleasure beckons the moneyed classes. An aura of "historicality" encapsulates his stroll down Villiers Street with the contentedness that established capital affords. "Urban nothing" does not conjure ideas of historic lesbian Manhattan.[54] It only offers solace for the loner who feels alienated from all Culture. Though she grew up in a lower-middle-class family from the Boston suburbs, Eileen feels most connected to big-city trash:

> piles of
> trash. Impersonal

street is a lover
to me.[55]

This is because (as her stories testify) as a young woman coming into her sexuality, she was repeatedly "trashed" by guardians of the all-American ideal.

A city poet, Eileen collects junk from the streets in the tradition of making *trouvailles*, which began with dada and evolved into Joseph Cornell's boxes and Mina Loy's Bowery poems and collages. Eileen associates herself most closely with James Schuyler, one of the "leading first-generation New York School poets," whose poetry is remembered for its quotidian "chronicle of days" and "unflinching portrayal of homosexuality."[56] She meets Schuyler in 1979 just as he is moving to the Chelsea, where he lived until his death and which on occasion is the subject of his verse:

This old hotel is
well built: if
you hold your breath and make a wish you'll meet Virgil
Thompson in the elevator
or a member of a punk rock band.[57]

In Schuyler, Eileen finds a model for using the recent and past refuse of everyday life as a medium of recollection.[58] She also senses in him a kindred dereliction that draws out her abject eroticism. Partly because Schuyler dwells here, the dilapidated hotel makes her feel at home. She is thus ecstatic when a woman she picks up in a bar points the taxi in the hotel's direction: "We were going up Eighth Avenue in a cab. You know where we were going? We were going to the Chelsea Hotel. I loved the moment when Mary said we should go to a hotel. She kind of snickered like a dirty girl. . . . Because of my job with Jimmy Schuyler I was very familiar with the place, its smells and sounds and the degree of dilapidation, the ugly art in the lobby that wasn't distractingly exotic or worthy of note at all. It was normal. It was like fucking at home" (268–69).

In the Chelsea, Eileen abandons herself to the vagrancies of her desire, free of domestic anxieties and buoyed by the hotel's wanton familiarity. Here she recognizes her need to have a room of her own. It is thus not until now, in the last chapter, that she points to the space in the future from where the entire narrative of *Chelsea Girls* is told: "Chris used to live here. For a couple of years. There's a character now called Eileen's apartment and perhaps she remembers everything I don't" (267). The first chapter, "Bath, Maine," recalls "three years ago" (12) when she was "living with [her] ex-girlfriend [Chris] and her new girlfriend, and *her* girlfriend" in an emotionally impossible and dangerous situation: "I could be writing this from a jail cell" (11). She, in fact, is writing three years hence from Eileen's apartment, which having been vacated by Chris, affords sexual freedom and freedom to reflect. With few possessions, the apartment has an ambience made of "floors of old wood," "a tree outside her window," and enough late afternoon light "to illuminate my place." After two years of residence, space becomes place. The apartment acquires sufficient "character" to recall memories of what she, her "self," has forgotten.

The narrative shift from hotel to apartment is a critical passage in Eileen's spatial configuration of memory. The historical connection that the Chelsea inspires is foundational to her connection to her own unremembered past. *Now*, in the space of the present—in the combined aura of apartment, hotel, and three dyke bars—is when and where they come back to her. Hence, all the girls of memory are *Chelsea* girls.[59] As Chelsea girls they recall figures of erotic rebelliousness from obscure memories of sexual victimization.

Cruising

The cruising scene of the last chapter is a *mise-en-abyme* where the memory of space solicits the memory of desire and desire's longed-for deliriums. Here Eileen and Mary cruise each other over a hot summer's night, moving from dyke bar to dyke bar and taking in the details of each other's situation before making a proposition and arriving at the Chelsea. After fucking with abandon, they enjoy a postorgasmic embrace until Eileen has to leave to attend to Schuyler two floors below. Charmed by her situation, Jimmy coaxes her delinquent independence. The scene sets the scenography, or mind-set, for Eileen's remembering all those other girls—girlfriends and love—with whom she shared sexual (mis) adventures.

Some girls are remembered from her Boston childhood and young adulthood; others, from New York's urbane dyke scene. She remembers them with sympathy and with latent excitement for their daring against all odds. It is not narcissistic hubris that moves her so much as an identification with the victims of history, her gaze falling less (if at all) on their beauty than on their ugly clash with sexual conformity. Tracing the details of each girl's disposition (whether she is a reckless junkie, a survivor of gang rape, an ambivalently married avant-garde poet, or a crudè working-class schoolgirl), Eileen brings into scope the cultural landscape of her sexual (un)becoming.

Collecting

A critical component of remembering is collecting. What Eileen's memory collects is the trash of history, along with the traumatic memory of being trashed by history. Eileen's apartment contains no treasures that assert the individuality of her taste or worth. But it houses memories that Eileen forgets or might forget if she is not vigilant. These are memories of "stray" women whom she has let in for a night and girls of long ago whom she befriended in the early stages of her sexual self-discovery. They are nobodies, not to be found in the *Who's Who of America.* Knowing that as women and/or dykes they count for nothing in the history of greater America, Eileen collects their memories against oblivion—as if her own life depended upon it.[60] The chapter "Mary Dolan: A History" makes this clear. Her "best friend from fifth grade until she graduated from college" (171), Mary spans a substantial period of Eileen's past and is her primary link to the world outside her home. It is with Mary that Eileen first discovers her erotic proclivities and in whose gaze she looks to see who she, Eileen, "really" is, a speculative process that continues through the formative years of their schoolgirl romance and well after

Mary abandons Eileen for a conventional career of nursing, marriage, and mothering.

Re/collecting

For Eileen, collecting further entails recollecting. Her memory of girls being trashed is not directly accessible. She remembers girls by remembering things that were sensually and emotionally close to them and by narrating a thread of association that invokes memory involuntarily.[61] These are the material things—commodities—of everyday life, primarily music and clothes whose brief but trendsetting popularity locates memory in the history of mass culture. The chapter "Madras," for example, begins with colorful, if superficial, memories associated with the fashion of wearing Madras shirts during a turbulent period of Eileen's adolescence. The shirt figures as a nexus of phantasmagoric memories whose entanglements she threads metonymically from thing to thing, thing to person, and person to event, until a detailed pattern of 1960s youth culture emerges. Out of the pattern appears Tootsie, a girlfriend with a car and a reputation for being wild. Tootsie figures as the central character in memory's reenactment of a shock experience. The scene recalls the two girls in Tootsie's car, with Tootsie at the wheel, Eileen in the back seat, each accompanied by a male stranger that they picked up along the way, and all are drunk. Tootsie drives into the woods and hits a deer and kills it. The scene shifts abruptly to Tootsie's confrontation with her father, who is cruel and abusive.[62] Having arrived at the climax of Tootsie's story, Eileen's memory fades into vague traces of Tootsie's decline into drug addiction and gradual self-destruction.

The chapter "Popponesset" similarly weaves its way through memory. Memory's free association recalls Eileen to the scene of her gang rape by male strangers, acquaintances of girlfriends whom she joins on vacation. Against her girlfriend's disavowal of rape and her own confusion (she passed out drunk while it was happening), Eileen sees *now* what she could not see *then*, that she had indeed been raped, that by being a "black out drinker" (108) she had opened herself to rape, and most critically, that the culture to which she struggled to belong condoned the "trashing" (190) of unclaimed women by propertied men ("good looking suburban guys . . . who all owned cars" [190]).

Recollecting things entails their interpretation. For Eileen, interpretation is part of the act of reliving past experience; it is presented in a flash of recognition, not in explanatory metanarrative. "Toys Я Us," for example, relates a moment in the life of Sarah, an ex-girlfriend, another girl who is trashed by society. But this trashing reverberates allegorically. Sarah "was currently battling her seventy-year-old father who treated her like a taxi or simply one of a chain of female ears and hands and arms that served his needs" (145). Her father "had been in a concentration camp, Auschwitz" (145), and yet he refuses to understand Sarah's need to be housed securely by her family: "It was clear to Yanik that Sarah was a lesbian, though the only way he acknowledged her difference was his financial unwillingness to buy her a house" (146). Treated like a thing and dispossessed of her patrimony, Sarah is expected to help Yanik buy a birthday gift for his grandson and join the party at her sister's expensive suburban home, paid for by her father. Eileen accompanies Sarah as her unacknowledged partner, regarded as a tagalong by the other, to Toys Я Us. There, in this megaspace of mass consumption, she sees with sudden illumination the ironic historical conjunction between fascism's and capitalism's dehumanization: "We walked down a long hall with our numbers. It was then that I thought about a century that could exterminate millions of people and then create such huge dehumanizing toy stores that would both serve and frustrate the survivors of those same camps. It seemed like a single impulse to me. I almost had to laugh as we walked down a brightly painted concrete hall, earnestly holding our number hoping our scooter would come up" (147).

"Toys Я Us" appears midway in Myles's narrative recollections, where it ends with a parable. Returning to Manhattan, Eileen and Sarah "felt sick" and wanted desperately to console themselves with "heroin" and "whiskey" (152). What awaits them is no opium dream but the stark and gritty reality of the East Village. Struck by its dinginess, after so much abundance, the girls soberly see their way "home" to the unassigned "lot on 7th between C & D," where Sarah parks her car, and on foot to "her street, 9th" where they "spend the night" (152).[63] The girls themselves figure in an allegory of the wake of the city. Framed in melancholy urban space, their memory is yanked out of suburban complacency and awakened into history's appalling dialectics.

Flights of Memory on the Main

Like *Who Was That Man?* and *Chelsea Girls,* Scott's *Main Brides* performs narrative, drawing attention to the narrative act itself. The act is a composite one of recollecting, involving memory, history, and fantasy. The narrator is a fictional persona, though she figures predominantly as the subject and object of a gaze—a focalizing point from which the universe of the Main is seen and to whom this world looks back in turn.[64] The gaze onto the boulevard projects lesbian desire. The look back is not one of reciprocation; it is the gaze of the other, coming from nowhere in particular, a mix of objectification and abjection, threatening to reduce the subject to "a pair of eyes," or worse, to a "thing." Whereas Bartlett and Myles allow their narrators an asylum from the world outside their recollection, Scott exposes hers to all the vulgarities and brutalities of the street that regularly intrude on her thinking. Storytelling places Lydia so precariously off guard that she is startled by the chaos of the heckling crowd.

Lydia tells her tales of coming out in the big city, though they are not her tales per se. Her narrative enters so profoundly the reminiscences and the dreams of other women of other times that it might best be described as "flights of memory." Only gradually does she emerge as a character at the scene of the present. The opening scene is a derelict, crowded bar on the Main, where Lydia, sitting at a table beside the window and consuming the ambience along with the alcohol, watches the sunset over the city. She finds her way there, we discover later, after wandering in shock since morning. The belatedness of our discovery, through the detours of many stories, makes it seem that she comes to the present from afar. Her catching up to the present, and the merging of fantasy and memory with exterior reality, is part of her story of coming out.

Coming out, for Lydia, entails spacing out. The reality of urban violence, especially violence against women, is too brutal and too obscene to allow her mobility and passage without a tremendous effort of imagination. Her present state of mind, split between dreaming and waking, gradually assimilates the horror of the morning and throws it onto the city as an image for critically distanced regard. Walking through a park at dawn, she stumbles across the corpse of a young woman. In shock she wanders the neighborhood until sunset, when she retreats to the bar on the Main and spends the rest of the night "composing" herself in drunken reverie. The scene comes back to her in partial flashbacks—a lumpy blanket and a girl's naked knee, veiled fragments of screen memory. Hours later, she can fully recollect the murder site. Aided by drugs (wine, beer, caffeine, nicotine) and the atmosphere of the bar (smoky, funky, heady with aromas of food, sex, crime), she opens herself to the city and begins to drift. Gazing and absorbing distractedly, she is able to "create a state of somnambulism preferable to drunkenness . . . in which there's incredible ease of movement regarding all whims unconnected to signs of what's-to-be-forgotten" (33).

Spacing out in *Main Brides* is a more radical act of fiction and fantasy than it is in the narrative productions of *Who Was That Man?* and *Chelsea Girls*. Lydia's state of mind is one of "'deliquescence'" (208) or a "kind of like blacking out. . . . 'like dissolving into essence,' she thinks . . . 'An essence, escaping into air. Making love to the city. Tasting, sucking, smelling'" (199).[65] Lydia "enters a spell. Until all she sees is the exterior of things" (99). Bartlett's narrator and Myles's Eileen retreat to various interiors (the British Library, the Pleasure Dome, the Chelsea Hotel, Eileen's apartment) whereas Scott's narrator turns her gaze outdoors, intending her "somnambulism" to "permit enlargement of exterior perception without interior disturbance" (100). She believes that the exteriorization of her senses opens her to realities other than those that trouble her inwardly and obsessively, *dis*pelling specters of urban terror: "exterior equals real" (99). The fine balance that she struggles to achieve between intoxication and perception requires a hyperwakefulness, "as if the eyelids had atrophied, letting in an overdose of impressions" (99).

Moreover, Lydia "loves to think architecturally":

> Different ways of light on pediments in different parts of town. In the better French parts, the gracious greystones, façades all symmetrical, yet

has never been made safe since the nineteenth century when women migrated en masse in search of economic and sexual independence.[70] As a final setting, it offers "Main Bride," a vantage point for recollection that is in keeping with Benjamin's view of history, namely, that "the 'state of emergency' in which we live is not the exception but the rule."[71]

Re/collecting

The final act of *Main Brides* is a complex performance. The present is "closing time," when the narrator must collect herself and prepare to leave the bar. To do so, she re/collects the tropes of previous stories to compose "Night Music," the collective last portrait of the city. One of these tropes is a "walking woman," who could be any of the brides or the Main Bride herself. Another is a male stalker, whose apparition looms repeatedly in "Canadian Girls" and "Dis-May." The object of recollection is itself a performance, a tango, choreographed and danced by a trio who explore the delinquent deliquescence of a lesbian love triangle. The voice of the lead performer, Cello, is now heard over the bar's radio, announcing the next song—a tango—recalling Lydia to the earlier scene.

Memory, once again, gives way to fantasy. The studio's "deliquescent tango" (227) evokes a dream tango on the Main, choreographed by the very intoxicated Lydia. Into the dream enters the walking woman, who as Lydia prepares to do, heads out into the city late at night in an effort to exhaust her loneliness and despair. She paces a rectangular pattern of side streets running parallel and perpendicular to the Main, and repeats it twice. Her lead is followed closely by a stalker. When the stalker overtakes her and barges up the stairs to the studio, Lydia rouses to her worst fear. Terror and desire collide at the climax of her dream from which she awakens, inside women's space. The stalker is met by Cello, who in ready self-defense "takes something gleaming from her boot" and "kick[s] back her chair" (230). With this flash of insight Lydia kicks back her chair as she gets up to leave the bar.

The final act is territorial: the walking woman paces out her space in the city, the artist leaps to repel the invader from her studio, the brides on the roofs shake their spears, and Lydia is incited to *take back the night.*

In the end, spacing out mobilizes Scott's narrator into action with a reflex of collaboration. Collecting her portraits of the Main, Lydia is able to reconstellate the reified space of the city and to place herself as an actor on the stage of present history. That she must draw so heavily on fantasy to produce collective memory testifies to the isolation of the modern storyteller and the imagination required to overcome the geography of women's fear. Against the memory of the Montreal Massacre, the ongoing history of women's impoverishment and endangerment, she who dares forge a story of coming out in the city must deploy a battery of fictional devices. At the same time, she remembers history in "the tradition of the oppressed," never forgetting where she, and her sex, are coming from.[72]

CHAPTER 3

Queer Passages in *Gai Paris*; or, Flâneries through the Paradoxes of History

If London, Manhattan, and Montreal can be reclaimed for queer collective memory by a peripatetics of cruising, what prospective queer encounters are posed by *gai Paris*? Site of political, industrial, and surrealist revolution, Paris is modernity's exemplary dream city. Parisian cafés and cabarets, boulevards and bohemias have paid host to a century of erotic refugees and tourists, including such queer city lovers and English language writers as Oscar Wilde, Djuna Barnes, John Glassco, and Edmund White. Home of the illustrious Passages, Paris is the birthplace of the flâneur, the archetypal urban wanderer. If cruising is a distinctively queer spatial practice and Paris is the flâneur's historic terrain, what perceptions of the city might result when such a practice occurs in such a space? At the turn of the last millennium two literary experiments appeared that fuse yesterday's flâneur and today's cruising subject in a queer characterization of the late metropolitan era: Gail Scott's *My Paris* (1999) and Edmund White's *The Flâneur* (2001). How does Benjamin inform these experiments, and, vice versa, how do these experiments adapt Benjamin to meet the challenge of writing the postrevolutionary city of late capitalism?

By all accounts "the flâneur" originated in the physiognomies of early-nineteenth-century Paris. Today the figure is synonymous with the constellations of motifs that comprise Benjamin's "The Flâneur."[1] Like the original, Benjamin's flâneur is a literary practice, production, and performance. A physiognomy (a city type) and physiognomist, his aloof gaze is lured by the crowd and its intoxicating habitat, the arcade. For Benjamin the flâneur serves as a device of "seeing" (and citing) the metropolitan space of history. He models his device on the peripatetic subject of Balzac's novellas, Baudelaire's prose poems, Proust's rambling sentences, and Aragon's impressionistic narratives. In "Paris Diary" (1930), for instance, he imitates and modifies, as he reflects upon, Proust's method of flânerie:

> As I walked along, my thoughts became all jumbled up as in a kaleidoscope—a new constellation at every step. Old elements disappeared, and unknown ones came stumbling up—figures of all shapes and sizes. If one remained, it was called a "sentence." And among thousands of possible ones, I found this one, for which I had been waiting for many years—the sentence that wholly defined the miracle that the Madeleine—not the Proustian madeleine, but the real one—had been from the first moment I saw it: in winter the Madeleine is a great furnace that warms the rue Royale with its shadow.[2]

Later, in "Hashish in Marseilles" (1932), Benjamin impersonates the surrealist flâneur, mixing narcotics with sleep-walking as a recipe for heightened perceptivity.[3] In "A Berlin Chronicle" (1932), "Paris" is the drug that illuminates the role played by city semiotics in conducting the daily life of a dreaming collective:

> I tell myself it had to be in Paris, where the walls and the quays, the asphalt surfaces, the collections and the rubbish, the railings and the squares, the arcades and the kiosks, teach a language so singular that our relations to people attain, in the solitude encompassing us in our immersion in that world of things, the depths of a sleep in which the dream image waits to show the people their true faces.[4]

Earlier, in his review of Franz Hessel's *On Foot in Berlin*, Benjamin commends a fellow Berliner for bringing home the specifically Parisian art of flânerie by turning it into a strategy of memory: "To depict a city as a native would calls for other, deeper motives—the motives of the person who journeys into the past, rather than to foreign parts."[5] "The Return of the *Flâneur*" (1929) signals a new dimension of flânerie, revealing what the flâneur has always been seeking: "namely, images, wherever they lodge."[6] It anticipates the experimental narrative of "A Berlin Chronicle," where thought is allowed to wander in the city of his childhood. In this "Berlin," Benjamin strolls across haunts of living memory that official history would have him forget. His passage through this city yields conscious memory to *mémoire involontaire* and spontaneous revelations of the present's past.

After "A Berlin Chronicle," Benjamin stops miming the flâneur's peripatetic narrative and shifts almost exclusively to the montage method of representing dialectics at a standstill. The Nazi seizure of Berlin forces him into exile in Paris. Leaving his homeland, Benjamin loses "that tension between distance and nearness from which the city portraits draw their life. . . . The emigrant's travels are not the kind one looks back upon."[7] If Benjamin devotes the rest of his life to writing on Paris, his perspective is now retrospectively removed. As Peter Szondi observes: "the projected book, a montage of historical texts presented *as if the city were writing its own memoirs*, was to be called *Paris, Capital of the Nineteenth Century*."[8]

The Paris of Benjamin's *Das Passagen-Werk* (*The Arcades Project*) is the subject/object of a thoroughly reoriented flânerie. The author still sees the city in terms of physiognomies, only now they belong not to *his* but the *city's* past. The art of losing oneself in the city is still in play, so that he continues to drift through an ambience of porosity and to absorb the fine details of his surroundings. But attention now falls on traces of the city of last century, still visible in dilapidated and renovated architectures. Historical sensitivity is heightened not by hashish, dream, or memory but by visits to the Bibliothèque Nationale where Benjamin spent his days collecting data for his *Project*. He fills convolutes with citations culled from every archival source, blasted out of context, and reassembled in emphatic antitheses. Montage becomes the critical counterperspective to dream and narcosis, and the optics with which Benjamin views the Paris of his (pre)occupation (or Paris before its occupation).

Benjamin collects his citations against the grain of historical narrative. A montage method structures their constellation, but the "chronicle" is absent. Susan Buck-Morss, however, finds sufficient trace of the author in *Das Passagen-Werk* to "reconstruct" a narrative subtext:

> It is not difficult through our own flanerie to reconstruct Benjamin's work schedule with the clues he left us. Arriving from the Left Bank by subway, he would have surfaced at rue 4 Septembre through the still-standing art nouveau portal. In bad weather (he preferred grey mornings) he would have sought the shelter of the Passage Choiseul (built in 1825) with its clothing and stationery stores catering to office workers; he would have turned left through its still-moribund extension toward the rue Sainte-Anne, exiting a block from the small, lush-green Square de Louvois, the quiet peace of which ends abruptly at the rue de Richelieu. Crossing its speeding lanes of traffic, he would reach the safety of the entry courtyard of the Bibliothèque Nationale. He worked "the whole day there" finally accustoming himself to the "annoying regulations" in the main reading room, with its 19th-century iron-and-glass dome, and on its ceiling, a "painted summer sky." Seated below, one hears the constant rustle of the dusty leaves of books. And when one tires of reading or waiting for a book, a short stroll from the library brings to view all of central Paris. Benjamin surely worked this way, uncovering in his research the history of those places through which he moved. The themes of the *Passagen-Werk* can in fact be mapped out typographically on a small section of Paris, with the Bibliothèque Nationale at its hub. In an era when Paris' first commercial airport was being constructed, and the ambivalent commodity culture was about to descend upon a still largely pre-industrial world, Benjamin found that culture's elements in their earliest, original form concentrated in a section of Paris easily reached by foot. He worked here like an ethnographer in a village, except that his informants were things and they spoke of a past life. Included within his walking terrain were, first and foremost, the surviving arcades which ring the B-N: Choiseul, Vivienne, Colbert, Puteaux, Havre, Panoramas, Jouffroy, Verdeau, Princes, Caire, Grand-Cerf, Vero-Dodat. A stroll through the Palais-Royal brought him to the Seine,

> on the banks of which, in 1937, as in 1867 and 1889, pavillions of the world exhibitions were built; to the north past the Bourse three passages—des Panoramas, Jouffroy, Verdeau—are linked together; in the Passage Jouffroy is an entry into the Musée Grévin, which houses wax figures in fashionable and historical tableaux. . . . To the east, Benjamin could walk from Les Halles to the Marais through a Parisian landscape which urban renewal has since totally transformed. But there is still the garment district, the backstage wardrobe for the Parisian scene, and naked mannequins in display windows selling themselves wholesale to the trade. To the west, along the boulevards toward the Opéra, Benjamin moved onto the Parisian stage proper. Fashionable shops and the *Grands Magazins*—Printemps, Galeries de Lafayette—line the Boulevard Haussmann. In the vicinity of the Gare St. Lazarre, an outmoded "factory of dreams," this display of commodities gives way suddenly to the display of women, prostitutes. The shock of the transition and its erotic effects are no less today.[9]

This reconstruction helps us imagine Benjamin's daily transposition of archival research into city walks. Elsewhere, in *The Dialectics of Seeing*, Buck-Morss elucidates the dialectical strategy of *Das Passagen-Werk* and, with a *colportage* of visual illustrations, demonstrates his montage technique. But she abandons the narrative of flânerie.

Recent city writing appears to have taken up that narrative where Benjamin (and Buck-Morss) leave off. Gail Scott's novel *My Paris* uses *Paris, capitale du XIX*[e] *siècle* (the French edition of *Das Passagen-Werk*) to guide her flâneries through fin de siècle Paris of last century.[10] Her flâneur/narrator wonders if reviving the nineteenth-century art of flânerie is still possible, given the pervasive pollution, congestion, and commercialization that makes serendipitous walking unlikely in today's city. At the same time, she is able to see beyond city traffic and commercial veneer to regions of cultural potential that lie dormant in last century's mass architectures. The erotics of this venture are doubly perverse. First, it is women's culture and a lesbian Paris that Scott's flâneur looks for on the city's horizon, though she is frequently, comically, disappointed. Second, it is through the lens of Benjamin's *Paris* that she sees her Paris, when she is not gazing in store windows at her own unconscious mirroring of *la Parisienne*. With artistic self-parodying reflection, the narrator displaces the author of direct observation. Edmund White's *The Flâneur* recasts Benjamin's Paris in idiosyncratic, documentary narratives.[11] *The Flâneur* models its perambulations on speculations of what flânerie might mean in the twenty-first century, thus qualifying as a fiction of flâneur realism. Invoking Benjamin as "the last of the great literary *flâneurs*" (45), White stylizes his flâneur in Benjaminian fashion, studying "The Return of the *Flâneur*" before launching the flâneur's return once again. *The Flâneur*'s subtitle, *A Stroll through the Paradoxes of Paris*, suggests a peripatetic dialectics, in keeping with Benjamin's critical method. If White's flâneur is as much of a dandy and collector as Benjamin's flâneur, he is also more queer. Reputedly "our greatest living gay writer,"[12] White views *gaiety* as the animus that drives the flâneur on, despite prohibitive urban development: "To be gay and cruise is perhaps an extension of the *flâneur*'s very essence, or at least its most successful application" (145).

The purpose of this chapter is to explore this latest, if not last, incarnation of the literary flâneur and to query the critical innovativeness of its queer adaptation. It also aims to compare the different uses to which Scott and White put Benjamin's constellations of Paris in their respective flâneries. I must say from the start that Scott is by far the more astute and ambitious practitioner of Benjamin's dialectics of seeing. Yet White provides a gay American counterpoint to her French-feminist rendering of the lesbian flâneur. How, then, does gender affect the political and historical vision of the cruising flâneur? What discrepant awareness is signaled by her possessive focus on the city object—*my paris*—and his universal emphasis on the city subject—*the flâneur*? How does *My Paris* reflect and/or recast "the lesbian" of Benjamin's "Modernity"? What paradoxes of liberated sexuality does *The Flâneur* stroll in that ambiguous, Parisian space of revolutionary history and capitalist totality?

Millennial Passagen: My Paris 1999/The Flâneur 2001

With publication dates that border each side of the millennium, Gail Scott's *My Paris* and Edmund White's *The Flâneur* present timely

directly, in an act of reading at the start of her text, where it has greatest potential for mediating forthcoming flâneries:

> Anyway—returning to divan. And lifting heavy volume of B's *Paris, Capitale du XIXe.* From turquoise roxy-painted bedside table. Subtitle *Le livre des passages. Passagenwerk* in German. Not yet available in English. Therefore weighing the more delightfully on wrists. *Not* a real history. Rather—vast collection of 19th century quotes and anecdotes. Initially seeming like a huge pile of detritus. But—on looking closer. More like montage. Possibly assembled using old surrealist trick. Of free association. I opening at contents' list. "*A*"—*Passages*—glass-roofed arcades, malls. —Hawking 19th century's new imperial luxury. Juxtaposed on "*B*"—*Mode*—Each new season. Ironizing time. Next to "*C*"—*Antique Paris, catacombes, démolitions*—Paris's underpinnings. Pointing to "*D*"—*L'ennui*—Eternal return. Present tense of dandy. Hovering over "*E*"— *Haussmannisation, combats des barricades*—Haussmann's wide boulevards. Versus the people. Progress's double coin. Segueing into "*J*"—Poet *Baudelaire.* First modern. Peer of "*M*"—*Flâneur*—whose initial post French-revolutionary languor not ultimately resisting rising capitalist market. "*X/Y*"—*Marx–realism.* Next to *Photography . . . Social Movements. Dolls. Automatons.*
>
> A person could wander here for months. (18)

Indeed, a person *does* wander here for months—the *personage* of Scott's flâneur whose study of Paris "constitutes," as Benjamin says, "a second existence, already predisposed toward dreaming." The Paris of *My Paris* is the millennial metropolis as Scott's flâneur strolls it with Benjamin's "eyes." Her entry into historic city space is mediated by her passage through the French edition of *Das Passagen-Werk.* But she is no scholar. With characteristic happenstance, she stumbles on the tome, left behind by the previous occupant of the writer's studio that she now inhabits. Impressed by its "weightiness," she scans its contents, compelled to comprehend its representational device. Her gesture of lifting the volume and browsing through its pages becomes a morning ritual in preparation for braving the traffic-choked streets. The more she browses, the more her dream city is reconstellated by Benjamin's strategy of juxtaposing images. Benjamin's *Paris* absorbs her as much as the city outside her window. She delights to discover that its voluminous contents are "*not* a real history" but a "vast collection of 19th century quotes and anecdotes" through which one can rummage "like a huge pile of detritus," lending imagination to "free association." If not a real history, it is a virtual *flea market* that the surrealists themselves might have gleaned. Eventually, she frames her strolls in dialectical images. She cultivates a presence of mind that apprehends real, historical contradiction as she moves through the phantasmagoria of Paris passages.

The Return of the Flâneur

The flâneur is the consummate modern, who resides outside in the city's stimulating environs. Baudelaire explains that "'for the perfect *flâneur*, for the passionate observer, it's an immense pleasure to take up residence in multiplicity, in whatever is seething, moving, evanescent and infinite: you're not at home, but you feel at home everywhere.'"[17] But can today's Paris accommodate this perfect flâneur? "We must bear in mind," White cautions,

> that the cosy, dirty, mysterious Paris Baudelaire is discussing (or Balzac or even the Flaubert of *Sentimental Education*) is the city that was destroyed after 1853 by one of the most massive urban renewal plans known to history, and replaced by a city of broad, strictly linear streets, unbroken façades, roundabouts radiating avenues, uniform city lighting, uniform street furniture, a complex, modern sewer system and public transportation (horse-drawn omnibuses eventually replaced by the métro and motor-powered buses). (37)

Nonetheless, White ardently contends that "more than any other city Paris is still constructed to tempt someone out for an aimless saunter, to walk on just another hundred yards—and then another" (38). He evokes the "intoxication" that overcomes Benjamin's flâneur—"with each step, the walk takes on greater momentum; ever weaker grow the temptations of shops, of bistros, of smiling women, ever more irresistible the magnetism of the next streetcorner, of a distant mass of foliage, of a street name" (AP 417 [M1, 3]). Despite the ready convenience of rapid transit, the city can still charm its travelers into walking: "Although the métro is the fastest, most efficient and silent one in the world, with stops that are never more than five minutes' walk from any destination, the visitor finds himself lured on by the steeple looming over the next block of houses, by the toy shop on the next corner, the row of antique stores, the shady little square" (White, *The Flâneur*, 38–39). And though given to unfathomable expansion, *The Flâneur*'s Paris remains porous and luminous as ever: "The city, which has grown so large it is incomprehensible, can suddenly be deciphered by the seer-drunk-genius in search of little miracles" (39).

Scott's Paris assaults the senses with relentless intensity. The pace and volubility of traffic shatters the walker's reveries at every step, and her frailty at day's end is a visceral indicator of how menacing the city has become. If flânerie is possible, there is no escaping the din—either by device or acclimatization. "Sitting with my earplugs. Music turned up high. Still I hear the racket" (11), she testifies in her first diary entry. "Traffic honking and screeching" (17), she notes six entries later; while six months down the road, the perpetual rush-hour roar of roundabouts and boulevards continues to punctuate her prose. Nor is traffic the only havoc the big city throws at her: there is a daily pandemonium of demonstrations, strikes, construction sites, and a resounding calamity of street hawkers, storefronts, and billboards "screaming ESCOMPTES. RABAIS, DISCOUNTS. RÉDUCTIONS" (21). Retiring to her divan in the evening, she sees the "same panic repeated on TV. Fluctuating franc. Endless company layoffs" (21), noting ironically—"At apogée of passages it fashionable to walk. Leading a tortoise" (21). The flâneur's famed maneuver is, by now, inconceivable.[18] The Paris of *My Paris* reverberates with the hazards of "the last *flâneur*," whose plight Benjamin quotes from *Le Temps* (May 1936):

> A man who goes for a walk ought not to have to concern himself with any hazards he may run into. . . . If he tries to collect the whimsical thoughts

> that may have come to mind, very possibly occasioned by sights on the street, he is deafened by car horns, stupefied by loud talkers ..., and demoralized by the scraps of conversation, of political meetings, of jazz, which escape slyly from the windows. In former times, moreover, his brothers, the rubbernecks, who ambled along so easily down the sidewalks and stopped a moment everywhere, lent to the stream of humanity a gentleness and a tranquillity which it has lost. Now it is a torrent where you are rolled, buffeted, cast up, and swept to one side and the other. (AP 435–36 [M9a, 3])[19]

Paris traffic affects the *idea* of the flâneur that *My Paris* entertains. Its racket drives Scott's visitor indoors. If she is a "sort of flâneur," then she must qualify her pose as a "flâneur (of interior!)" (14). Benjamin's flâneur finds "the temptations of shops, bistros, smiling women" grow "ever weaker," whereas Scott's flâneur succumbs increasingly to their allure as sites of refuge. In reaction to the hectic tempo, she is perversely disposed to *oisiveté*—an idleness that is essential to flânerie.[20] Her idleness is exaggerated, aspiring more to the ease of the early-nineteenth-century flâneur, or to his decadently relaxed, *Belle Époque* counterpart, than to the enterprising flâneur of the Second Empire: "Clearly *not* flâneur. In later 19th-century sense of industrious strolling" (15).[21] "Like a heroine from Balzac . . . on a divan" (11) or like Proust on his bed, she "prefer[s] to lie back in interior of peluche" (15), her idleness accentuated by her fatigue from battling the traffic.[22] On the one hand, she hails "the return of the *flâneur*" with anti-industrial vengeance, personifying Benjamin's idea that "the idleness of the flâneur is a demonstration against the division of labour" (AP 427 [M 5, 8]). On the other hand, she marks the exhaustion of a tradition: "But exhausted. So late again when slipping off cushion. Clearly *not* flâneur" (15).[23] In any case, she is not "at home" in Paris, as Baudelaire once dreamed of being.

White's flâneur is also "like a Balzacian hero" (192). His similarity with Scott's flâneur does not extend very far.[24] Scott's character looks back to Balzac's flâneur in defiance of postmodern velocity. But her failure to act heroically parodies Balzac's heroic flâneries and alerts her character to the flâneur's anachronism. White mimes the heroic flâneur in earnest:

> The *flâneur* knows where to find the best sashimi and the best couscous, but he is not just awash with *bonnes adresses.* Like a Balzacian hero he has seen all of Paris stretching out at his feet as he stands on the steps of that mortuary chapel to French military ambitions, the Sacré Coeur. He knows his way around the parks and marketplaces, the book stalls and the *grands magasins*; these are the world's first department stores, celebrated in Zola's novel *Le Bonheur des dames*, which ends with a massive white sale. (192–93)

Though White applauds his heroics, the department store flâneur is a farce. Priscilla Ferguson's history of the type reads Zola's flâneur as degenerate, having devolved from the aloof maverick of the arcades to the pathetically seduced shopper of the *grands magasins*:

> *Au Bonheur des dames* recounts an epic battle of modern merchandising, which culminates in the decisive victory of the colossal department store and the death of small-scale retail establishments in the neighbourhood. In contrast to the arcades, where the *flâneur* could enjoy the show without involvement on his part, consumption is the only motivation for anyone's presence in the department store. Where the *flâneur* could once discreetly negotiate the ins and outs of the city, the department store presents an extravagant display that seals *flânerie* with an almost hermetically sealed universe, a hothouse from which no one escapes unaltered. There is no standing apart from the exhibition for the customers whom Zola presents as increasingly frenzied, increasingly liable to seduction by the ever changing displays of merchandise. From the "fever of spending" of the bourgeoisie to shoplifting by the aristocracy, Zola hammers away at the renunciation of responsibility on the part of these women who live to satisfy the desires that are roused by the capitalist seducer. . . . The *flâneur* "gives himself [who is now a "herself"] over entirely to the phantasmagorias of the market" from which there is now no escape.[25]

Still, White asserts that "Paris is the shopping city *par excellence*" (11). Shopping, cruising, and flânerie are equally at home here, and the consuming conflation of these activities embellishes the author's idea of the flâneur. The opening chapter of *The Flâneur* defines what constitutes the big-citiness of Paris, guiding readers on a tour of fashion fads and figures with Parisian savoir-faire:

> Women who want to be dressed by couturiers can still find them in Paris if they're willing to pay up to $35,000 for a frock. . . . A ritual of Parisian life is trading *les bonnes adresses*—the names and locations of some talented upholsterer or hatmaker or re-caner of straw-bottomed chairs or of a lovely little neighbourhood seamstress. Or the best places for buying whatever details of home decoration that will prove one is *à la page*. . . . Above a certain level of income and social standing every detail of life follows a fad. For a while everyone had to serve dinner in the kitchen, which meant entirely redecorating the kitchen so that it would be Philippe Starck sleek and preparing nothing but cold food. (11–13)

If tempered by a bemusement befitting his love of American casualness, White's descriptions of Paris markets are idylls to consumerism:

> In Paris you can buy anything. At Izrael's Le Monde des Epices you can find tequila and tacos, pancake mix and black-eyed peas, popcorn in heat-and-serve silver foil bags and the best plum slivovitz. There are four major English-language bookshops (the most *sympathique* is the Village Voice at 6 rue Princesse on the Left Bank), two or three for the German language, one in Catalan and Spanish—and two French bookshops that sell nothing but old Jules Verne books in the original bindings. Fauchon, the famous grocer and caterer on the Place Madeleine, offers Skippy's peanut butter, not to mention all the edible delights the mind can imagine or remember, including a pale-green pistachio cake. In a Japanese women's shop around the corner from the Village Voice you can find the soaps and perfumes produced in Florence by the *farmacia* attached to Santa Maria Novella; the *farmacia* has been in business since the seventeenth century. The best

> silver (Puiforcat), the best sheets (Noel and Pourthault), the best florist (Lachaume, in business since Proust's day, or Christian Tortu near the Odéon for something more up to date) . . . Oh, it's all there— (14–15)

With irony, White notes that all that is missing is "a truly refined and elegant Italian meal (the French think all the Italians eat is pizza) [and] . . . a decent public library system" (15). But he does not criticize the Republic for veiling its failure to meet the masses' literary needs with the "phantasmagorias of the market."

Scott's flâneur adjusts nervously to what she perceives as a bewildering barrage of things. To savor the abundance of delicacies, she must first overcome the traffic and, then, open her senses to the commodity:

> What is it about Paris. Trying to see past sleepless nights from traffic. Choking on pollution. Overly self-conscious of appearance. Hair neat and smooth. Shiny shoes. Then one day noticing "one" standing automatically straighter. The way Parisians do. Noticing the earthy naughty odours of a hundred different cheeses. Wafting entwined from a cheese shop. One alive and oozing through its wax paper in her bag. Plus a lambchop so pink she could kiss it. Nice olives. Smiling she enters the lobby of her building. This nourishment of senses conferring on her. A surface more shiny— (14)

But even when treated by "this nourishment of senses," she is acutely aware of the market "conferring on her. A surface more shiny—." The enjambment of sentence fragments signifies that her flânerie is at once *critically transitive* (that is, alert to how city sensations aim at "conferring on her. A surface more shiny—" than revealing), and *uncritically intransitive* (that is, open to the "nourishment" of superficial sensation—full stop). The jerkiness of her prose is reflected in the awkwardness of her pose. Whether passing as a *Parisienne* or acting the flâneur, she expresses a perpetual ambivalence between resisting and succumbing to phantasmagorical temptation. When she does attempt to stomach the all-consuming consumer culture, her body betrays her with irritating symptoms (rashes, headaches, eczema); her physiology resists assimilation, revolted by the killing ecology.[26] Still, she covets the fastidious French facility for balancing poisons with pleasures:

> Not having entirely mastered. French pleasure-balancing trick. E.g. countering hangover. Like woman leisure lottery director. With simple filet mignon. Light sauce. One glass of right wine. Taken in deep insistent breath. No distractions. No deep-fried onion rings. Thousand Island dressing. Similar specialized well-being. Served as l'onglerie, for nails. La parfumerie, for perfume. Le bottier, for boots. La ganterie, for gloves. Even men wearing perfume. Purses. Little tootsies cosseted in nice silk socks. (33)

At the same time, she internalizes a panopticon of Parisian haute couture, confusing the gaze of fashion with that of patrolling gendarmes, who she fears will discover her missing papers: "Straightening in boutique façade mirror. Then passing cops by café—I whispering speak French so they not asking for visa. Forgetting québécois accents" (32). Forever the stranger despite her masquerade, she turns the gaze on herself and thereby inhabits a state of (self-)surveillance.

The flâneur's preoccupation with Paris fashion reflects what Benjamin diagnoses as an "empathy with the commodity [which] is fundamentally empathy with exchange value itself. The flâneur is a virtuoso of this empathy. He takes the concept of marketability itself for a stroll" (AP 448 [M17a, 2]). "This empathy" is facilitated by hard-selling consumerism that targets women especially for wholesale submission to fashion. Benjamin further infers how fashion constitutes a carceral specularity, where "'mannequins become the model for imitation, and the soul becomes the image of the body'" (AP 78 [B8, 4]).[27] He observes how *la mode* so "revolutionized" *les bourgeoises* of the Second Empire that "'it became difficult to distinguish an honest woman from a courtesan on the basis of clothing alone.'"[28] As if to confirm these conjectures, White observes how *les poules de luxes*, "those upscale whores who stand in the doorways [of Avenue Foch]," copy the haute couture worn by *les bourgeoises* of their neighborhood,[29] asserting that "Paris is the one city left

> Sitting in café at Sèvres-Babylone. I.e. at corner of Exquisite China and Pursuit of Sensuous Pleasure. Homeless guy selling *Macadam, Pavement.* By métro. Thinking time to start wandering. From present bifurcation. Toward Hermit's Well. Stone's throw from Buffoon Street. Down Beaujolais Alley. Through Wolf's Crack or Breach. Hot Cat Road. Passage of Desire. Magenta Boulevard. Where walking *Nadja* towards *Hôtel Sphinx.* Little Girls' Impasse. Saint-Jacques' Ditch. B saying "one's" perception of Paris streets. Based on sensuality of names. Adding *we* (sic) never having felt sharpness of pavement stones. Under bare feet. *We* never having to check uneven flagstones. To see if suitable for bed. (25–26)

The sensuality of names brings with it a cornucopia of sense: "Sèvres-Babylone" (a métro stop at the corner of two boutiques) connotes Sèvres, the place where exquisite china is made, and Babylon, archetypal site of the pursuit of sensuous pleasure. A man selling a homeless newspaper called *Macadam, Pavement* connotes the tiles that were used to pave the first boulevards, named after the Scottish engineer who invented them.[34] These rich connotations of other times and other places abut onto bucolic village landscapes conjured by "Hermit's Well," "Buffoon Street," "Beaujolais Alley," "Wolf's Crack," "Breach," "Hot Cat Road," "Little Girls' Impasse," "Saint-Jacques' Ditch." The name of the hotel from where Breton and Nadja launched their wanderings evokes Egyptian mysteries, together with the rune/ruin of surrealism's drift. Yet the hard reality that lies at the base of this dream is not lost on the historical unconscious. As Benjamin reminds her, the flâneur is afforded perceptions not afforded by those who must sleep on the street.

Benjamin stresses that the flâneur is drawn most compellingly to public spaces where memories of the collective are housed:

> The street conducts the flâneur into a vanished time . . . into a past that can be all the more spellbinding because it is *not his own, not private.* (AP 416 [M1, 2], my emphasis)

> Streets are the dwelling place of the collective. The collective is an eternally unquiet, eternally agitated being that—in the space between the building

> fronts—experiences, learns, understands, and invents as much as individuals do within the privacy of their own four walls. (AP 423 [M3a, 4])

> The most characteristic building projects of the nineteenth-century—railroad stations, exhibition halls, department stores . . .—all have matters of collective importance as their object. The flâneur feels drawn to these "despised, everyday" structures, as [Siegfried] Giedion calls them. In these constructions, the appearance of great masses on the stage of history was already foreseen. (AP 455 [M21a, 2])

Scott's flâneur feels drawn to spaces where the collective "dwells," including exhibition halls ("le Grand Palais," "Centre Pompidou," "l'Institut du Monde Arabe"), public and popular museums ("Musée Carnavalet," "Musée Grevin"), train stations, parks, and department stores. She frequents those nineteenth-century spaces that, like the arcades, assembled the first urban masses, enjoying their haunting ambience. She highlights these spaces in bold lettering, as if to signpost her flânerie with stops she makes along the way: "*Gastronomie Cosmopolite*" (21), "*Opéra*" (25), "*gare du Nord*" (29), "*Prix Unique*" (33), "*Hôtel Lutétia*" (43), "*Tour Eiffel*" (57), "*Au Bon Marché*" (64), "*Passage Vivienne*" (66), "*Canal de l'Ourcq*" (69), "*gare d'Austerlitz*" (77), "*Bibliothèque Nationale*" (111), "*Cirque d'Hiver*" (113), "*Folies-Bergere,*" "*Les Temps des Cerises*" (131), "*Passage Des Princes,*" "*Passage Des Panoramas*" (138), "*Passage Jouffroy,*" "*Passage Verdeau*" (139), "*Madeleine*" (144). White steers shy of mass spaces in favor of out-of-the-way places that house precious collections and/or memorabilia of the city's great dandies and eccentrics. Benjamin's flâneur is "'happy to trade all his knowledge of artists' quarters, birthplaces, and princely palaces for the scent of a single weathered threshold or the touch of a single tile—that which any old dog carries away'" (White, *The Flâneur,* 46). White's flâneur delights in guiding us around artists' quarters and sharing obscure biographical details. He dwells on Colette:

> From St-Germain I like to work my way down the rue Bonaparte past the furniture and fabric stores, the Académie des Beaux Arts and the shops

> selling prints, finishing at the Institute, the building that houses the French Academy and its library, the Bibliothèque Mazarine. . . . From there I like to go to the Palais Royal, an oasis of silence and elegance in the heart of the old city. Once you get past the tacky silver balls or the striped columns by Buren, you're back in the world of Colette and Cocteau, the two most famous denizens of the Palais in the twentieth century. They were neighbours and could wave to one another from their windows. Colette liked to look at Cocteau in his low-ceilinged entresol apartment lit from below by the sunlight bouncing up from the pavement, as though he were an actor illuminated by footlights. (23–24)

From here he commences a lengthy digression on Colette's life, full of "juicy details" (as the book jacket intimates) including surprising facts concerning her "mixed African descent," her "unidiomatic affection for strange words," her "'baroque transvestism'" ("'she is a woman writing as a man, who poses as a boyish girl, Claudine, who marries a "feminized" man, the ageing Renaud, who pushes her into the arms of a female lover, Rézi, with whom she takes the virile role'"[35]), and her and her mother's lesbianism. Returning to the present where "the magic still radiates from Colette's apartment on the second floor of number 9 rue de Beaujolais" (33), he notes a minor renovation by Jacques Grange, "the famous decorator" and present owner, who otherwise keeps her space unchanged (33–34).

The city rarely strikes Scott's flâneur as unchanging—except where one expects it least, say, in fashion or in war, where, instead of "revolution," she sees things "eternally returning" (35, 38). Change comes to her in colliding images from different eras that she perceives simultaneously. For her, the city is a "landscape" whose layered history she experiences en passant.[36] Embedded in this landscape, "Colette" appears before her as a living specter, the product of an association of concrete objects:[37]

> Former home of Colette. Old hedonist! Knowing how to take pleasures of the body. Without ruining her skin. Pale-with-something-darker-under.

> She grooming 50 minutes daily. Standing by mirror. Automatically straightening sagging hip. Raising drooping neck. Before sitting at her desk. And writing 50 books.
>
> I entering from behind. Through crumbly passage end. . . . Across rue de Beaujolais. . . . Fountains gurgling lazily. Birds singing everywhere. Old Colette's magnificent aubergine head. Above. Sniffing. Touching. Listening. To very end. Despite pain of arthritis. Heavy immovable body. Irritating boys. Shitting below. (37)

Here Colette is as present to the eye as the crumbling Palais Royal passage. The "old hedonist" appears at the end of a "crumbling passage": both are wrecks. The flâneur's sensitivity to anachronistic contiguity conjures forth a fantasy of the arthritic writer. Amidst real fountains and birds, Colette's head appears—not a portrait of the author in cameo—but a thinking, sensing, organic presence. In another diary entry, the flâneur lounges on a café terrasse, contemplating the label "*ORANGINE*" on a bottle and thinking how the design—"simple outlines on plain or empty backgrounds"—resembles a historic, avant-garde art form (50). This, in turn, solicits another memory of Colette:

> I ordering more Kir. Sky paling behind la Gaîté. Where old Colette formerly performing. Her early turn-of-20th work Modern Style too. Les *Claudines* emphasizing silhouettes. Projecting in simplicity of appearance. Some new kind of writing. Walking up Raspail in pinkness of dusk. I musing whether all ends of centuries requiring—résumé of surfaces. Back in studio. Looking out at façade opposite. . . . Its indeterminate pasted-on decor. Rejection of periods. As if time adrift. A bastard. (50)

The flâneur's drifting thought throws Colette's literary profile into relief, connecting her writing to the visual art of "Modern Style" and visualizing her formal inventiveness. Thought continues on this drift as the flâneur walks back to her studio, the range of her reflections gathering metaphysical scope. The resulting vision is a constellation of colliding "ends of centuries"—a vision that confronts her concretely in the "indeterminate pasted-on decor" of the postmodern facade opposite her studio window.

Melancholy/Story/Allegory

For Edmund White, the return of the flâneur is inexplicably sad. The last pages of his opening chapter introduce his palpable melancholia:

> Imagine dying and being grateful you'd gone to heaven, until one day (or one century) it dawned on you that your main mood was melancholy, although you were constantly convinced that happiness lay just around the next corner. That's something like living in Paris for years, even decades. It's a mild hell so comfortable that it resembles heaven. . . . If so, then why is the *flâneur* so lonely? So sad? Why is there such an elegiac feeling hanging over this city with the gilded cupola gleaming above the Emperor's Tomb and the foaming, wild horses prancing out of a sea of verdigris on the roof of the Grand Palais? . . . Why is he unhappy, this foreign *flâneur*, even when he strolls? (50–51)

The question is subtly rhetorical and the answer may lie in its posing. Does the flâneur's sadness not issue from the fact that today's Paris no longer lives up to the dream that its imperial past inspired? Earlier, White notes the loss of "intellectual lustre" that has accompanied the "boutiquification" of St. Germain-des-Prés and that "everyone is lamenting" (18).[38] Moreover, he notes that the disappearance of what was once "Intelligence Central for the whole world" is not confined to that neighborhood alone: "If Saint-Germain is now less interesting, it's because Paris itself has become a cultural backwater" (22). In other words, *gai Paris* is *gai* no longer.[39]

The *gay* flâneur resuscitates the intellectual and cultural image of Paris by returning to its otherness—to the city *not* yet depleted by renovations and tourist venues. Leaving the vacuous center for the colorful margins, he reorients his flâneries to the "strongholds of multiculturalism rather than to the headquarters of the Gallic tradition" (52). He contends that "the real vitality of Paris today lies elsewhere—in Belleville and Barbès, the teeming *quartiers* where Arabs and Asians and blacks live and blend their respective cultures into new hybrids" (52). Yet, instead of visiting these vital, new communities, he tells the histories of deceased contingents of others, focusing on African Americans who once lived in Montmartre. "Black Paris" is the Paris of Josephine Baker, Sidney Bechet, Richard Wright, Langston Hughes, Chester Himes, and James Baldwin—revisited (65–87). If Black Paris is animated with colorful characters, "Jewish Paris" is haunted by doleful tales about Alfred Dreyfus and Léon Blum. Noting the historic Jewish quarter of the Marais, White detours to Parc Monçeau where he finds "the most impressive museum—and one that tells a melancholy tale" (106). This is the museum and the tale of Nissim de Camondo, the last of the Camondos, a line of Jewish bankers who emigrated from Constantinople in 1867 to Paris, "where the Jewish population was the most perfectly integrated one in the world and the most stable" (108). As White tells it, the Camondos' story is that of a wealthy, assimilated, immigrant family that is ultimately betrayed by its adoptive country, the members of the last generation having been deported to Auschwitz. What he finds particularly sad is the loss of "personal memorabilia" from the family's vast collection of precious art (119). The story of gay Paris is also depressing. The disproportionate number of AIDS-related deaths among gays may, White claims, be attributed to French republicanism's reticence toward recognizing a distinctively gay society, thus undermining (that) society's ability to organize against the disease. Paradoxically, his next chapter traces a queer tale of Royalist survival in republican France. "In Paris there is even room for *socialist* monarchists," White claims, though he delights in telling how one of the last Bourbon heirs was beheaded on a skiing accident when someone "put an invisible wire across his path that sliced off his head—exactly on the centennial of the Revolution" (184). The failure of proletarian revolution is not what saddens this flâneur. Indeed, he makes his last stop of his stroll through Paris at the *Chapelle Expiatoire*, erected by the Restoration to absolve the nation for its insurrectionist sins (174–75).

Scott's flâneur is likewise melancholic. More precisely, she oscillates between expectation and disappointment, a dynamic ambivalence that adds to her fatigue. She senses a resurgence of political resistance stirring in the ambience of a new café—"Espresso machine bubbling. Delicious nape of redhead across room. Eating pommes parisiennes, parsley fried potates. . . . Publisher deploring epoch's cynicism. Citing fashion industry. . . . Subject changing to ambiguous article in *Libé.* On gay rights" (35). This is "*the Paris I expecting,*" where she finds the city to be both *gai* and gay. Yet she wonders if, in her dream-state of suspended commitment, she is sensing not what is actually happening but what has in advance been arranged for one's attention. "It occurring to me—state of feeling-less. Precursive to state of floating. Possibly problematic. Because in hovering/observing. 'One' *arbitrarily* gathering little external details. In part pre-selected" (49). Alternatively, she is confronted by what "I not at all in Paris I expecting. Having imagined things less glossy. More comfily dilapidated. As in *Hôtel Sphinx* where *Nadja* used to live. Or old shops. Teeming with 'marvellous' detritus. Such as Breton's strange curved spoon with tiny woman's heel holding up the handle" (13). Hoping for an encounter with the "'marvellous,'"[40] she happens upon the "polished Faubourg Saint-Germain [where] nothing [is] left to chance" (13). Beyond the Paris she is expecting or not expecting, there is the Paris that abolishes all illusion. This is the city of *un*marvelous detritus, much of it *human*, that confronts her on the street when she is least prepared for it. Floating in insular fantasy, she is jarred into brutal awakening by *clochards* in the métro (36), a starving young beggar (37), prostitutes openly turning tricks in alleys near porte Saint-Denis (39), a person with AIDS taking a shit in park bushes (94), a raging, homeless drunk on the train (144), a suicide on the tracks (144). Dream Paris crumbles into *real* Paris—repeatedly—so that "one's" flâneries are disjointed trajectories of urban consciousness. Every diary entry records a confrontation with the real in a moment of re/cognition. The second entry, for example, begins:

> Now on canapé near window. Listening to some radio station. Not Ferrat singing Aragon. Nor Satie nor Barbara. The new France. Conjuring up mint in the margins. Rosewater. Orange. Sweet nutcakes of the medinas of Morocco. Looking out at chic boulevard Raspail. (11)

But her reverie collapses with

> Cops everywhere in the neighbourhood. A block away they're posted beside a rather nice café. I refuse to go there. S saying I'm ridiculous. Failing to mention the new strictness regarding visas. Will normalement be applied selectively. To people from "the south." I.e. Africa. Maghrebia. (12)

Set adrift on the "oneiric ambiance" wafting over the radio waves, she is awakened by a glance out the window down the boulevard that reveals, despite the pooh-poohing of her Parisian friend, that the "new France" is a reincarnation of the old Empire.[41] In a later entry, she is "Strolling to Pont-Neuf. . . . Leaning over bridge. Taking in sunset. Through partly cloudy sky. On glass-and-iron roof. Of magnificent Grand Palais. Built for 1900 World Exhibition. At curve of river" (33). Just as she becomes absorbed in the city's Imperial dream (with the same grandeur that captivates White's flâneur), she is "abruptly" disillusioned: "Then strolling back again. Walking up Rennes. Sudden cold rain. Abruptly showering half-naked torso. Of young man sitting. Bent forward. On cement promontory. Near *Prix Unique*. Displaying back scored with large deep scars. Likely burns. I hurrying down curved white Grenelle" (33). Repelled by the sight of such exposure on rue de Renne's commercial thoroughfare—what has been described as "the most desolate, inhuman street in Paris"[42]—she retreats, leaving the reader in her wake to interpret the signs of human suffering as a blazon of capitalist devastation.

White's flâneries lend themselves to melancholy *tales*. Scott's lead to critical *allegories*. Allegory barricades Scott's narrative drift with heaps of detritus that are the waste products of urbanization—detritus that the dream cannot assimilate. Syntactical fragmentation, the juxtaposition of partial images, the montage of freeze-framed gestures: these stylistic devices of *My Paris* serve allegory's destruction of urban mythology cast by capitalist phantasmagoria. They frame perception in what Benjamin describes as "topographic vision":

> There is the Place du Maroc in Belleville: that desolate heap of stones with its rows of tenements became for me, when I happened on it one Sunday

vexed by the fact that "the country that produced some of the most renowned pioneer homosexual writers of this century (Marcel Proust, André Gide, Jean Genet, Jean Cocteau and Marguerite Yourcenar, just to begin the list)—is also today the country that most vigorously rejects the very idea of gay literature" (162). As corrective, White recovers the presence of gay writers, artists, and politicians at every turn of his stroll. After Colette (24–34), he sights/cites Cocteau (24), Proust (26), Genet (58), Elise Sargent—"la Pomaré" (Baudelaire's friend [134]), Jean-Jacques de Cambacérè (Napoleon's "hand-picked Second Consul . . . a notorious homosexual . . . who incorporated the 1791 measure decriminalizing homosexuality into the new Napoleonic constitution" [151–52]), Astolphe de Custine (a popular novelist, best known for his book *Russia in 1839* and possibly one of the models for Proust's arrogant Baron de Charlus [152–54]).

The flâneur of *My Paris* also strolls into the paradoxes of history. What, in part, makes her so sensitive to contradiction is her own contrariness. Firstly, she does not view the city as a foreign nationalist. She knows, like Virginia Woolf, that as a woman she has no country—no place that recognizes her citizenry with the same public authority as men. As a native of Quebec, she senses the city's disdain for colonials. As an *Anglo*-Quebecker, she cultivates the sensitivities of a divided subject. She writes her diary in her native tongue, but with a subversive awareness of linguistic imperialism. Sketching the city in participles instead of proper English and supplementing Parisian French with idiomatic Quebecois, she minoritizes the official language of two first-world nations. As a lesbian for whom the city offers few cruising spaces or (affordable) bars, she seeks other lesbians in unlikely places. Hailed ubiquitously by the city's seduction, she is everywhere met with frustration.

Paradoxes are not presented discursively, as they are in *The Flâneur*. Scott's flâneur does not step out of her flâneries through Paris to protest that postrevolutionary history that denies women the *liberté, egalité, fraternité* that their male compatriots enjoy. Instead, she acquires the art of "dialectical movement . . . of montage history method" (59) that she models on Benjamin's *Paris*. This is a method of sighting (and citing) history "wherein author saying nothing. Only endlessly oneirically conjuncting" images of different epochs against each other "for purposes of shocking unconscious knowing. Into realm of conscious recognition" (27). She develops Benjamin's thesis that "the most heterogeneous elements . . . coexist in the city" (AP 435 [M 9, 4]), and she transforms his "montage history method" into a *praxis* of postmodern *flânerie.* We might recall her first take on "B's *Paris*" (18, cited above) and the way the prepositional phrases of that passage—"juxtaposed on," "next to," "pointing to," "hovering over," "segueing into"—accentuate the "dialectical movement" of Benjamin's *Paris,* while indicating the gestures of seeing that are in motion as she strolls.

Benjamin's montage is "*not* a real history" but a radical re/presentation of history that embodies a critique of bourgeois historicism and a method of recollecting dispersed revolutionary impulses. If a concept of history informs *The Arcades Project* it might be summarized as thus: the aims of Revolution had been obscured, as Marx demonstrated, by postrevolutionary developments. Counterrevolution, restoration, and bourgeois imperialism are factors of *political* obfuscation. But a more insidious, *cultural* distraction was afforded by the installation of mass urban architectures. These architectures transformed Paris from a space of battlefields into a space of boulevards too wide to effectively barricade, and too entertaining to afford bourgeois support for the Commune. New commodity markets, novel commercial constructions, and spectacular exhibitions distracted, seduced, and consumed bourgeois masses, stimulating their forgetting of the people's revolution. The luxury arcade was a cornerstone in this forgetting. If liberty, fraternity, and equality were etched into its blueprints (as Fourier's *phalansterie* envisioned), bourgeois imperialism became its manifest destiny. Archetype of capitalist globalization, the arcade recast the city-in-miniature, exhibiting for consumption all the treasures of the industrial empire: manufactured merchandise from adjoining factories, together with artifacts extorted from the colonies. Encapsulated in the arcade's panoramas, dioramas, and wax museum, *history itself* became a commodity exhibit.

To negate this development, Benjamin invents a technique that houses, the museum multiplies the effects of interiorization. The arcade reproduces the city in miniature with its gas-lit streets and shop-lined promenades. The wax museum restages world history in miniature. The museum's arcade-like corridors guide visitors past dioramas of history's most memorable spectacles: "'All history' being laid out for consumption" (140). With comic irreverence, the flâneur observes the histrionic historicity:

> Grévin a scream. Distorting mirrored labyrinth. Presenting history backwards. Modern retreating toward mediaeval. Starting off with Fonda. In *Barbarella* space suit. Surprised multiple orgasm expression of 60s film. On physiognomy. Michael Jackson moonwalking. Backwards. Towards Communards. Napoléons. Jacobins. Several Louis. And queens. . . . Head of some noble on pole. Being waved by victorious sans-culotte at incestuous lesbian Marie-Antoinette's window. She falling naturellement in faint. (140)

The museum maps a backward passage in time so that history is framed by the space of contemporaneity. Scott's flâneur notes the relapse of "Fonda" into "Marie-Antoinette." If Barbarella's "liberated" sexuality personifies the climax of modernity, the queen's shocked physiognomy caricatures the terror of insurgency. The constellation of images affords a spectacular view of the historical suppression of lesbianism: women are no more free to explore lesbianism in Barbarella's space age than in Marie-Antoinette's age of terror.

The spectacle fails to seduce the flâneur who looks on from the margins. As "one" whose desires are nowhere represented, except by the queen who, for her libertine sins, is beheaded by revolutionary moral agents, she is mindful of the phantasmagoric device and how shabbily dated it (now) appears:

> Labyrinth ending in Palais des Mirages. Small room. Belle-époque. Columns of entwined snakes. Masks. Lights going out. Darkness slowly filling with lit-up butterflies. And stars. Stiffly rising. Descending. On faintly visible wires. "Beautiful." But technology so dated. Being chiefly conceived.

> Like old panoramas. For spectators. Watching from immoveable centre. (140)

Once again, history ends where it is encapsulated in bourgeois illusion. But the technology of "Palais des Mirages" is so obsolete that its aura fails to charm. A more effective production is found in a restaurant directly opposite the museum, where the flâneur joins her gay friend for a drink. In his cruiserly company, she recovers the distraction once becoming of the old arcades:

> Happily—I distracted by R's pleasure in glimmering tight-jeaned ass of young man. Commenting—as we exiting—that arcade life reviving. Compared to first visit 20 years back. Young man heading for *Hôtel Chopin.* Through open door. We glimpsing dark pink lobby. Campy lampshades. Men coming down stairs. We entering café with real wicker chairs. Opposite Grévin. With handsome male waiters. Little red kerchiefs knotted round necks. To drink fine porto. Out of lovely porto glasses. Beige palm trees in relief. Climbing up beige wall. R taking in male fauna. I the porto. Sinking by osmosis. Into roof of mouth. (140–41)

From the *musée* to the restaurant opposite, the flâneur traverses the passage from past to present. Yet the progress of this passage is ambiguous. At best it traces the dialectics of entrepreneurial development. The restaurant embodies the charm of the arcade by enhancing the technique of display. "At this turning point of history, the Parisian shopkeeper," Benjamin observes, "makes two discoveries that revolutionize the world of *la nouveauté*: the display of goods and the male employee" (AP 52 [A8, 3]). Just as the shopkeepers of the arcade were first to use male employees to "replace the seduction of man by woman—something conceived by the shopkeepers of the ancien régime—with the seduction of woman by man" (AP 52 [A8, 3]), the managers of the *gai* (gay) restaurant use them to replace the seduction of woman with the seduction of man by man—another twist in the perversity of capitalist modernity. If the restaurant is a favorite cruising site for gay men, in the eyes of Scott's flâneur it is just another case of bourgeois spectacle, "opposite Grévin." She is not seduced by the "male fauna" cast among exotic flora. But her gay friend is infatuated. *Gai Paris* undergoes its latest transformation. Is it sexual emancipation or the eternal return of the same?

Angelus Novus: Angela Lesbia

If the greatest similarity between *The Flâneur* and *My Paris* is the gaiety with which they cruise historic Paris, the greatest disparity lies in how differently they view the city's futurity. White ends his gay flâneries with parting glances at his Paris past. The only future he foresees is the one he offers in his list of guidebooks for "Further Reading." In contrast, Scott ends her six-month flânerie in Paris with a break of uncertain time followed by a return. The last diary entry figures her flâneur back home, "trudging in snow down Saint-Denis. Montréal. Québec" (152), absorbing the discrepancies of social space. Two pages later, she is once again in Paris, drinking in the ambiance of a New Year's Eve in a "dark over-crowded square" near Notre-Dame, "looking toward (fog-erased) Grand Palais" (155). Instead of an ending, we are given a coda, a formal device that functions here, like in music, as "a passage added after the natural completion of a movement, so as to form a more definite and satisfactory conclusion."[53] At once repetitive and visionary, the coda stages a final flânerie that, drifting as before but at an accelerated pace, exchanges catastrophe-ridden glances for glimpses of utopia.

The coda, like the diary, is punctuated by reports on the ongoing war in Bosnia. War is the state of emergency that raises specters of crises through the mists of phantasmagoria, if with unheeded alarm. Ellipses between diary entries are enjambed with the refrain, "raining [or snowing] in Bosnia," updating the carnage with the regularity of a weather report.[54] Though it is a foreign war, the disaster in Sarajevo strikes the flâneur in Paris as the universal condition of late metropolitan modernity. The space she wanders in dream is repeatedly shattered by the horror taking place next door. Subjected again and again to rude awakening, she discovers that the real catastrophe is that *the war just keeps on going*, despite the efficiency of postmodern communications in raising public consciousness through televised trauma. As antidote to her own disposition to distraction, she locates a passage in Benjamin:

> *Que les choses continuent comme avant: voilà la catastrophe.*
> I taping it to TV screen. (69)

The war is no less present in the coda, though in the fog-drenched streets of a Paris January at the end of the millennium, its presence is felt more directly:

> —Sauntering—Silent—Sky. . . . Out into street—Dogcatcher truck. Buses—Taxi. Cruising past Odéon columns. Actors fasting. For Sarajevo—Leaving enclave. Dissatisfied—Suburbs—Cement saucer of airport—That dogcatcher truck. Pulling up behind. Woman stepping out. . . . Saying I come from war. And here is confusion. Handing out pamphlet. Saying les Bosniennes, Bosnian women. Saving culture. In chaos. With 100 small attentions. Presenting selves impeccably. Best food. In worst situations—Pink lips ahead. Pointed boots forward. Towards boarding gate—I turning. Once. Looking— (161)

The last image to be added to the constellation of *My Paris* is a dialectical image. At once, looking ahead/looking back, the flâneur presents a Janus-faced glance at contemporaneity. What she sees is not a specter of hope or ruin but a real woman, from Bosnia, bringing tidings of resistance. Against catastrophic "chaos" she beholds a figure of salvation, a collective image of "les Bosniennes. . . . Saving culture." But the realism of this image is animated by a dream-wish, the dream of social transformation that revolutionary modernity inspires (and is inspired by). On the outskirts of the city, past the historic center (where actors stage a fast for the war), past the dismal, sprawling suburbs, onto Charles de Gaulle airport, the flâneur is borne by a cumulative vision of unactualized possibility beyond all materialized disappointment. The capacity to see utopia is, as Benjamin observes with retrospective foresight, the affirmative dimension of metropolitan phantasmagoria. Besides veiling catastrophe and sidetracking revolution, phantasmagoria harbors a wish-fulfilling impulse to transform. In the end, Scott's flâneur is invested with this impulse.

In the coda, a new intoxicant has been added to the dream in her drift through Paris. That intoxicant is lesbian love. Paris is still a primary passion of the flâneur, who, on return from Montreal, picks up where she left off, reengaged. But her engagement with the city is affected by the presence of a lover who joins her from Canada. "Love" scores the text both figuratively and syntactically. Where there were once only periods there are now, periodically, "orgasms," crossed out as perverse slips of speech:

> She beside me saying. Very pink lips. Initially not wanting to come. Preferring riding horses—Still what ~~orgasms~~ angels popping up. Mid walls. Near Louvre's small eyes. Looking in. Or out. She asking— (155)

Though reluctant to visit Paris, preferring amazonian adventures in wilder country, the lover is the cue to the flâneur's final revelation. "Pink lips" appears "ahead" of the flâneur like a star on the horizon, illuminating the erotic orientation of the scene, "pointing forward" in a gesture that confirms that *the future is women.*

"Pink lips" appears in every coda passage as a corporeal gesture. A synecdoche of the lesbian body, she, like all bodies caught in the flâneur's field of cruising, is erotically moving. An unassimilable fragment of (lesbian) sexual difference, however, "Pink lips" defies commodity fetishism that, as Benjamin notes, is the charismatic appeal of "the girl with the golden eyes." Nor is she like the dispensable Nadja, Breton's esoteric love with whom the surrealist flâneur is less intimate than the marvelous things she connotes. For Scott's flâneur, "she" is "she beside me" (155) who, in arousing proximity, initiates the metonymic drift that constitutes a lesbian semiotics. If, as Benjamin perceived, the "sexual shock" to which the big-city dweller is subjected is the violent effect of the commodity's division and appropriation of sex from Eros,[55] then their unmarketable, *lesbian*, reunion is our redemption.

A figure also of communication/communion between women, "Pink lips" is the flâneur's closest interlocutor. When accompanying her on flâneries, "Pink lips" speaks her desire, proposing alternatives to "femmes légitimes" (159), ridiculing "Natalie Barney" (158), one of Paris's notoriously "out" lesbians, and protesting the marginality "of girls like us" (159). Laughing at the cowboy drag of Parisian gays (158), she scorns their simulation from the perspective of authentic cowgirl knowledge (155). Like the horse-riding amazons of Cirque d'Hiver (159), her androgyny contests the gender status quo that Paris so artfully and artificially preserves.

"Pink lips" signals "~~orgasms~~" that keep "popping up" in the text, reflecting her subliminal effect on the flâneur. Thinking "orgasms," she sees "angels" sculpted into the Louvre's baroque facade—"mid walls" (155). These imaginary, or visionary, angels suggestively allude to Benjamin's angel, or the seraphic motifs in Baudelaire that Benjamin reads as figures of baroque modernism. Scott tempts us to read her orgasmic angel as a perverse and provocative adaptation of Benjamin's theses on the future of history.

Benjamin's most famous allegory—"the angel of history"—takes Paul Klee's painting of *Angelus Novus* as referent. For Benjamin, Klee's angel looks "toward the past" where he sees catastrophe "piling wreckage upon wreckage."[56] The angel "would like to stay, awaken the dead, and make whole what has been smashed," but he is caught in a storm "blowing from Paradise" that "irresistibly propels him forward into the future to which his back is turned, while the pile of debris before him grows toward the sky. What we call progress is *this* storm."[57] Benjamin, moreover, characterizes this *Janus-faced* angel of history as *androgynous*, alluding to "sources in the Jewish kabbalist tradition in which God is feminized, bisexualized,"[58] as well as sources in Baudelaire to whom prostitutes and lesbians appear as seraphic androgynes. Reappraising Baudelaire's idealization of outcast women in materialist terms, Benjamin explains that the prostitute of *Les Fleurs du mal* is angelic because she displays the "holy prostitution of the . . . commodity-soul"[59] and because she affords the insular, alienated big-city dweller a form of "communion with the masses."[60] As regards the lesbian, "the woman who signifies hardness and virility,"[61] she is angelic for she is an emblem of sexual purity even if she is damned by society. Benjamin discovers this *amour pur* of lesbianism to be a primary motif of *Jugendstil*, "Modern Style": "The Lesbian woman carries spiritualization [*Vergeistigung*] into even the womb. There she plants the lily-banner of 'pure' love, which knows neither pregnancy nor family" (AP 558 [S8a, 3]).

To the lesbian's angelicism, Baudelaire adds her heroicism. "The lesbian is the heroine of *la modernité*," Benjamin reiterates, explaining "why Baudelaire long considered using the title *Les Lesbiennes*" for *Les Fleurs du mal*.[62] Benjamin reads this heroism as a resistance to the "impotent" ruling class, which "ceases to be occupied with the future of the productive forces it has unleashed" and, instead, preoccupies itself with "the wish to have children."[63] Recognizing that these tropes should not be mistaken for Baudelaire's commitment to women's emancipation, Benjamin attributes the poet's sources to utopian socialism, whose manifestos were "in the air," in particular, those of Claire Démar:

> In the widely ramified literature of those days which deals with the future of women, Démar's manifesto is unique in its power and passion. It appeared under the title *Ma loi d'avenir*. . . . Here the image of the heroic woman—an image that Baudelaire absorbed—is seen in its original version. Its lesbian variant was not the work of writers but a product of the Saint-Simonian circle.[64]

By recovering these sources, Benjamin points to a forgotten—*lesbian feminist*—dimension of revolutionary history, taking pains to cite whatever archival remnants he can find in his reconstellation of "modernité":

> Whatever documentation is involved here surely was not in the best of hands with the chroniclers of this school [the Saint-Simonian circle]. Yet we do have the following peculiar confession by a woman who was an adherent of Saint-Simon's doctrine: "I began to love my fellow woman as much as I loved my fellow man.... I conceded the physical strength of men,

> as well as the kind of intelligence that is peculiar to them, but I placed alongside men's qualities, as their equal, the physical beauty of women and the intellectual gifts peculiar to them."[65]

Connecting the Saint-Simonians to "the Vésuviennes" whose movement "supplied the February Revolution with a corps composed of women," Benjamin conjectures that "such a change in the feminine habitus brought out tendencies capable of firing Baudelaire's imagination"; if Baudelaire "reached the point where he gave a purely sexual accent to this development," Benjamin reaches further, resurrecting the political alongside the sexual with a retrospective glimpse of *the coming community of women.*[66] Christine Buci-Glucksmann raises the radical implications of Benjamin's feminist speculations:

> Female culture is ultimately universal culture, which makes it possible to confront difference within the self and the other. In this respect we should bear in mind Benjamin's words: "All rulers are the heirs of those who conquered before them. Hence, empathy with the victor invariably benefits the rulers. Historical materialists know what that means. Whoever has emerged victorious participates to this day in the triumphal procession in which the present rulers step over those who are lying prostrate."[67]

Buci-Glucksmann urges us to not overlook the mystical dimension of the "angel of history" in our focus on the allegorical. If read in light of Benjamin's kabalistic sources, his "angel" becomes a visionary rendering of history's repressed potential—a feminine, androgynous, and bisexual potential to absorb the fragmentation that issues from the sexual division of labor and commodity fetishism. And, if read in context of neglected historical sources in women's revolution, Benjamin's angel takes on a *lesbian* face. It is the lesbianism of utopian socialism that commands a change in "feminine habitus," so radical that woman should love her fellow woman as much as her fellow man, "mak[ing] it possible to confront difference within the self and the other" without hegemony.

Benjamin's reclamation of the revolutionary history of women is not lost on the flâneur of postmodernity. The last image of the constellation of *My Paris* is an image of women, "Bosnian women," who emerge from history's ongoing catastrophe, "presenting selves impeccably," while attending others "With 100 small attentions." Women's culture, were it to survive its repeated defeat, is (a) "Saving culture." Or so Scott's flâneur urges us to see with vision, prompted by love of woman for woman.

CHAPTER 4

The Lesbian Bohème

As popular stereotype, the bohemian was to have a long and continuous history, from Mürger's popular *Scènes de la Vie de bohème,* which became the hit of the Parisian theater season in 1849; through Puccini's *La Bohème,* first performed in Milan in 1896; all the way to *Rent,* the contemporary version of the bohemian legend transposed to the New York of the 1980s. Behind all these images, there continue to hover the charismatic figures of the first bohemians who used costume and lifestyle to define a cultural alternative to bourgeois modernity.

—Mary Gluck, "Theorizing the Cultural Roots of the Bohemian Artist"

The representations of the East Village spun by *Rent* and its boutique, formed through the daily exploits in cyberspace and on television and chronicled in trend-setting magazines, yield a specific rendition of the neighborhood and the everyday experiences of its residents. Primarily through media exposure, middle-class visitors encounter, become familiar with, and appreciate an illusion of the East Village lifted from bits and pieces of an otherwise complex interplay of ethnic, racial, class, political, and sexual social relations.

—Christopher Mele, *Selling the Lower East Side*

Rent had two plots: the straight half was from Puccini, and the gay half was from me. . . . Larson . . . transformed it into a dominant-culture piece by removing the lesbian authorial voice. . . . It was a hit made possible only because of the groundwork set by actual gay and lesbian artists who had taken such pains to familiarize the heterosexual majority with our own existence. It was like a Mississippi bluesman having his song ripped off by Pat Boone. The very thing about it that made it commodifiable was the mediocrity that remained once the music's soul was stripped.

—Sarah Schulman, *Stage Struck: Theater, AIDS, and the Marketing of Gay America*

Reading these statements, one is struck by the conflicting perspectives on *Rent*, Broadway's hit musical that stars East Village bohemia. For the cultural theorist, *Rent* signifies the latest production of a long and continuous history of bohemian resistance to "bourgeois modernity."[1] For the urban sociologist, *Rent* signifies an aesthetic obfuscation of East Village social relations that exploits bohemian images to entertain middle-class spectators and investors.[2] For the resident artist, *Rent* signifies a betrayal of gay and lesbian artists who laid behind-the-scenes "groundwork" for Jonathan Larson's popular staging of their bohemian community.[3] Perspectives collide even where they would imply common interests. Both cultural theorist and resident artist support bohemia's "cultural alternative." But the former sees *Rent* as a culminating moment of bohemian production, whereas the latter discerns in it a wholesale recuperation that divests subculture of its subversive "soul." Both resident artist and urban sociologist express concern for the neighborhood. But the former champions bohemian sexuality and artistry as productive counterculture, whereas the latter criticizes bohemian self-promotion as counterproductive to the struggle of ethnic and/or working-class residents against urban redevelopment.[4]

Rent may be the object of these colliding perspectives, but the nucleus of conflict is the idea of bohemia (or bohemian, or bohemianism). For the cultural theorist, bohemia is the historic beginning and ongoing source of metropolitan subculture. For the urban sociologist, bohemia is a transitory occupation of low-rent districts by cultural and sexual dissidents, who recast the neighborhood in their image and neglect to represent long-term residents, who, in turn, are subject to displacement by bohemian-inspired trendiness.[5] The question that arises in this clash of opinion concerns the nature of bohemian resistance. *Who* is served by bohemia's subversive (self-)representation, if not bohemians themselves? Are bourgeois audiences not simultaneously insulted and entertained, offended and enticed by bohemian prospects of living otherwise? On this point, the cultural theorist and urban sociologist may agree: from low rent to *Rent* on Broadway, the route of bohemian resistance is ultimately mainstream popularity. But the East Village artist voices a dimension of bohemia that remains off-stage and outside the markets and institutions of culture. The lesbian component that *Rent* "removed" to take bohemia to Broadway is, she argues, integral to East Village social infrastructure. What role, then, does *lesbian* bohemia play in the making of subculture and community? If it has a hand in producing and staging East Village life, why is it largely *excluded* from the Broadway plot and yet *implicated* in the story of selling out the neighborhood?[6] Against the massive success of dominant culture's misrepresentation of East Village bohemianism, the resident artist calls for recognition of lesbian and gay presence. She raises public awareness of the queer character of that space that has generated images of counterculture worldwide. Meanwhile, the cultural theorist and the urban sociologist critique dominant discourse, calling for consideration of cultural factors that are overlooked in the history of urban development.[7] But if the academics narrate a more inclusive history, the artist exhorts us to think of the excluded other whose character is too off-Broadway to sell or simply *too* other to be history's "corrective" factor.

This exhortation raises questions concerning the ambiguous character of bohemia, in general, and of bohemian perversity, in particular, as well as questions concerning strategies of historiography. Is failure to enjoy cultural ascendancy not the capital, psychological, and moral price bohemia must pay for resisting bourgeois modernity? Is bohemia's conundrum not death by success whose vitality is surpassed only by its survival in dereliction? How does the East Village lesbian artist exemplify (hyperbolize) the antitheses that characterize the city's most enigmatic type: the bohème? What role does *lesbian* bohemia play in the history of urban development and the making of the gay metropolis? If the history of lesbian bohemia is not continuous with the plot of global gentrification and cultural triumph, then how is it (to be) documented?

Sarah Schulman's representations of East Village life deploy various forms, reflecting her different occupations as community activist, journalist, historian, playwright, and novelist. If narrative is a preferred form, it is variously and experimentally constructed, defying traditional paradigms and inventing new models of exploratory realism. As Schulman observes, the East Village is a diverse collectivity of city actors and agents whose varying commitments and productions demand "novel" documentation. Bohemia and bohemians occupy center stage in her New York. Erected against backdrops of midtown and downtown, on site of the historic Lower East Side and casting racial and economic disparity in its space, this stage englobes an *era*:

> Life in the East Village . . . is thoroughly documented in my first six novels, which detail the neighborhood from the years 1981 to 1995. Suffice it to say that the East Village was a center for the production of global ideas. It was filled with varied races of immigrants, homosexuals, working people, bohemians, and artists working in both traditional and emergent forms, most of whom had no institutional training or support. . . . It was destroyed by AIDS, gentrification, and marketing. Now the East Village is primarily a center of consumption for the wealthy. (*Stage Struck*, 42)[8]

"A center for the production of global ideas," the East Village marked a temporary mobilization of local subculture on the world scene. It was destroyed by a (mismanaged) AIDS epidemic, "systematic and policy-driven gentrification," and "the marketing of false bohemia" that bolstered local real estate markets:[9] three fronts of social violence that were instrumental in clearing productive, heterogeneous space for a space of homogeneous, bourgeois consumption. Schulman's stress on the demise of the East Village as a site of cultural production contradicts *Rent*'s celebration of *la vie de bohème* that happily and miraculously survives all three fronts and enjoys a lengthy run on Broadway long after the real, referential bohemia dies out. Omitting the "lesbian authorial voice" from its representation, *Rent* loses a prime vantage from which to recast the experience and perception of actual urban devastation.

Schulman's witnessing of the destruction of East Village bohemia challenges the view that bohemia serves the deleterious restructuring of the neighborhood by generating trend-setting images and lifestyles for laissez-faire consumption. Christopher Mele includes queer artists and bohemians among East Village subcultures whose symbolic dissidence, he argues, paves the way for gentrification: "representations that imaginatively venerate the ethnic, racial, sexual and cultural diversity of place but intentionally understate the material dimensions of structural inequality have become increasingly prominent in forms of urban development in New York and similar Western cities."[10] By omitting bohemian representations that *do* document "the material dimensions of structural inequality" from his investigation, he overstates the case against bohemian complicity with real estate speculation and downplays bohemian struggle against colluding fronts of gentrification, marketing, and urban policy. He misrepresents bohemian constituencies that are composed of not just middle-class dropouts but also outcasts, including émigrés and refugees from all classes and castes who seek community and asylum from social/sexual persecution.

How do Schulman's novels document an era of bohemian New York that both venerates diversity *and* critiques inequity? What model of critical historiography could we use to foreground and discuss the complex interaction between bohemian production and urban development that we might find represented there? Walter Benjamin's "The Paris in the Second Empire in Baudelaire" readily suggests itself, most obviously the critical physiognomy of "The *Bohème*" that he presents in the first section of that essay, as does his concept of history as a "constellation" of epochal space.[11] Against the prevailing idea of history as "progress" and the additive method of "mustering . . . a mass of data to fill the homogeneous, empty time," Benjamin views history monadologically, that is, as a space of heterogeneous and antithetical forces that crystallize into eras. As he sees it, the task of the historical materialist is to "blast a specific era out of the homogeneous course of history"[12] and reveal its "dialectics at a standstill" (AP 462 [N2a, 3]).

Spanning a decade, three of Schulman's novels, *Girls, Visions and Everything* (1986), *People in Trouble* (1990), and *Rat Bohemia* (1995), construct imaginary constituencies of city types that characterize the rise and fall of East Village bohemia.[13] The *lesbian* characterization of this "era" demarcates not just the latest or last incarnation of bohemia but, more significantly, a radical revelation of the material paradoxes that drive urban production to catastrophic resolution. As a "trilogy," these novels illuminate the phantasmagoric making and unmaking of lesbian mecca, minus gay capital to "sell out" to niche marketing or invest in fetishistic nostalgia. Most provocative is the destructive character of "rat bohemia" as a strategy of negation of total domination by commodity space. Just as Benjamin sought to recover the trash of history and to represent modernity from the victims', not victors', perspective, so Schulman foregrounds a caricature of the lesbian bohème to raise the *refuse* of abjection.

The aim of this chapter is to reread the history of bohemia together with the history of urban development as represented in Schulman's fictions and viewed through the lens of Benjamin's dialectics. The critical optics applied in this reading are not superimposed on the primary text but are intended to bring out the materialist analyses that are already embedded in Schulman's literary production. Schulman's peripatetic narrators walk the city alert to social reality at base level, as made explicit by a citation of Marx in the epigram to *People in Trouble*: "'It is not the consciousness of men that determines their being, but their social being that determines their consciousness.'" Schulman's bohemian is a dissident, self-marketing subject *and* consumer object, whose *bohemian* social being raises awareness of our immersion in commodity culture.

Schulman's protagonists update the dilemma of the boulevard poet. "'Cette bohème-là, c'est mon tout' ['that bohemian woman—she means everything to me']," Benjamin cites Baudelaire, referring to the figure of the streetwalker whom the poet "casually includes . . . in the brotherhood of the *bohème*. Baudelaire knows that the true situation of the man of letters was: he goes to the marketplace as a flâneur supposedly to take a look at it but in reality to find a buyer."[14] If Benjamin's bohème caricatures the paradox of producing poetry only to sell one's soul, Schulman's bohème caricatures the paradox of producing art only to find no market, or to be sold without soul—or even to be remaindered after being made commodifiable. Her *lesbian* bohème personifies the constellation of critical themes that Benjamin started to explore in "Central Park" and that view Baudelaire's "heroic" lesbian as an instance of Art Nouveau resistance to bourgeois cultural reproduction.[15] Like Benjamin, Schulman takes sexuality to be a key aspect of Marx's discovery that the "commodity . . . is, in reality, *a very queer thing.*"[16] Beyond Benjamin, she populates the queer space of the East Village with a mélange of dyke types to represent the real and phantasmagorical, subversive and seductive, libidinal and (un)marketable character of urban reality.

A Fictive Constituency

> With *Un Prince de la bohème* (1840), Balzac wanted to portray a . . . characteristic of this nascent *bohème.* The amorous preoccupations . . . of Rusticoli de la Palférine are only a Balzacian expansion upon the triumphs of [Mürger's] Marcel and Rudolphe, which would soon follow. . . . This novel contains a grandiloquent definition of bohemianism, . . . the first: "The *bohème*—what should be called the doctrine of the Boulevard des Italiens—consists of young people, . . . all men of genius in their way, men as yet little known, but soon to become known. . . . Here one meets writers, administrators, soldiers, journalists, artists!..." . . . During this same period, George Sand . . . and Alphonse Karr ... initiated bohemian circles.... But these were imaginary bohemias; and that of Balzac was entirely fantastic. (AP 763 [d10, 1])[17]

From the beginning, bohemia was a product of radical self-fashioning and fantastic fabrication. Founding and future members of the bohème are the authors and bearers of stereotypes and myths.[18] Their agency as cultural subversives is mediated and performed by the fictions by which they image themselves and/or are imaged. These fictions feature, above all, *storybook cities.*[19] "Paris" sets the stage for *la vie de bohème.*

The bohème recasts Paris in its likeness. A production of social space, bohemian Paris forges an imaginary constituency of "types" and "places" to which no formal, symbolic, or political representation is assigned, yet which mobilize dissident identifications and collaborations. Driven by desire for self-representation, yet subject to the exploits of market reproduction, the bohème is facilitated and betrayed by the popularization of its images.[20] This is no less the case for *lesbian* bohemians.

But what "types" and "places" comprise a *lesbian* bohème and where do they arise? Who, what *real* constituency of city dwellers, do they serve?

Benjamin emphasizes the imaginary character of the bohème in his archive of "Literary History" (Convolute "d"). Elsewhere, he elaborates upon the aura of the "fantastic" derived from artists and also theorists, like Marx, who analyses the nebulous social forces astir in postrevolutionary Paris. He cites Marx's description of the bohème as a haven for "'professional conspirators'" and their incendiary "'inventions'"—"'fire bombs, destructive machines with magical effects, riots which are to be the more miraculous and surprising the less rational their foundation'" (Benjamin, "The *Bohème,*" 4). Invoking the wine cellar as unlikely headquarters where conspirators meet among "'all sorts of dubious people'" (3), Marx amplifies the bohème's motley aspect and pictures intoxicated, rabble-rousing plebeians in pointed contrast to the sober, theoretically-enlightened proletarians led by Louis Blanqui's *habit-noirs* (4). Discerning false from true revolutionaries, he casts the bohème in a phantasmagoria of aimless demagoguery and mob mystique.

Though persuaded by Marx's description of political instability, wavering class loyalty, and a tendency to provoke "revolution for revolution's sake," Benjamin implies another reason for the bohème's problematic subversiveness. If Marx interpellated the bohemians as a gang of "terroristic pipe-dream[ers]" (5), an emergent popular media obscures its reputation even further. When the bohème entered the public sphere as a recognizable Parisian "type," it had already been domesticated for the mass market. The taming of bohemia was a condition of its rebellious popularity. The "physiologies" were the taming mechanism:

> From the itinerant street vendor of the boulevards to the dandy in the opera-house foyer, there was not a figure of Paris life that was not sketched by a *physiologue.* The great flowering of the genre came in the early 1840s—the period that marked the *haute école* of the feuilleton. Baudelaire's generation went through it. . . . It was a petty-bourgeois genre. . . . The long series of eccentric or appealingly simple or severe

> figures which the physiologies presented to the public in character sketches had one thing in common: *they were harmless and perfectly affable.*[21]

The physiologies were designed to sell the city to leisured, moneyed, and entrepreneurial city readers, while quelling consumer fear of the city's "dangerous classes."[22] Their most obvious function was to "give people a friendly picture of one another. Thus, the physiologies helped fashion the phantasmagoria of Parisian life in their own way."[23] "*Physiologues*" neutralized the big city of strangers by presenting taxonomies of benign and pleasing caricatures. After physiologies of types, there appeared physiologies of the city: "Paris la nuit, Paris à table, Paris dans l'eau, Paris à cheval, Paris pittoresque, Paris marié," where, in each case, "innocuousness was of the essence" (Benjamin, "The Flâneur," 18). Benjamin prompts us to consider how the physiologies conditioned the production and reception of the bohème as a harmless stock character.

Henri Mürger is credited with casting the bohemian prototypes that would be proliferated and embellished in novels and operas, and imitated in real life. But his "originals" were already cast in the physiologues' standard mold. Drawn from his life among bitterly poverty-struck artists, Mürger's stories of "Marcel" and "Rudolph" radiate the aura of *bonhomie* as befitted the feuilleton (*Le Corsaire*) to which they were sold. Revised for the stage, they reflect "various concessions to 'good theatre' and bourgeois susceptibility."[24] The success of *La Vie de Bohème* in 1849 follows the defeat of the revolution of 1848, dispersing antibourgeois feeling in an aura of mystique, and redeeming the bohemian author with substantial proceeds. A source of subsistence and recognition, the fiction in turn hails the author with demands for further phantasmagoric self-reproductions.[25]

Echoing Benjamin, historian Christine Stansell stresses that an international implementation of the physiologues' domesticating strategy mediated the bohème's popularity. "In the 1890s, bohemia was on everyone's mind because of the English and American publication of the runaway best-seller *Trilby* (1894), a novel . . . that updated the Mürger prototype."[26] A further updating, Puccini's *La Bohème*, premiered in Turin in 1896 before touring to Los Angeles the next year. The characters these productions promulgated so appealingly were "thwarted male genius, impoverished creativity, doomed love affairs, and *perpetual bonhomie*," cast by a "habit of mind already attuned to discovering and observing stock 'types' in their particular metropolitan niches" (Stansell, *American Moderns*, 17). City guides helped forge this habit of mind. *New York by Gas-Light* (1850), to take a famous example, illuminated such types as "the courtesan," "the newsboy," "the seamstress," "the fashionable assignation house," "the saloon," "the tenement lodging" (Stansell, *American Moderns*, 17–18). Added to this gallery of innocuous rogues, "the *bohème*" was easily placed and contained.

Adapting European prototypes, an American bohème went into production on the site of Greenwich Village.[27] Promoted by artists and speculators alike, "the Village" was an idealized urban geography that attracted middle-class migrants from uptown New York and small town USA who sought escape from petit-bourgeois life and a role on the metropolitan stage that they themselves were casting and consuming.[28] A "selective vision of city life that installed some people in the foreground as protagonists and shunted others to the background or offstage altogether," the bohemian Village foregrounded the newcomers but overlooked working-class, Black, and ethnic residents, tenements, and sweatshops (41–43).[29] Stansell concedes the white, middle-class bias of this enabling fiction but stresses the invention of bold new types: "the revolutionary worker," "the 'rebel girl' worker," "the intellectual," and "the Jewish working-girl militant."

Villagers looked for radical cultural alternatives in the Lower East Side where Russian Jews and other, mostly eastern European, immigrants and refugees carried on their commitment to revolutionary art and politics. Among these displaced peoples were bohemians of a different kind, whose "intellectual and cultural life . . . encompassed Yiddish newspapers and theaters, literary societies, clubs, night classes, discussion groups" (22). Here WASP explorers discovered another universe where "socialist, anarchist, and Zionist controversies reverberated through . . . lecture halls, saloons, and tenements [and] . . . Yiddish was [the] primary means of expression" (22). Harboring a heterogeneous population of urban aliens

market invisibility, and corrosive poverty that cannot be transformed or redeemed by bohemian love alone. For the *lesbian* bohème, love arouses antagonism to the metropolitan status quo against the ideal of romantic transcendence that *Rent* popularizes.[43] Stereotyping bohemia as an enclave of self-absorbed artists whose passion revolves around a crisis of heterosexual love, *Rent* pays lip-service to the resistance and abjection that Schulman's low renters struggle to articulate and act out on the urban stage of political economy.[44] By marginalizing the lesbian character of East Village bohemia, *Rent* minimizes and simplifies the complex material struggle for collective and communal survival that is experienced by erotic outlaws and other resident aliens.

Schulman's bohème stereotypes lesbian love as a critical agent of urban production. As Schulman tells them, the superficial pleasures of *la vie de bohème* are troubled by a darkening, subterranean humor that makes strange bedfellows of community activism and amorous acting out. Where *Girls, Visions and Everything* reflects a vibrant arena of local theater, *People in Trouble* stages a riotous conflict between city developers and queer militants on site of art's duplicitous collaboration. *Rat Bohemia* recasts bohemia after epidemic homophobia and gentrification have destroyed its vibrancy and undermined its resistance. The rat bohème figures the lesbian bohème at its most repellent, as what remains of bohemia in the wake of the city after public space and the basis for community is systemically eroded. A rising and falling constellation of the capital of late capitalism, Schulman's bohème deploys a representational strategy we might discern more tellingly in light of Benjamin's constellation of motifs.

Situating Bohemia, Citing Antitheses: Benjamin/Schulman

To cultural historians, bohemia is the first instance of what we now call *subculture*, "a society within society."[45] It rises in the wake of the French Revolution in perpetual reaction to the expanding bourgeois establishment. A motley gathering of petit-bourgeois defectors, bohemians forge testy alliances between poor artists, dissolute vagrants, and professional conspirators. For Benjamin, the emergence of this unconsolidated class is less a historic turning point in revolutionary politics than a constellation of postrevolutionary space whose agents provocateurs and shifting arenas merely recast themselves, repeatedly, on the volatile stage of urban political economy.

Yet Benjamin's constellation of postrevolutionary history contests historicist models that interpret this age in terms of "progress" and that assimilate the antitheses of metropolitan society in a unifying idea of bourgeois development. Mary Gluck would correct Benjamin's representation of bohemia by recovering a dimension of history that it overlooks—namely, the insurgence waged by cultural and artistic dissidence that has "roots" in populist romanticism and that continues to mobilize anti-bourgeois art as a collective alternative to aesthetic individualism.[46] Defending these roots, she obscures the target of Benjamin's critique, which is the *spectacle* of revolution—the artful deployment of an *aura of insurgency* that presages and embellishes the space of commodity. Is it not the case that, from Mürger to Puccini to Jonathan Larson, the historic staging of *la bohème* displays the "continuity" with which populist romanticism is packaged in revolutionary fantasia for mainstream consumption?

Benjamin's constellation of nineteenth-century Paris makes visible the ur-forms and wish-images that mobilize revolutionary energies that were released by the French Revolution but never actualized in a proletarian transformation of society. It also reveals the ruin that comes of the bourgeoisie's fetishistic harnessing of these energies in the voracious expansion of industry. In this constellation, bohemia signifies a postrevolutionary sector of Paris that embodies revolution in perversely counterproductive productions aimed to defy the bourgeois ethic of industriousness and aesthetics of good taste. Discord is its primary expression, while its tactic is to appropriate metropolitan space to act up and act out, to (melo)dramatize the internal contradictions of postrevolutionary society. Benjamin held out no hopes for bohemia's instigation of *real* revolution. But he shifted the focus of historical materialism from proletarian-bourgeois opposition to the irresolute dialectics of bohemian insurrection.

Schulman expresses bohemia's categorical instability with critical irony. If lesbian love figures in her novels as a primary mediator of discordant factions, it does not resolve the dialectics of East Village life.

Love raises the aura of contradiction that envelopes the urban theater of emancipated desire, revealing the passionate antitheses between producing Lesbiana as an image of alternative community and marketing it for mainstream metropolitan consumption. In light of Benjamin's constellation, the categorical instability of Schulman's lesbian bohème is dialectically illuminated.

A Class and/or Not a Class?

> By 'bohemians' I mean that class of individuals for whom existence is a problem, circumstances a myth, and fortune an enigma; who have no sort of fixed abode, no place of refuge; who belong nowhere and are met with everywhere; who have no particular calling in life but follow fifty professions; who, for the most part, arise in the morning without knowing where they are to dine in the evening; who are rich today, impoverished tomorrow; who are ready to live honestly if they can, and otherwise if they cannot. (AP 428 [M5a, 2])[47]

> To tell the truth, [Théophile] Gauthier and his friends ... did not realize right away, in 1833, that they were bohemians; they were content with calling themselves "Jeune France." ... Their poverty was merely relative. (AP 764 [d10, 1])[48]

> RITA: I can't figure out what category I'm in.
> KILLER: Category?
> RITA: Yeah, I mean, I don't have any money but I'm not *poor*. I have aspirations but they're spiritual ones, not careers. I look around at how people are really living and I can't identify. But when I turn on the TV I don't understand that either. What the hell is going on, Killer? . . . Who the hell do we think we are?
> KILLER: We're bohemians. (Schulman, *Rat Bohemia*, 29)

Reading Schulman's fiction, we realize that bohemians form an inscrutable class of city dwellers whose most distinctive character is resistance to being placed in the reified scheme of capitalist production. At the same time, they instigate a small-scale, heterogeneous, and autonomous production of their own. That production is a mix of rogue art and everyday life, energetically conceived and collectively assembled at low cost. A conspiracy of neighborhood artists, bohemia sets no limit on outrageousness in its productive antagonism to elitist and generic markets. East Village lesbians make art for each other in disdain for dominant culture, acutely aware that their renegade sexuality lowers their marketable notoriety. As the protagonist of *Girls, Visions and Everything* reports, "there was no support outside of that tiny community of downtown dykes who understood being compelled towards an unlikely goal" (67).

Lila Futuransky, Schulman's archetypal dyke-about-town, is certain of her sexuality, her outlawry, her youthful and carefree vagrancy. She

> always knew she was an outlaw, but she could never figure out which one. She wanted to be free but couldn't decide what that meant. Yet, endlessly persevering, she continued to believe that she could construct any kind of life that she desired to live. And, because she both understood the phenomenon of process and felt that, at twenty-five, she was still young and had time, she continued to be a general dyke about town, alternately entertaining and antagonizing the people she bumped into, tripped over, walked with and the women that she slept with. (*Girls, Visions and Everything*, 3)

Her certainty affords her a future of *uncertainty*, free of the security provided by traditional assets, money, marriage, profession, gainful employment—everything the ambitious entrepreneur ought to possess. If this uncertainty is welcome, it is not a matter of gambling for future prosperity. The *lesbian* bohemian knows her resistance to reproducing heterosexuality makes her art of loving socially marginal and commercially improbable. Yet she goes into production anyway, eager to alter the norms of erotic entertainment and join in the neighborhood theater of everyday bohemian life.

Futuransky's friends and lovers, including the "Kitsch-Inn crowd" of writers, theater designers, and performance artists, cultivate a vision and practice of alternative, yet basic, living: "[they] understood about uncertainty and experiment and unreasonable expectations. They were trying to do good work, have good sex, make meaningful friends, and do all this with no impetus except their own ambition and desires" (67). To afford to materialize this living, they double their labor for half the remuneration. A typical bohemian like Isabel Schwartz "worked forty hours a week slinging burgers and saving her quarters until she had enough to put on a show. Her plays were tales of average lesbians and the little things they knew and cared about. Then it was back to the burgers" (17). A typical bohemian *writer*, Futuransky suffers twice the obscurity that accompanies the solitariness of her medium: "a writer who never published anything had a hard time convincing other people that she was really working. . . . She thought of her ideas alone, wrote them down alone, took them to the post office alone and got back the rejection letters alone" (16).

Futuransky greets rejection by projecting her ambition on a grand plane. The contrariness of this response is characteristic of her hubristic economics. In postrevolutionary Paris it was the bohemian's incoherence of class identity and oscillation of political allegiance that made him so perversely resistant to categorization and so potent an agent of destabilization, as exemplified by the (mis)rule of Napoléon III.[49] In late capitalism, what makes Schulman's bohème so unclassifiable is an incoherence of "vision": unviable speculation. Futuransky dreams futuristically of lesbian subculture on the metropolitan stage, of exploiting the contradiction between being sexual outlaws and becoming sexual icons. With political irony, she

> had often considered the question of marketing lesbian popularity. She looked at other groups of outcasts who had managed to make a name for themselves. The ultimate failures were Communists. In America, they were still at the bottom of the charts. After considering various historical examples, she concluded that the most successful model was that of the Beats. . . . They had made a phenomenon of themselves. They made themselves into the fashion, each one quoting from the other, building an image based not so much on their work as on the idea that they led interesting lives.

> Lila firmly believed that was exactly what lesbians needed to do. Why not make heroes out of Isabel Schwartz and Helen Hayes, and make The Kitsch-Inn the new mecca? Let kids from all over America pack their bags, sneak out at night and flock to the East Village to hang out with the lesbians. Soon there'd be lines around the block for the Inn's midnight show bringing those hungry for stimulation flocking to catch the last word in Lesbiana. They'd have magazine covers, syndicated situation comedies, do the lecture circuit, maybe even walk down the street without being afraid. Who knows? In Amerika, anything is theoretically possible. The next time she saw Allen Ginsberg buying cannollis at Veniero's, she would be sure to ask him how he did it. (59–60)

Schulman parodies the dream that possesses her as that which possessed the brotherhood of Beats, namely the dream of making a success on bohemian terms. As sociologist Pierre Bourdieu confirms "one of [bohemia's] major functions is to be its own market. . . . The rewards of this privileged market, if they do not manifest themselves in cold cash, have at least the virtue of assuring a form of social recognition for those who otherwise appear (that is, to other groups) as a challenge to common sense."[50] Futuransky's retrospective fantasy of Beat success *screens* the image of Beat mass marketing. It omits the conversion of utopian rebellion into fetish beatnik fashion and mobile, rebel homosexuality into a chic lifestyle option. "Rat bohemia" is the *real* future of Futuransky's "Lesbiana," testifying to its failure—like the Communists' "ultimate failure"—to attain the degree of market success that catapulted *and* ruined the Beat movement. Lesbian bohemia lacks sufficient capital to broadcast itself on public television but thrives anyway. It may survive mass marketing by eluding the global scene, but it is exposed to the rise in local cost of living that it helps bring about by enhancing East Village popularity.

Real and/or Phantasmagorical?

> [Théophile Gauthier's] bohemianism ... was the *bohème galante*; it could just as well be called gilded bohemianism, the *bohème dorée*.... Ten or fifteen

> years later, around 1843, there was a new bohemia..., the true *bohème*. Théophile Gauthier, Gérard de Nerval, Arsène Houssaye were then approaching forty; Mürger and his friends were not yet twenty-five. This time, it was a genuine intellectual proletariat. Mürger was the son of a concierge tailor; Champfleury's father was a secretary at the town hall in Laon;... Delvau's father was a tanner in the Faubourg Saint-Marcel; Courbet's family were quasi-peasants.... Champfleury and Chintreuil wrapped packages in a bookstore; Bonvin was a working-class typographer. (AP 763–64 [d10, 1])[51]

> KILLER: We're bohemians. We don't have those dominant culture values. . . . In the past there were decade-specific names . . . Like hippies, beatniks, New Age, punks or Communists. . . . Nowadays it's not generational. Bohemians aren't grouped by clothes or sex or age. Nowadays, it's just a state of mind. Anyone with a different idea is IN. (Schulman, *Rat Bohemia*, 29)

> LOURDES: I'm the New York bohemian just passing through.
> RITA: A real live bohemian?
> LOURDES: If this was the forties we'd be ... we'd be ... We'd be exactly who we are today. Our kind never changes. We're the international, eternal bohemia. (Schulman, *Rat Bohemia*, 36)

Benjamin's citation foregrounds generational and class differences that constitute a mythical divide between "true" or "real" and "false" bohemia that is advanced by historians, theorists, and bohemians themselves. Benjamin does not, however, articulate the vicissitudes of the bohème in oppositional terms. As he presents it, the constituency of this type is an unruly assemblage that, in its earliest formation, included professional conspirators among its plebeian carnival of rag pickers and prostitutes, wine-drinkers and wastrels. Even if antibourgeois conspiracy is its most defining feature, bourgeois features cannot be erased from its "true" physiognomy. As Bourdieu confirms, bohemia is "an ambiguous reality":

> near to the "people," with whom it often shares misery, it is separated from them by the art of living that defines it socially and which, even if

> ostentatiously opposed to the conventions and proprieties of the bourgeoisie, is situated nearer to the aristocracy or the grande bourgeoisie than to the orderly petite-bourgeoisie, notably in the matter of relations between the sexes, where it experiments on a large scale with all the forms of transgression (free love, venal love, pure love, eroticism) which it institutes as models in its writings.[52]

The Parisian bohème hosts a mélange of ambiguous types, notably "'proletariod intellectuals,'" who, like Mürger's water-drinkers, "are often so miserable that, in taking themselves for object . . . invent what will be called 'realism.'" And there are the "'penniless bourgeois'" who, like Baudelaire, are "poor relations of the great bourgeois dynasties, aristocrats ruined or in decline, foreigners and members of stigmatized minorities such as Jews."[53] In late-twentieth-century capitalism, the bohème is as ambiguous as ever. Schulman's bohème hosts successful artists ("Kate" in *People in Trouble*, "Muriel Kay Starr" in *Rat Bohemia*), aspiring but unrecompensed artists who hold poor-paying day jobs, low-life activists, and jobless, slum dwelling, shock-artists. Embodying the relative poverty of women and lacking institutional support, Schulman's artists are "directly subject to the laws of the market and often obliged to live off a second skill (sometimes with no direct relation to literature) in order to live an art that cannot make a living."[54]

At the heart of lesbian bohemia are "hardcore New Yorkers" (*Rat Bohemia*, 4) who cast themselves on their local stage, inventing a "realism" that reflects their own quotidian reality *and*, at the same time, contests the encroaching "art scene" that is part of the plan to gentrify the neighborhood. Among these "hardcore" city types are Lila Futuransky (*Girls, Visions and Everything*), Molly (*People in Trouble*), and Rita Mae Weems and Killer (*Rat Bohemia*), primary protagonists who present eyewitness reports from the site of confrontation. Hardcore bohemians are profoundly attached to the New York that they help to produce, to their staging of city life that specifically images the East Village and their place in it.

In *Girls, Visions and Everything*, the bohemian East Village is *in*

> small. . . . Lesbian playwrights have faced a special history of isolation and obstruction. . . . Because we were out, we were institutionally underdeveloped. (Schulman, *Stage Struck*, 65–66, 70)

The "bohemian woman" is a figure of down-and-out existence. A destitute street person, she makes the gutter her home with her few "appurtenances" of domestic habitation. So mean a refuge, yet this dwelling out-of-doors possesses an aura of interiority. "With an air of intimacy," she lays out her belongings under the bridge of the Seine that serves as her domicile, or so it strikes the eye of the bourgeois dialectician who has never not had a roof over his head. But if Benjamin exaggerates the coziness of this scene, he raises awareness of the bohemian use of space, a use we might interpret as *appropriative*. Instead of a fallen bourgeoise who imposes her household order by recasting the city in the image of her class, we might see a type of gypsy-rebel who accommodates her restless desires with makeshift resourcefulness.

That the physiognomy of bohemian misery should be female, in any case, reflects the poverty of the bohemian *woman*. Her male counterpart is the rag picker. In Benjamin's constellation, the rag picker "cannot, of course, be part of the *bohème*." He falls out of society just too far to make an entry into bohemian circles, though "from the littérateur to the professional conspirator, everyone who belonged to the *bohème* could recognize a bit of himself in the rag picker. Each person was in a more or less obscure state of revolt against society and faced a more or less precarious future" ("The *Bohème*," 20). If every bohemian *man* could identify with the rag picker, what of this bohemian *woman* who, by defecting from domesticity, would have crossed all proprietary limits of bourgeois femininity? In nineteenth-century Paris, this woman may have resembled a derelict housewife; more likely she was a streetwalker. Stepping out of the paternal domicile, she abandoned cloistered decency for the liberation of the gutter.[62]

Schulman's bohème typically has no money though she is not poor. Her relative poverty is due, in part, to the comparatively lower wages that society awards women as a class. There is, moreover, the unmarketability of *lesbian* cultural production. For the *lesbian* bohemian, being out *sexually* inevitably means being down *economically*. Schulman explains:

> There are fewer and fewer pockets of American culture that exist subculturally without a marketing influence. Probably the categories that remain untapped are dominated by people with little discretionary income. . . . Marketing can now use the existence of nondominant experience to two lucrative ends: it can sell products directly to minority groups, and it can repackage minority expressions and ideas for voracious consumption by a dominant culture that can't come up with its own innovations. . . . We live in a society deeply conflicted about homosexuality but no longer able to deny its existence. This combination makes gay people simultaneously an ideal group for niche marketing and for the containment inherent in commodification to straight consumers. . . . Lesbians represent one of the few subcultures that are still too underground to be fully seen by marketers, including gay male marketers. (*Stage Struck*, 104–08)[63]

While she works to have a roof over her head, the lesbian bohemian pays dearly for her sexual outlawry. Moreover, she pays in excess of what a gay bohemian pays for his, hustled as he is by niche marketing and commodified mass consumption.[64] Hustling the streets is not a viable alternative for lesbians, as Michelle Tea testifies in her streetwise journal *Valencia*. Hooking has none of the swaggering mobility and (literary) marketability that it has for the gay hustler (so richly described in John Rechy's best-selling *City of Nights*[65]). The price for being/acting lesbian on the metropolitan stage is greater than that of being/acting gay[66] (and bohemian), demanding immense moral and spiritual investment just to survive.

Nor are the times propitious for bohemian survival. New York in the 1990s is much more expensive than New York in the 1950s, whose "Beat hotel" (actually in Paris but figuratively in any inner-city low-rent district) recalls the easy vagrancy of bohemian New York in the 1920s (epitomized by Charles Henri Ford and Parker Tyler's modernist narrative of queer hobohemia in *The Young and Evil*[67]). The girls of *Girls*,

> living. . . . The park was so clean it was only a dream. The homeless were out of consciousness now. Then I remembered that, actually, they're living on our front stoops now, but the landlords live in Nyack. (Schulman, *Rat Bohemia*, 96–98)

If *Girls, Visions and Everything* documents the lesbian production of bohemian social space, *Rat Bohemia* documents the city's reappropriation, gentrification, and evacuation of that space for middle-class consumption. In the first instance, bohemians occupy the Lower East Side as creators of an East Village scene. Generating "visions" of urban reality, they transform the local landscape. The garden at Avenue B and East Sixth Street emblematizes their cultivation of Village community, a coming together in diversity to plot a common green.[73] In the second instance, bohemians are "exterminated," along with the homeless, by a systemic drive to beautify Lower Manhattan and spur real estate speculation. Renovated in the wake of the riot that took place on its grounds, the new Tompkins Square Park emblematizes the city's cosmetic revitalization. The utopianism of the former contrasts, in extremis, with the fascism of the latter, though both are phantasmagorical fabrications: the "visions" that transpired in the lesbian Lower East Side are obliterated by the city's "dream" of urban cleansing.

From utopia to ruin, the short history of the lesbian Lower East Side maps a space of violent contradiction. Schulman demarcates this rising/falling constellation of urban reality against the chronology of metropolitan "progress." Her bohemians testify to their success at creating a local self-image *and* at the same time to the destitution of their community. The city that hosts bohemia destroys its viability. At times, in complicity with homogeneous heteronomy, the bohemians are protagonists of their own demise. More often, they are the abject, autonomous antiheros of heterogeneous homosexuality. The crisis that signals the turning point of their communal resistance is not constituted by AIDS alone. The AIDS crisis is critically caught up in the antitheses of urban (re)production, as illustrated by the abyssal climax of *People in Trouble*. The visionary bohème of *Girls, Visions and Everything* becomes, in *Rat Bohemia*, the allegory of plaguing emergency.

Aspiration: Girls, Visions and Everything, 1986

The lesbian production of East Village bohemia is set by what, in the 1980s, was an established, working-class neighborhood of colorful ethnic and cultural diversity that offered low-rent housing, as well as abandoned buildings and vacant lots for creative squatting. It is historically preceded by the Jewish women's bohemia of the Lower East Side in the 1920s, and by the Beats' in the 1950s, whose "success" is the source of Lila Futuransky's aspirations (17, 56).[74] Lesbian prehistory also includes such disaster zones as the junkies' shooting gallery that Futuransky's fellow bohemians convert into a garden. Schulman's lesbian bohemians show how regeneration does not entail gentrification and turn derelict space into bohemian space in a manner that respects the older, residential character.[75] They deplore the "ARTS SCENE" that has been encroaching upon the neighborhood ever since the Beats:

> "The arty types were all over America sucking its blood," said Jack Kerouac to Carlo Marx in Denver. From Lila's East Village vantage point, she could see that he was right. At least as pertained to the ARTS SCENE which was oozing its slime all over Second Avenue. The upscale New Yorkers who cabbed it down to the fancy spaces to see performers on tour from Europe, ate out afterwards in restaurants where Lila couldn't even get a job. It was an invading homogenous monster composed of a lot of boring people thinking they were leading wacky lives. (43)

Gentrification looms on the horizon and pushes the lesbian bohemians further east of the Beat's Eastside, toward Hispanic Loisaida.[76] Futuransky retreats down Sixth Street to Avenue B, observing that

> things were so bad that even Avenue A was unlivable. The Good Humor man had been replaced by tofutti-selling teenaged boys in teased Mohawks. Polish and Puerto Rican mom and pop soda fountains featuring Breyer's ice

> cream, vanilla or chocolate, bowed to the pressure of imported ices. Tanned Europeans in skimpy t-shirts sold one dollar and fifty cent scoop-du-jour. (19)

It is the neighborhood's quotidian heterogeneousness that inspires Futuransky—"the beauty of the Lower Eastside everyday." She feels that she "needed to take a look at everything. . . . the Polish butcher and the Korean fruit stands and the Chinese take-out and the Arab deli and the Greek coffee shop and the East Asian newsstand and the Jewish bakery" (97). It is this thriving diversity that she loves, opening her to whatever further love/r might come her way. "Her city," she muses, "was the most beautiful woman she had ever known" (177). Yet she is protective of this first love, wary of "getting lost in the world of romance" (97). She considers heeding the warning of her bohemian comrade to not get "settled in your own little hole" and lose sight of the city's greater scene, so that "by the time you wake up, she won't be yours anymore" (178).

The opening scene of *Girls, Visions and Everything* locates Futuransky at the front row of "The Pyramid Club" where she watches Helen Hayes do her "East Village dead-pan" to insider audiences (4). Dazzled by this star performance, Futuransky pursues Hayes for a date. But Hayes stands her up and the romance is suspended. It is the play *between the acts* that keeps Futuransky in suspense. More than a love story, the novel lends the scene of romance to frequent interruption. Urban fantasy and phantasmagoria are *rent* by realism at critical narrative moments, thereby prompting Schulman's readers to see the shocking disjunction between what makes subculture thrive and what threatens to kill it.

Gentrification is clearly a prime killer, one that threatens to colonize the city with its glossy extravaganza. But it is not the only scene downtown. "At the same time . . . —a depression culture was rising on the streets. There was better dancing in Washington Square Park by Black boys or Puerto Rican faggots than in any performance space. There was Doo-Wop under the Washington Arch and excellent fusion jazz every night for free on Astor Place" (65). "Noticing these contradictions" (65), Futuransky and her friends dream of a theater that displays cultural antitheses with candid abrasiveness. They invent "The

Worst Performance Festival" with the rationale that "we want to look at both sides of what it means to be the worst. Some performers are bad because they're about nothing but the audience loves them because the audience is also about nothing. Other performances are bad because they're really about something but that makes the audience uncomfortable, so they don't like it. That is the dialectic of worst" (66). "The Worst Performance Festival" parodies the dialectics of Brecht's epic theater. Though, like Brecht, Kitsch-Inn dramaturgists stress "the functional connection between stage and public," and they "portray situations rather than develop plots" by "interrupting the plot" with "the procedure of montage," true to the historic avant-garde, Futuransky's bohemian avant-garde is—to quote Benjamin on epic theater—"concerned less with filling the public with feelings, even seditious ones, than with alienating it in an enduring way, through thinking, from the conditions in which it lives."[77] Futuransky works the play between performers and viewers so that the distance of spectacle breaks down. This is how Schulman's novel works overall. Whatever future prospects urban planners have been plotting, *Girls, Visions and Everything* delights in exposing in the worst possible light, showcasing the production with comic nihilism. For Schulman's thespians, the critical agent is laughter, a convulsive gaiety that lesbians also take to bed.[78]

Conflagration: People in Trouble, *1991*

The first view of the Lower East Side in *People in Trouble* looks on "the Tompkins Square Park riot" (13) of summer 1988 as a dramatic turning point in the history of the neighborhood.[79] It is a local, epochal, production. But the lesbian bohème is not a principle actor. Instead

> there were a lot of skinheads but also many regular neighbors plus punks and aging hippies. There were officers on the edges grabbing others arbitrarily and kicking them or hitting them with police sticks. It was more police than Kate had seen since the sixties. It was real violence in the midst of great confusion. It was not a movie of the week. It was hot. It was stylized. It was unbelievable when it happened so openly. (12)

Viewing the scene is "Kate," a resident artist, who watches at such proximity that "a helicopter hovered outside almost level with her windowframe" (12). Framing Kate's perspective are fantasies of memory and media that, despite her sense of closeness, distances her awareness of the crisis. If at first it seems real "like a war movie" (12), in retrospect it seems eerily surreal. "Now that it was September, that hot night had become a screen, another newscast, a spectacular event. . . . Girls and boys with bleached blond military haircuts were hanging out again wearing T-shirts claiming I survived the Tompkins Square Park Riot" (13). As a "screen memory," the riot assumes the character of a commodity. Yet Kate is shaken: "something was changing in the way she was seeing and it had started to affect her drawing" (14). Arising in the wake of a "hallucinatorily hot summer with AIDS wastes and other signs of the Apocalypse washing up on the beaches" (12), the riot stirs the "fragments," "shreds," and "partial phrases" of a perception that forms the basis of her artistic breakthrough.

The battle over Tompkins Square Park is not the novel's only scene of war. AIDS is killing the gay community with the collaboration of genocidal policies and practices, including the treacherous eviction of PWAs from tenements targeted for redevelopment. If in *Girls, Visions and Everything* gentrification is an encroaching terror, in *People in Trouble* it penetrates the heart of the gay Village, and even the Lower East Side.[80] Threatened with displacement or even homelessness, and grieving the mounting deaths of gay friends and neighbors, Schulman's lesbians join forces with gay municipal activists. They meet at an underground gathering where they become outraged at the disclosure of a development scam:

> This week many of you received eviction notices from Ronald Horne's development company. This is the man who has warehoused thousands of empty apartments while ninety thousand people live in the subways and stairwells and public bathrooms of this city. Now we have learned that he has purposely bought buildings with more than fifty percent gay tenants in the hope that we will drop dead and leave him with empty apartments. He files these eviction notices anticipating that some of us will be too ill

> to contest. Now let me ask you, what are we going to do to get *justice*? (118)

With gathering militancy, a disparate conglomerate of queer types is mobilized:

> Attendance at meetings had grown to well over five hundred and numbers like that meant all kinds, all kinds. There were the tough street Furies who had all been around the block a couple of times. There were distinguished homosexuals with white-boy jobs, who had forgotten they were *queer* until AIDS came along and everyone else reminded them. . . . There was also a contingent of old-time radicals of various stripes who had rioted in the sixties at Stonewall, in Newark, with the Young Lords, with SDS, and hadn't done a goddamn thing since. . . . There was a band of veterans from the now defunct women's liberation movement who were the only ones who had been consistently politically active for the last decade. (158–59)

Though gay men comprise the vanguard, lesbians count among the most active (and robust) members.[81] "'We like dykes,' the guys would chant every once in a while when the women did something really great" (159). In bohemian style, they stage their outrage outrageously, parading their anger and mourning with increasing volume and visibility.

"Molly" is a furious type of lesbian bohemian, an East Village dyke who casts her lot with the gay militants. She engages Kate in a love affair that enhances Kate's exposure to the city. Their love-making is a revelation to Kate, a straight woman, who, while she remains emotionally aloof, has never enjoyed such bodily rapture. At the same time, Molly introduces Kate to queer sites of urban trauma that put Kate in touch with her own embodied memories of urban violence (16). Where before Kate kept aloof to what was happening outside her studio, "stay[ing] at the window watching and . . . decid[ing] not to enter into it" (12), she is prompted to look again. In Molly, she finds someone to help "search . . . for the particles of physicality that captured the fear, the pain" that, presently, she can only articulate as "*chaos*" (16). The bohemian activist couples with the avant-garde artist in a productive moment of embracing conflict. The two types do not merge into a composite one but, instead, present dialectical components in an enactment of contemporary urban space. Ultimately, the avant-garde artist abandons the affair to pursue her sky-rocketing career. The bohemian activist retreats to the trenches of the Lower East Side, where, for her, love and life converge in ongoing acts of resistance.

Through the interactions of these two types, we see colliding visions of the city. Communication between Molly and Kate is often stated to such cross-purposes that conversation devolves into contention. Narrative breaks into episodes that are orchestrated, *dialogically*, from one or other contesting third-person points of view, each episode headed by the name of the character from whose perspective it is represented. "Molly" views the city at street-level in daily encounters with the poor and homeless, whom she treats with sober resourcefulness. She is an insider eyewitness to the underground organizing and above-ground militating of queer city activists. She leads us, with Kate, on "a guided tour of all the lesbian bars below Fourteenth Street" (81), highlighting the effects of gentrification/commodification:

> "This is the Cubbyhole," Molly had said, starting with a loud, overpriced butcher-block place on Hudson Street. "It should be called the Glove Compartment. It mostly attracts graphic artists and luppies. That's lesbian yuppies in case you didn't know." . . .
>
> "This is Kelly's," Molly told her, bringing them to a remodeled overpriced bar across Seventh Avenue. "It used to be exclusively for jocks. But since the renovation it got taken over by collegiate dyklings. Everyone here is femme." . . .
>
> "This is the Duchess. . . . This dive is world-renowned for being overpriced. . . . There is usually some girl on black beauties breaking up with her girlfriend over the pay phone. It happens so often I used to think it was the same girl and they put her on salary for atmosphere."
>
> . . . They ended up at Tracks, a three-story gay entertainment emporium in the middle of nothing over by the river. . . . "It's gay-owned," Molly

> said. "Unlike some of those previous establishments. This is a chain . . . like a homosexual Howard Johnson's." (81–83)

As Kate withdraws into her art, Molly retreats into an affair with "Sam," an unpretentious and sexually unambiguous butch. Molly's first view of Sam's Lower East Side south-of-Houston apartment reveals what is to Molly the last authentic remnant of bohemian space:

> It was a fifties' dime-store novel about a pregentrification bohemia that no one could live in anymore because of high rents and lack of inclination. Sam led her up rickety stairs past a front door with a busted lock, past the beat-up mailboxes hanging open on mangled hinges. Everyone in the building was Chinese. The hallways were decorated with red hanging things left over from the New Year and all the apartment doors were open so they could see old-world grandmothers in quilted jackets and white T-shirts cooking rice on hot plates. There were lots of beds in each room and walls papered with magazine covers, calendar pages and red fringe. Tired men shuffled to bathrooms in the hall, barefoot on the torn linoleum.
>
> It was one room. It was spare. There was no refrigerator. Her beer was sitting on the windowsill trying to keep cool in the June rain. There was a bulb from the ceiling, a bed she had built, a TV. . . . There were no chairs. There was an ancient stove. . . . The window faced a wall, so there was no breeze and no light. . . . Sam . . . was a memory from another time. (179–80)

An anachronism, Sam's dwelling compels us to see the displacement of lesbian bohemia to the last frontier of gentrification, the poorest area of the tenement district in, or bordering, Chinatown.

Drawn to Molly, Kate follows her into her world but does not dwell there. She returns to her studio and works her sensation of exposure into expression. When that expression takes the shape of a large art installation, her agent suggests that she exhibit with the city's arts project that, wishing to decorate recently expropriated public space for private development, will supply her with "large areas of park and sidewalk" (99). Through Kate, we see the racket behind the city-sponsored arts scene.[82]

To these conflicting visions, Schulman adds a third through the eyes of "Peter," Kate's estranged husband. Determined to succeed as an independent, solo designer, Peter looks on the city with formal and competitive interest. He is oblivious of ubiquitous poverty and homelessness and only vaguely conscious of the massive orchestration of gay funeral processions. But when Kate commences her lesbian affair, he feels "slapped in the face by homosexuality practically every day" (13). Alternatively, he is readily, if disdainfully, impressed by the designs of archdeveloper Ronald Horne. On his daily jog around Lower Manhattan, he serves as the vehicle through which we see the city of renovation:

> Downtown City's main drag was called Freedom Place. . . . The buildings were mostly sky-rise condominiums, although there were a few newly constructed waterfront townhouses reminiscent of Henry James's Washington Square. That way the truly wealthy could stare out at Ellis Island through their bay windows as they drank down their coffee every morning. The only visible storefront was Chemical Bank. . . . Liberty Avenue was designed to replicate the solid turn-of-the-century Rockefeller-style riches usually found on Fifth. There was a square, pre-Depression, old-money austerity; an impenetrable magnificence. No expense had been spared and yet there was nothing garish; imported marble, tasteful ironwork, elegant windows. It had all the elements of a made-to-order American shrine. . . . Peter ran on through Battery Park past all the signs warning of rat poison and past all the homeless people avoiding the lines of tourists waiting to see the Statue of Liberty. He sprinted through the South Street Seaport, Manhattan's only shopping mall, down around the big Pathmark where every morning black men and old Chinese women in straw hats stood together on line waiting to cash in the empty cans they had collected for the five-cent deposit. The river smelled of abandoned cars, old fish and stale beer. Peter turned up East River Park, under the Manhattan Bridge, and jogged slowly back over to the West Side. (27–29)

Peter recognizes "how Downtown City was advanced capitalism's version of the company town" (28). With further insight, Schulman prompts us to see how advanced capitalism erases all traces of depression from its catastrophic history, ensuring that history will repeat itself on a grander scale.[83]

What is common to all three visions is the appalling sight of *people in trouble*. The novel stages their explosive coming together on site of Kate's installation. If the set is avant-garde, the *stage-off* between city development and queer processions is high melodrama. The AIDS activist groups "Justice" and "Fury" are representatives of *Good* in a battle against *Evil*, supremely represented by Ronald Horne (Donald Trump). Trumpeting family values and aggressive privatization, Horne's most diabolical scheme is to convert New York's beloved Public Library into a luxury health club for wealthy midtown businessmen (220).[84]

Melodrama, Mary Gluck explains, is counterculture's original medium. For bohemians of postrevolutionary Paris, "the melodrama was an object lesson in revolutionary justice, transposing onto the plane of private life the abstract moral and ideological values of revolutionary politics."[85] Schulman uses melodrama to amplify the camp/kitsch of Socialist Realism, the tradition out of which she explicitly writes, and to foreground a "lesson in revolutionary justice," transposing *sexual* politics onto the plane of private, *erotic* life (Kate's, Molly's, Peter's), while performing public justice with dissident homosexual antics.[86] "Justice" is bohemia's last stand against advanced, laissez-faire capitalism, a gay commune that arises in the wake of the AIDS epidemic and the Tompkins Square Park riot. Deploying spatial strategies, "Justice" reappropriates "the abandoned Saint Mark's bathhouse, closed down by the mayor" (156) for its underground gatherings. When membership outgrows the bathhouse, it crashes "The Saint"—"a three-storey nightclub, former gay bar extraordinaire," which housed "three generations of underground people" before selling out to the "Business Association of Single Traders and Retail Distributors of Saccharine" (206).

Schulman's eponymous novel names the victims of urban violence who take part in plotting justice. Kate uses the same name as the title for her installation.[87] Erected on site of the *new* Public Library, at the intersection of Horne's opening ceremonies and a Justice-led funeral procession, her installation literally sets the stage for a riotous conflagration. A spontaneous "happening" of street art and life, the two fronts converge in chaos against the specter of "People in Trouble." Bodyguards flee "against the background of her collage," leaving Horne to be "wrapped by her images" (221) of inflammable artwork. With impulsive intervention, Kate sets the work ablaze, engulfing the tyrant in flames just as he pulls his gun.

If Horne is brought down, the victory is pyrrhic at best. The artwork is destroyed and the marchers are dispersed. In the fallout of confrontation, the primary actors go their disparate ways.[88] Art and bohemia have their dialectical climax, leaving the ruins of both in its wake.

Decimation: Rat Bohemia, *1995*

Schulman's third and last novel of bohemian New York opens on a cataclysmic scene of erratic and lethal violence, abyssal unemployment, epidemic homelessness, an HIV-ridden gay body politic, and an out-of-control rat infestation. Protesting the killing of lower Manhattan ecology, the novel makes explicit the cause. Municipal and federal governments are to blame for the atrophy of social infrastructure. President "Reagan [is] held . . . directly responsible" (*Rat Bohemia*, 5) for social policy that "exterminates" the poor and the sick who are dying in the streets from a flawed administration of public health.[89] But if the villain is boldly outlined, there is little melodrama. Narrative and dialogue comprise the libretto of a wake, an unremitting dirge.

By the early 1990s the East Village has become a stage for daily funeral processions. The scene is a sorry parody of gay pride:

> The official stepping-off spot for the funeral was at Houston Street and First Avenue at one o'clock. But, the organizers forgot that about twenty-five homeless people sold their stuff on that very spot every day. . . . So we all had to kind of stand around them, step over them and refuse them nonchalantly while crying and comforting each other at the same time. . . . A

> bunch of big, strong gym queens in tiny cutoffs lifted the coffin onto their shoulders and all two hundred of us walked behind it up First Avenue. There were some Radical Faeries with bells on their toes. . . . There were not many observers on that strip of First Avenue as we walked past some funeral homes and into Tompkins Square Park. We ended up in the void where the bandshell used to be. (155–57)

Since public space has been privatized, mourners must compete with homeless people for a place on the street. The procession arrives at Tompkins Square Park, the site of the squatters' defeat and where, now, gay villagers park their dead, marking the void of public care against the backdrop of gentrification.

From such dereliction arises the last generation of the lesbian bohème. Occupying center stage are two antithetical types. There is "the international, eternal bohemia," caricatured by "Lourdes," who, "glamorous," "worldly," and "really sexy," offers erotic sanctuary to lesbians less mobile in the global city (35–36). Lourdes is a survivor of Cuba's postrevolutionary fallout, including a violent crackdown on gays. A veteran sexual fugitive, she knows how to enjoy sex *sans* emotional bondage. Her apartment, though "cozy" and "tasteful," is also spare and impersonal, a space where all that matters is the act of inhabiting the moment (33). True to her namesake, Lourdes brings her city-weary lover a glass of water after therapeutic love-making (36).

On the other hand, there is "rat bohemia," comprised of indigenous, "hardcore New Yorkers" (4). A type that has never appeared before, the rat bohème is more destitute of means and hopes than Mürger's "water-drinkers." Harboring "liars and believers, tops and bottoms, butches and femmes, doers and wannabes, yuppies and deadbeats, mommies and daddies, enemies and friends," rat bohemia is a duplicitous and imperiled "lesbian community" whose consensus is that "the more you hide, the safer you are" (113). Lila Futuransky makes a furtive reappearance as a murder suspect before she has "the charges dropped under mysterious circumstances" (166). She is replaced by a trio of antagonistic understudies.

Daughter of a Jew from Bremen who found a way to Queen's from Thereisenstadt (a Nazi concentration camp), "Rita Mae Weems" is a survivor of today's urban holocaust (11).[90] She acts as a "witness to her own time," in belief that she's "gonna live a lot longer than most of the people [she] meet[s]" (6). Cast out on the streets by her Catholic father who learns of her lesbianism, she finds refuge in gay nightclubs and bars. But yesterday's sanctuary is today's graveyard:

> La Femme . . . The Dutchess . . . the west side of Washington Square Park . . . Bonnie and Clyde's . . . Chaps and Rusty's by Chrystie Street . . . the pier on West Street [with] the leather queens getting blow jobs or fucking in the open at all hours. . . . Now, they're ghosts. That's where the gay children were—kids like me with nowhere to go. (195–96)

In the wake of the gay Village, stricken by disease and expropriation, Rita retreats to the lesbian ghetto to make a subsistence living among friends. Her creative potential is reduced to imagining unimaginable ways to exterminate rats. Working for the city's pathetic "Pest Control," she pays the rent and spends most of her spare time with her best friend "Killer," "just walking around because [they] didn't have any money" (4).

Killer recognizes that "you can't drop out or you'll be homeless" and that "you gotta function to be a boho" (30). Like most rat bohemians, she is minimally functional, "except," as Rita remarks, "when it came to finding a place to live. She couldn't imagine her way out of that slum" (41). Jobless for two years during a crisis of severe unemployment, Killer "had forgotten how to even look for a job" (4). Her flat on Avenue C and East Seventh Street is "a good example of urban blight" (41). Fearing Killer's tendency to "sit around and deteriorate due to lack of realistic planning," Rita tries to drive home a sense of emergency. She finds an accomplice in Killer's girlfriend; "Troy Ruby," like her father, "Jack Ruby" (109), would rid the nation of its worst enemy (111). Besieged by a bourgeois soullessness, she attacks patriotic platitudes with the vitriolic dissent of Allen Ginsberg (110). A reverse Futuransky, she foresees the abysmal danger of future progress:

> Future is a scary word here in America. . . . Americans are dangerous. . . . We destroy the earth, mind and lymph node and then market that

> destruction. . . . I have a lot of predictions about the future of America. Predictions that might have already come true. . . . I predict that there will be a new kind of cancer and advertising executives will name it Lymphomania. I predict T-shirts that say *I want to rape you.* I predict haphazard memorial services at every hour of the day and night because too many people are dead. Their ghosts have to compete wildly for remembrance. I predict that homeless people will piss on bank machines like storefronts lined with urinals. (127)

The most terminal case of bohemianism is "David." An avant-garde writer and sex radical, David's artistry and gaiety are both cut short by AIDS. Suffering illness with fatalistic ambivalence, he denounces the all-American family (87) while confessing a desire for "normalcy" (89). Reacting to having HIV, he views the history of AIDS activism with cynical negativity: "First, Sex Positive was the movement. Now, it's a sex movement. Sex, sex, sex. There's a lot of copulating going on out there. It's all come full circle back to 1984. Apocalypse Now! Paradise Now! Apocalypse Now! Paradise Now!" (58). Though he rants against homophobic epidemiology and homocidal society, his outrage is undialectical. Instead of militating against social and sexual abjection, he internalizes it, betraying the revolution that he helped to mobilize and being repeatedly betrayed by his straight family to whom he ultimately appeals.[91]

The plot of *Rat Bohemia* is to present the truth of Now for future generations of rat bohemians. Lacking a unifying vision, the narrative devolves into a constellation of voices, whose dialogism *is* dialectical.[92] The critique of bourgeois America is raised not in unison but with differing ideas of what it means to be bohemian and alive in this deadening era of urban history. Yet if voices are not heard in harmony, nor do they sound as soliloquies. Each voice interpenetrates the other, in speech acts that couple diversity in love and animosity. Spontaneous intercourse between Rita and Lourdes incarnates an antithetical communing between gritty Lower East Side realism and global city savvy in an aura of good sex. The love affair between Killer and Troy enjoins one bohemian's self-defeatism with another's artistic activism. Killer's candid connection with

David affords his devastated life unsentimental testimony, whereas David frankly resents Rita, blaming her for living while he is dying, and Rita disparages (David's) familial desertion. The conflict of dialogue is productive, if pessimistic, generating a bohemian conspiracy that takes the form of strategic ressentiment—or "conscientious abjection."[93]

The novel ends with a view of Lower Manhattan from the collective perspective of the lesbian bohème. Conspiring to recover Rita's "lost love" who is married and residing in the suburbs, the bohemians drive through the city in a budget rental car en route to Delaware. The drive takes them through different neighborhoods from the East to West Village, after leaving the congested freeway of the "FDR" (Franklin D. Roosevelt Drive). What they see is not a scenic panorama but a montage of colliding New York images, as disparate as the Lower East Side's Cherry Street projects (215) *and* South Street Seaport. If the former is exemplary for its local ethnicity and precapitalist porosity, the latter is a paragon of commercial homogeneity and luxury interiority:

> Everyone is outside, all those Dominican men with their cotton shirts open and women sitting on stoops and folding chairs. Radios. Water streaming from fire hydrants. Kids, jumping in front of the car chasing balls, so you have to be on alert at all times. Everyone's got a Budweiser. The garbage never gets picked up. Sirens. Yellow lights from hallways, open windows with TVs flickering unattended in the background. Dogs without leashes. Skinny legs on small boys. Pir Agua for the Latinos, and greasy meat on skewers for everyone else. . . . We ended up in the middle of incredible congestion around South Street Seaport. Between the cars and the cabs and the tourist buses, you couldn't move a muscle. Plus, all those Americans and their families dodging in and out. Thank God for South Street Seaport. Now, when Americans come to New York they have a place to go. Everything is the same as their luxury malls back home and it keeps them all together in one spot. (211–12)

The bohemians finally run out of gas at Fourteenth Street and the West Side Highway in the vicinity of the "Clit Club" (218). Diverted from their plan, they watch the young dykes lining up outside the Club's door. They notice "a bunch of guys in suits . . . pleading for admission" knowing that "this was the only place on earth where [guys in suits] were not going to get in" (218). They do not join the line but return to the East Village "with the needle on empty" (218).

The Return of the Real (Bohemia)

> If I make my contribution to truth, some Rat Bohemian down the line will notice and appreciate it. She'll be sitting in a city strewn with rats and rat carcasses and come across my petite observation. That's the most amazing relationship in the universe. The girl on rat bones who knows that she is not alone. She is not American. (Schulman, *Rat Bohemia*, 53–54)

> The tradition of the oppressed teaches us that the "state of emergency" in which we live is not the exception but the rule. We must attain to a conception of history that accords with this insight. Then we will clearly see that it is our task to bring about a real state of emergency, and this will improve our position in the struggle against fascism. (Benjamin, "On the Concept of History," 392)

Rat Bohemia stages real catastrophe behind illusory progress. Cast among detritus such as AIDS victims and rat carcasses, the real remainders of urban "development," Schulman's bohème signals the alarm that "teaches us that the 'state of emergency' in which we live is not the exception but the rule." A didactic tale, the novel sheds all hope, faith, and belief in American prosperity, which it is the duty of every patriot to uphold. Cherished institutions of family, nation, and religion are relentlessly exposed and found horribly wanting by these rebels, who are in the first place refugees from abuse and intolerance, and who now feel the double betrayal of society's moralizing homeostasis in the face of crisis. Rat bohemians do not stoop to consolation. Instead, they glean among the corpses hard evidence of an unchecked, man-made disaster that plagues the heart of urban America.

If this generation of bohemians is a degenerate—ratty—one, that is because programs of renewal breed unlivable misery for inner-city populations that have been targeted for expropriation and relocation. Yet Elizabeth Wilson views the growing economic disparity between elite art markets and underfunded local production as ripe for bohemian resurgence: "notwithstanding the astonishing wealth of the few, we see the return of the impoverished artist and intellectual, in a world not unlike—although so different—from the café culture of the 1830s."[94] For Wilson, bohemianism survives such disparity by paradoxically—parasitically—proliferating antibourgeois lifestyles for bourgeois consumption: "bohemians haunted and still haunt capitalist society, their dissidence, far from being recuperated, is feasting vampiristically on the lifeblood of contemporary bourgeois society."[95] If Wilson regards bohemian viability with guarded optimism, Schulman remains intransigently pessimistic. Her bohemians find nothing in contemporary bourgeois culture on which to feed their souls or even sustain basic biological needs. The image of "a city strewn with rats and rat carcasses" nurtures no (bohemian) illusions about the catastrophe of history; no future is posed that might alleviate the present.

Allegory is Schulman's prime strategy of signaling emergency. Her narrative erupts into graphic reports on the city's flourishing rat infestation and its grotesquely ineffectual methods of eradication. Rat sightings are matched by equally graphic updates on David's advancing disease (149–52), as if the urban body and the gay body were one and the same. "Rats" allegorize a host of pestilence: the AIDS virus, the vehicle of colonialism through which infectious diseases were first transported, ruthless developers and criminal administrators whose project of gentrification taxes and destroys social infrastructure, a voracious market in global communications that disenfranchises local arts communities, parents who refuse to help their dying gay children, and hack physicians who sell expensive placebos to despairing PWAs—PWLOPWAs—"People Who Live Off People With AIDS" (153). Yet, like the Holocaust survivors of Art Spiegelman's *MAUS*, Schulman's bohemians identify with the rodent (in this case, "super rat") who survives concerted efforts by family members and civic authorities to exterminate their kind.

An overdetermined symbol, the rat dispels sympathetic identification with any aspect of the situation, including bohemia itself. There is no redeeming conclusion, though narrative recuperation is bohemia's bestselling fiction. Anticipating *Rent*, Schulman illustrates the betrayal of bohemia by bohemians in her "appendix," where excerpts of Muriel Kay Starr's top-of-the-charts novel are cited for critical consumption. A soap-opera revision of *Rat Bohemia*'s preceding chapters, *The Good and the Bad* converts hard-core urban realism into a straight and saccharine fantasy of bourgeois assimilation (219–31). But bohemia's self-parody is profoundly anticlimactic. The crux of the plot is the allegory of eternity that ends the story of bohemia's ever fashionable recycling. It appears ex nihilo in the middle of the story:

> Eternity is a hooded skeleton, a human tiger with a butterfly on his scalp. A bespectacled burro waving a death's-head flag. Dried bread. A one-armed Inca with tattooed knees, his sister plays the mandolin with artificial fingernails. A uniformed pig holds his hand down a wooden pile. The scarecrow is bleeding. My tongue is too big. There a swastika in red, white and blue. A bag of gold. A blank, open book. (99–100)

This is a figure of the death's head, embellished with the iconography of the Incas.[96] An exotic un-American emblem of futurity that seems, bizarrely, to fall from the sky, it recalls the figure that punctuates salvation narratives of the baroque seventeenth century—the figure wherein Benjamin reads the iconoclasm of an unquestioning Catholicism.[97] Raising its visage once again, Schulman confronts the "fascism" of capitalist orthodoxy that inspires and empowers the moral majority. Bohemia can regenerate (in) today's big city only as a degenerate version of cultural possibility. In Schulman's latest and last incarnation, one thing is sure: our time is come. The return of the real (bohemia) is at the point of no return.

CONCLUSION

Millennial Metropolis: Blasting a Queer Era out of Homogeneous History

> "The modern Babylon will not be smashed like the tower of Lylak; it will not be lost in a sea of asphalt like Pentapolis, or buried under the sand like Thebes. It will simply be depopulated and ravaged by the rats of Montfaucon." Extraordinary vision of a vague but prophetic dreamer! And it has in essence proven true.... The rats of Montfaucon ... have not endangered Paris; Haussmann's arts of embellishment have driven them off. . . . But from the heights of Montfaucon the proletariat have descended, and with gunpowder and petroleum they have begun the destruction of Paris that Gauthier foresaw.
>
> —Walter Benjamin, *The Arcades Project*

I

Benjamin's highlighting of Max Nordau's reading of Théophile Gauthier's *Caprices et zizags* captions the ironic truth of Gauthier's vision of Paris in decline.[1] The city is destroyed not by rats but by a sanitizing and aggrandizing urban renewal that drives them away only to generate a scourge of insurgency by the working poor whose slums have been razed in the process. His citation (of a citation) demonstrates the dialectical strategy of juxtaposing images. It prompts us to see the foundation and destruction of postrevolutionary development and an encapsulation of the metropolitan era: Paris artistically embellished with panoramic, rat-free boulevards (Haussmann's utopia) *and* Paris violently demolished by a displaced and betrayed proletariat (Gauthier's apocalypse).

Schulman's *Rat Bohemia* deploys visionary realism to image the material dialectics of urban development. In her fiction, rats *do* destroy Lower Manhattan's ecology but as a virulent by-product of policy and planning. Rats are systemic symptoms of a gentrification that, on the one hand, promotes neighborhood beautification to appeal to prospective property owners and, on the other, divests low-cost housing and public welfare of municipal funding. As the gentry moves in the poor are turfed out, either because their tenements are condemned or because they cannot afford the rising rents. Newly created homeless populations join the throngs of rats in the poorest and most neglected inner-city neighborhoods, wastelands of future redevelopment. But where Benjamin foresees a revolutionary return of the repressed, Schulman envisions a decline of bohemian protestation into material and spiritual destitution.

No proletarian armies descend on the East Village. Lower Manhattan's industrial working class has been irreversibly dismantled by postindustrialism's real estate elites. The renovation of Tompkins Square Park marks the triumph of the city's planning authority and the erosion of what was, in the first place, a shaky alliance between long-term (ethnic and working-class) residents and more recent arrivals, including artists and/or queers. There arises a shabby contingency of "rat bohemians," whose greatest weapon of insurrection is to demonstrate their abjection. Rat bohemians are hardcore New Yorkers who struggle to maintain creative community and minimal city living while resisting the status quo of commodity culture. Terrorized by poverty, corruption, and disease, rat bohemians die out or concede defeat and succumb to the pressure of market forces, except for one who conspires to survive and witness the city's historic undoing. Schulman's nihilism is a primary provocation of her realism. But is it dialectical? Yes, if we accept Benjamin's conceptualization of history as dialectics *without progress*. Like Benjamin, Schulman imagines a negative dialectic that "ends" with an eternal return of the same. Her postindustrial New York reproduces and aggrandizes the antitheses of industrialism minus the transformation that would eliminate poverty and disparity. Against the suspension of proletariat revolution she wages "revolutionary nihilism" such as Benjamin extolled in surrealism, deploying a soul-wrenching pessimism against the spellbinding optimism with which capitalism veils its inflationary catastrophes.[2]

Rat Bohemia is radically out of synch with the ethos of gentrification that has conquered lower Manhattan. But does it not divine a future Lesbiana? A queue of young dykes appears outside the "Clit Club" (218) in the novel's final scene. Yet rat bohemians do not see themselves in this "new generation" (218). Nor do they envision cultural rejuvenation. Instead of advancement they discern novelty—"They're not better or worse. Just new"—and novelty is not sufficiently revolutionary—"They're freer. . . . But not enough" (218). Uncoupling the fetish of newness from the reproductive process, yesterday's insurgents look on themselves as "old meat" (218). The dialectics of sub/culture proceed without even the consolation of success(ors).

II

Schulman draws an era of bohemianism to a close rather than acclaim its eternal resurrection. In doing so she initiates the task that Benjamin set for the historical materialist. To elaborate this claim let us review Benjamin's thesis:

> The historical materialist approaches a historical object only where it confronts him as a monad. In this structure he recognizes the sign of a messianic arrest of happening, or (to put it differently) a revolutionary chance in the fight for the oppressed past. He takes cognizance of it in order to blast a specific era out of the homogeneous course of history; thus, he blasts a specific life out of the era, a specific work out of the lifework. As a result of this method, the lifework is both preserved and sublated *in* the work, the era *in* the lifework, and the entire course of history *in* the era.[3]

The task of the historical materialist is threefold: he (1) approaches a historical object as a monad, where it confronts him as such; (2) recognizes "the specific era" wherein this historical object comes into being, and *of which* that era is traced in the object in miniature; (3) blasts that era out of "the homogeneous course of history" into a constellation of antitheses or "configuration saturated with tensions." The historical materialist substitutes teleology—narratives of progress—for monadology. Conjoining the metaphysical and the material, he apprehends the dialectic that "is crystallized as a monad." What specifies the era are its modes of production. The metropolitan era is marked by its dialectics of urbanization. The "lifework" of this era is "preserved" and "cancelled" in artifacts and architectures of urban industrialism that are prematurely and wastefully remaindered or fetishistically renovated and aggrandized.

Schulman's East Village fictions manifest Benjamin's critical historiography. They document a decade of urban development and reveal its negative dialectics. And what Schulman initiates as a writer, I complete as a reader (of Benjamin). She chronicles East Village life in three novels that confront me as the monad of a specific era—as a "trilogy" that traces the (late) rise and fall of revolutionary bohemianism and the structural paradoxes that constitute "the bohème." What she presents as fictional encapsulation of the Reagan/Bush years, I read as a queer constellation of metropolitan modernity. Her fiction, as I see it, blasts the era of lesbian bohemianism out of the historical continuum and figures the heterogeneous forces of (its) urban production. Lesbianism is a device of perspective through which extreme and antithetical difference is brought into view against mainstream culture and the homogeneous course of history. Situated on center stage of bohemian happening, Schulman's "Village" mirrors what is/is not happening culturally in extremis and at large. Reading her novels side by side, not in order of publication, I see "dialectics at a standstill."

To summarize: viewed through Benjamin's monad-montage, Schulman's East Village Lesbiana reveals the (un)making of metropolitan culture and/as the seductions of revolutionary fashion. The character of revelation is visibly and viscerally contradictory. *Ruinous* sites/sights (of the infestation and destitution of lower Manhattan, the graveyard of West Village gay bars and clubs, funeral marches in memoriam to AIDS victims, slum-living lesbians, the abysmal disappearance of public space) collide with *utopian* sites/sights (Sally Liberty's community garden on Sixth Street between Avenues A and B; an early Pride parade down Fifth Avenue; the spontaneous, low-rent, make-shift community theater). These, in turn, collide with *fetish* sites/sights of renovation (gentrification of Tompkins Square Park and South Street Seaport, appropriation of The Saint by wealthy businessmen, conversion of the New York Public Library into a mens' exclusive health club, encroachment of the bourgeois

Arts Scene) and *fossil* sites/sights of revolutionary foundations (P.S.122 and the continuing avant-garde scene, the militant gay reoccupation of the closed St. Marks Baths, the lesbian occupation of pregentrified Chinatown).

III

> Where a chain of events appears before *us*, *he* sees one single catastrophe, which keeps piling wreckage upon wreckage and hurls it at his feet.
>
> —Walter Benjamin, "On the Concept of History"

> She'll be sitting in a city strewn with rats and rat carcasses and will come across my petite observation. That's the most amazing relationship in the universe. The girl on rat bones who knows that she is not alone.
>
> —Sarah Schulman, *Rat Bohemia*

The view taken by Benjamin's angel of history is reiterated by Schulman's hardcore New Yorker. From the ruins of the present she looks to the future and beholds a "bohemian down the line . . . sitting in a city strewn with rats and rat carcasses."[4] This decadent bohemian is another *rat* bohemian. She is no better off than today's bohemian. But from her vantage on "rat bones" she has a greater view of the city's accumulating wreckage. The future offers no promised land. If the retreat of bohemia to pregentrified slums is now becoming unviable, there will be no refuge from catastrophe down the line. As Tony Kushner observes: "The country-within-a-country these people inhabit, of which the feral rodent is both emblem and curse, is a beleaguered, incomplete refuge, in which the validity of refuge is constantly questioned, in which exile is both embraced and recoiled from."[5]

Schulman's politics of vision makes no concession to progress. Her rat bohemians defy to the end the encroachment of bourgeois culture that threatens to privatize or aestheticize every vestige of public space and convert inner-city diversity into homogeneous prosperity. They foresee no place for themselves in a coming community that is founded on commodity consumption, and they disdain the market's catering to queers. Such hardline rejection of American socioeconomic liberalism ensures the novel's unpopularity in the land of the brave and free, especially after the resounding success of *Angels in America* (1992). The triumph of *Angels* may be attributed to its transcendental plot. Conversely, *Rat Bohemia*'s morbid realism welcomes ideological dismissal.

Kushner's prophetic drama performs a queerly-updated adaptation of Benjamin's theses of history. The "angel" that appears in the play's dying moments bears thematic comparison with Benjamin's angel.[6] Yet, as various critics have observed, this adaptation is performed in the spirit of redemption as if history could be saved in good faith. Art Borreca, for example, points to the "play's blasting of an era—mid-1980s Reaganite America—out of 'homogeneous' history" and to how this era is shown to "'preserve'" and "'cancel'" the dialectical forces of "absolute conservatism" and "pluralist liberalism."[7] But he concludes that this "is by no means a purely Benjaminian play" and that "paradoxically, the work adapts Benjamin's visionary materialism to a historiography founded on faith in enlightened historical progress."[8] Likewise, David Savran notes that the play bases its "'theory of history and utopia' [in] Benjamin's theologically inflected historical materialism," while fostering an Enlightenment tradition that believes in progress.[9] By fitting sexual radicalism into a "comfortable and dominant tradition of liberal pluralism," *Angels* shows how the catastrophe of AIDS and other storms of history are ideally surmounted, thus cultivating hope in the future of metropolitan America.[10]

There are two antithetical endings to *Rat Bohemia*, and both omit teleology. The "Appendix" that features excerpts from Muriel Kay Starr's best-selling novel is one ending. A parody of consumer culture's assimilation and betrayal of rebel subculture, it displays a cynical vision of history. Starr's *Good and Bad* retells the story of *Rat Bohemia* minus homosexuality and catastrophe, domesticating the era's shocking dialectics and converting them into the "good and bad" competitors of bourgeois progress. For Schulman, as for Marx, history that repeats itself to accommodate change is a farce. *Rent* is Broadway's farce of East Village bohemia and the legacy of success bequeathed by *Angels in America*. In tragic contrast, there is Schulman's "girl on rat bones" (*Rat Bohemia*, 54) who rejects all accommodation. She signals the other ending to *Rat Bohemia* and she heralds an apocalyptic vision of history.

Who is this girl? She is the visionary in the vision who "will come across [the] petite observation" (54) left by today's rat bohemian who had elected to be "a witness to [her] own time" (6). She is a foil to Muriel Kay Starr and the selling out of bohemia. She sees from this "observation" of the past, as well as from the wreckage heaped before her eyes, that the "truth" of progress is disastrous (53). In sharing this truth she "knows that she is not alone" (53), though she is also "not American" (53) in not believing in the future. Sitting among carcasses, she aligns herself with history's devastated oppressed. And, like the Jews, she receives the covenant of remembrance. This bohemian pact between the dead (but not gone) and the living (yet to come) is the "most amazing relationship in the universe" (53) and the only realistic prospect of redemption.[11]

IV

Queer Constellations blasts the specific era of queer modernity out of capitalism's homogenizing universe and throws the late(nt) dialectics of urban reality into radical relief. The "trilogy" of Schulman novels constitutes one constellation. The montage of images of the gay bathhouse constitutes another. Just as Schulman's "trilogy" appears ready-made, so also do the constellations of memories and flâneries that comprise the documentary fictions of Gail Scott, Eileen Myles, Neil Bartlett, Edmund White, and David Wojnarowicz. Other fictions, like those of the gay bathhouse, suggest a montage-in-the-making. The montage of *Queer Constellations* reassembles the montage embedded or implied in these fictions with heightened illumination and reflection; it constitutes a visionary prosthesis that enables us to see the dialectical trappings of our own age. The materials recollected here are not the only materials that could be used to forge this perspective, and other constellations could be constructed with which to perceive "the end" of the metropolitan era. But the contradictory extremes with which they plot their urban encounters supply a most radical adumbration of Benjamin's critical optics.

Each chapter of this book performs a different blasting of the queer era by sighting/citing a different object of history through a different variation of montage. The chapter on gay baths views the gay bathhouse as historical object, blasting the specific era of gay bathhouse culture out of the narrative of progress—an era that, in terms of chronology, amounts to roughly a century (mid-1890s to mid-1980s). Spatial, not chronological, framing is applied. Focus turns from the proprietary and liberatory evolution of gay bathhouse culture over time to the mobilization and collapse of revolutionary gay culture in bathhouse space. The (gay) space of (gay) history is held up to view. History is contained and excavated in the space of social architecture. Now dilapidated, or displaced by newer, more fashionable, global architectures, the gay bathhouse becomes a dinosaur on the city's landscape. Montage views the passing of its emergence on the scene and its most progressive antitheses. Against the wish-images and fossils of the gay bathhouse's revolutionary prehistory, we see the fetishes and ruins of its revolutionary posthistory. A viewing of dialectics in extremis, the montage of the gay bathhouse draws on the extreme images of documentary fictions (far more extreme, and heterogeneous, than those presented by gay bathhouse histories), ripping them out of their narrative contexts and highlighting their historical disjunction.

The montage of the gay bathhouse differs methodologically from the montage of the East Village. The latter draws solely on Schulman's "trilogy" for its images and takes the lesbian bohème—not the gay bathhouse—as its historical object. Viewing the late-twentieth-century *lesbian* East Village in constellation with the early-twentieth-century *anarchist-socialist* Lower East Side, and viewing the rise and fall of bohemian "Lesbiana" in the space of a decade (mid-1980s to mid-1990s), Schulman's montage is more "ready-made" than the montage of the gay bathhouse. The bathhouse montage draws images from fictions of different cities, whereas the bohemian montage draws specifically on Schulman's New York. Yet, in each case, the construction of image-space from fiction is itself a fiction and not just a mirror reflection (of fiction). The montage of the lesbian bohème makes perceptible the dialectical unfolding of a

Notes

Preface

1. Beatriz Colomina, Dennis Dollens, Eve Kosofsky Sedgwick, Henry Urbach, Mark Wigley, "Something about Space Is Queer," excerpted from the program of the "Queer Space" exhibition, StoreFront Art and Architecture, 97 Kenmare Street, New York City, 18 June–30 July 1994, my emphasis. The exhibition featured installations by Jay Critchley, Michelle Fornabai and Mark Robbins, Rocco Giannetti, Blake Goble and Robert Ransick, Paul Haslhofer and Greg Tuck, Gordon Brent Ingram and Martha Judge, Tom Kalin, Jürgen Mayer, Brian McGrath, Mitchell Owen and Charles Renfro, REPOHistory, and Maureen Sheehan.

2. See, e.g., Sally Munt's oft-cited "The Lesbian *Flâneur.*"

Introduction

1. Delany derives his sense of "contact" from Jane Jacobs's *Death and Life of Great American Cities*: "Jacobs describes contact as a fundamentally urban phenomenon and finds it necessary for everything from neighborhood safety to a general sense of social well-being. She sees it supported by a strong sense of private and public in a field of socioeconomic diversity that mixes living spaces with a variety of commercial spaces, which in turn must provide a variety of human services if contact is to function in a pleasant and rewarding manner. Jacobs mentions neither casual sex nor public sexual relations as part of contact—presumably because she was writing at a time when such things were not talked of or analyzed as elements contributing to an overall pleasurable social fabric. Today we can" (Delany, *Times Square*, 126; hereafter cited in the text with page numbers).

2. Delany describes Times Square's cruising and commingling gay population as "white, black, Hispanic, Asian, Indian, Native American, and a variety of Pacific Islanders. In the Forty-second Street area's sex theaters specifically, since I started frequenting them in the summer of 1975, I've met playwrights, carpenters, opera singers, telephone repair men, stockbrokers, guys on welfare, guys with trust funds, guys on crutches, on walkers, in wheelchairs, teachers, warehouse workers, male nurses, fancy chefs, guys who worked at Dunkin Donuts, guys who gave out flyers on street corners, guys who drove garbage trucks, and guys who washed windows on the Empire State Building. As a gentile, I note that this is the only place in a lifetime's New York residency I've had any extended conversation with some of the city's Hasidim" (ibid., 15–16).

3. Concurrent with this transformation is the legitimization of (symbolic) violence: "In order to bring about this redevelopment, the city has instituted not only a violent reconfiguration of its own landscape but also a legal and moral revamping of its own discursive structures, changing laws about sex, health, and zoning, in the course of which it has been willing, and even anxious, to exploit everything from homophobia and AIDS to family values and fear of drugs" (ibid., xi–xii).

4. Chatting with customers in Times Square's remaining gay bars, Delany asks what they think of the New Forty-second Street. He cites vocal outrage at the prospect of redeveloping for safety's sake: "'For gay men in this city, it's a disaster! The city says it'll rezone all the sex-specific businesses to the waterfront. Here because there were so many other kinds of activity around, we were safe. The men who go over there looking for sex will be preyed on by muggers, bashers, not to mention all the legal forms of exploitation'" (ibid., 106).

5. "Take a walk through. *If you have any memory of what was there before, you'll see they've been largely successful. Legally, however, they've set gay liberation back to a point notably pre-Stonewall.* The talk now is of rezoning all such businesses over to the waterfront while Forty-second Street will basically be a mall" (ibid., 91–92, my emphasis).

6. Delany explains how owner corporations contract building construction to different and autonomous corporations where the major profit is to be made. "The Forty-second Street Development Project (I use this as a metonym for the hidden corporate web behind it) *wants* to build those buildings. Renting them out is secondary, even if the failure to rent them is a major catastrophe for the city, turning the area into a glass and aluminum graveyard" (ibid., 149–51).

7. Utopian projections of the city, often queer, feature in much of Delany's science fiction. See, e.g., *Dhalgren* (1974; reprint, New York: Vintage, 2001), *Trouble on Triton: An Ambiguous Heterotopia* (1976; reprint, Hanover: Wesleyan University Press, 1996), *Stars in My Pocket Like Grains of Sand* (New York: Bantam, 1984).

8. Though his memoir of Times Square is emblematic of the kind of historical materialism that I see being played out in the primary texts of this study, Delany's is the only writing represented here by an author of color. If the focus of *Queer Constellations* falls on the constellation of *queer* urban space, it is not meant to exclude focus on race. However, in my (albeit finite) reading of late-twentieth-century, urban narrative, Delany's writing is exceptional in its use of a *black* gay male perspective to view the dialectics of coming out in commodity space. Though this is not the place to elaborate speculation, a possible route to thinking about this is to consider how being black in dominant white culture imposes a hazardous negotiation of space—even queer space that, in its most public expression, is predominantly white. Black gay men may see and occupy queer space differently (Delany does not suggest how, at least not in his *Times Square*), or they may create an *other* queer space in the city that is differently, if dialectically, susceptible to commodity culture. For example, a recent news article reports an emerging black gay male underground. "Rejecting a gay culture they perceive as white and effeminate, many black men have settled on a new identity, with its own vocabulary and customs and its own name: Down Low. There have always been men—black and white—who have had secret sexual lives with men. But the creation of an organized, underground subculture largely made up of black men who otherwise live straight lives is a phenomenon of the last decade." See Denizet-Lewis, "Double Lives on the Down Low," 48, 52–53.

9. Despite the common assumption that Times Square is a prime space for hustling, Delany regards it as a prime cruising ground and for intermixing hustling and cruising. "While the lure of hustlers most certainly helped attract the sexually available and sexually curious to the area, a good 80 or 85 percent of the gay sexual contacts that occurred there (to make what is admittedly a totally informal guess) were *not* commercial. . . . Though the relation between commercial and noncommercial sex was not without its hostilities (occasionally intense), in such a situation there is a far greater interpenetration of the two modes than in other areas—due to contact" (*Times Square*, 145–46).

10. The cited phrases in this sentence are key concepts in Benjamin's historical

materialism. They will be elaborated in the course of this introduction and in the chapters to follow.

11. Edmund White quotes at length from Benjamin's "The Return of the *Flâneur*" in his own return to *The Flâneur*, 45–46) and he refers to *Paris, capitale du XIXe siècle: le livre des passages* (the French edition of *Das Passagen-Werk*) in his guide to "Further Reading" (199). Gail Scott's *My Paris* installs *Paris, capitale du XIXe siècle* in her fiction as figurative reader (a "guide" to the city) and structural allegory (a "montage-method" with which her narrator records city perceptions in her Paris diary).

12. Sarah Schulman's *People in Trouble* alludes to "Walter Benjamin" in a caricature of East Village bohemianism (74). I link this figure to Benjamin's study of "The *Bohème*" and with a radical, European, leftist, Jewish intelligentsia more generally. Eileen Myles makes no references or allusions to Benjamin whatsoever. Nor do Alan Hollinghurst and Gary Indiana, whereas Neil Bartlett's *Who Was That Man?* cites a passage from Benjamin's "Berlin Chronicle" in his epigram and refers to Benjamin's "Work of Art" essay in the notes, outlining a Benjaminian-inflected experiment in critical historiography (251). Robert Glück's "Long Note on New Narrative" lists Benjamin among those critics who were most formative in forging New Narrative experimentalism (6). In addition to alluding to Benjamin's "Paris, Capital of the Nineteenth Century" in *Times Square Red, Times Square Blue*, Delany names Benjamin's "One Way Street" as one of his "favourite autobiographical memoirs" and as possible model for his own autobiographical memoir, *Motion of Light in Water* (14).

13. For David Harvey, paradoxicality is what essentially defines the capitalist city—whether modern or postmodern. The "flexible accumulation" that characterizes postmodernity only intensifies the material antitheses of urban capitalism: "The city is the high point of human achievement, objectifying the most sophisticated knowledge in a physical landscape of extraordinary complexity, power, and splendour at the same time as it brings together social forces capable of the most amazing sociotechnical and political innovation. But it is also the site of squalid human failure, the lightning rod of the profoundest human discontents, and the arena of social and political conflict. It is a place of mystery, the site of the unexpected, full of agitations and ferments, of multiple liberties, opportunities, and alienations; of passions and repressions; of cosmopolitanism and extreme parochialism; of violence, innovation, and reaction. The capitalist city is the arena of the most intense social and political confusions at the same

time as it is monumental testimony to and a moving force within the dialectics of capitalism's uneven development" (Harvey, *Consciousness and the Urban Experience*, 229).

14. Sibalis, "Paris," 11.

15. Altman, *The Homosexualization of America*, 96. Altman, along with John D'Emilio and others, have long since observed a base, material relation between modern capitalism and modern homosexuality: "Not only does modern capitalism create the socioeconomic conditions for the emergence of a homosexual identity, it creates the psychological ones as well. In short, the new homosexual could only emerge in the conditions created by modern capitalism" (ibid., 93). Altman further observes the reverse impact on modern capitalism by the modern—*urban*—homosexual. "An excellent example of this is the vogue among gay men for self-improvement, both of the body and of the psyche. . . . There is a fascinating anthropological detective story to be written on the way in which running shoes and shorts moved out of the gay ghettos to permeate mainstream middle-class America with what Blair Sabol called 'phys. ed. fashion'" (96–97).

16. Betsky, *Queer Space*, 59.

17. Ibid.

18. Sibalis, "Paris," 18. Sibalis cites an angry citizen who, in 1850, wrote to the prefect of police to report the profanation of his evening stroll by "'those hideous hermaphrodites!' who make the boulevards 'the heart of Sodom and Gomorrah'" (18).

19. Ibid.

20. Ibid., 19.

21. Altman, *The Homosexualization of America*, 94.

22. Ibid., 82.

23. Ibid., 79, 80.

24. "It is this [promiscuity] that so enrages critics, who cannot imagine that the enjoyment of sex can coexist with long-term and committed relationships. One rarely finds the same vituperation directed against prostitution, although there is surely more degradation involved in buying a sexual partner than in freely choosing to take part in transitory sexual encounters. But the baths undermine conventional morality in that they are predicated neither on the subordination of women to men, nor on the direct exchange of money" (ibid., 81).

25. Ibid., 80.

26. Ibid., 79.

27. Chauncey, *Gay New York*. See especially chapter 8, "The Social World of the Baths."

28. Bérubé, "The History of Gay Bathhouses."

29. Tattelman, "The Meaning at the Wall."

30. Altman, *The Homosexualization of America*, 79–80.

31. See, e.g., the chapters on various modern cities that comprise *Queer Sites*.

32. Sibalis, "Paris," 14.

33. Ibid. "Even before Proust set pen to paper, minor novelists had already treated the subject and dozens more of varying talent would follow suit over the years. Some of their novels offer precious insights into past attitudes and sexual activities through their strong characterization of homosexual men and their evocations of urban gay spaces" (ibid.).

34. In his editor's "Introduction" to *Queer Sites*, David Higgs claims that the male-centeredness of the collection is simply due to the fact that the authors "have more evidence" on gay male urban life (2).

35. Choquette, "Homosexuals in the City," 157–58. Choquette reports the appearance of gay "haunts" and "nighttime cruising spots" in such publications as *Nuits à Paris*, 1889 "(essentially a naughty guidebook for visitors to the World Fair)" (157).

36. Ibid., 160, 152, 153.

37. Ibid., 155. A deposition on prostitution submitted to the Paris Municipal Council reports that "the Charbanais, the city's premier deluxe brothel, admitted not only *demi-mondaines* but authentic *femmes du monde*." Choquette also refers to "the *chroniques* (hybrids of fiction and reportage)" of journalist Cautlle Mendès that report "that aristocratic ladies also picked up prostitutes in the Bréda quarter's millinery shops." Accordingly, the lesbians who cruised the arcades for potential pickups were bourgeoise dressed "in wool jackets, starched collars, and straight, tweed skirts" (155).

38. Ibid.

39. Ibid., 158–59, 162, 156–57.

40. Koolhaas, *Delirious New York*. Among these phantasmagorical follies, Koolhaas includes "the Downtown Athletic Healthclub," "*a locker room the size of a skyscraper*" with twelve floors accessible only to men designed to cater to every masculine desire (157).

41. Chauncey, *Gay New York*, 212. Chauncey stresses the capability of the bathhouse to host mass sex in open space, as well as private sex in closed dressing

rooms. He describes in lavish detail the labyrinthine architecture that was designed to circulate and display cruising gay bodies in a steamy phantasmagoria of voyeurism and exhibitionism.

42. Sibalis, "Paris," 15.

43. I allude, of course, to Robert K. Martin's groundbreaking book, *The Homosexual Tradition in American Poetry.*

44. Whitman, "City of Orgies," in *Leaves of Grass,* 105.

45. "Yet comes one a Manhattanese and ever at parting kisses me / lightly on the lips with robust love, / And I on the crossing of the street or on the ship's deck give a / kiss in return" (Whitman, "Behold This Swarthy Face," ibid., 105).

46. Benjamin, "On Some Motifs in Baudelaire," 324. Benjamin may have perceived this contrast of gazes for, in "Central Park," he speculates that "compared to his [Baudelaire's] poetry of the big-city, later work of this type is marked by weakness, not least where it sees the city as the throne of progress. But: Walt Whitman?" (Benjamin, "Central Park," 185).

47. A literary antecedent of this motif may be found in Balzac's short novel "Girl with the Golden Eyes," where the golden age of postrevolutionary Parisian capitalism is reflected in the perversely avaricious and mutually destructive gaze of the lesbian protagonists.

48. Joseph Boone, "Queer Sites in Modernism."

49. See, e.g., Wright, "San Francisco."

50. Ibid., 164.

51. Fritscher, *Some Dance To Remember,* "Foreword" (n.p.), 3.

52. Siegle, *Suburban Ambush,* 3.

53. Ibid., 3, 8.

54. "Slumming realism" is how Kurt Hollander, editor of *The Portable Lower East Side,* describes the neighborhood writing that he collected and published over the years: "Instead of including exclusively 'literary' writing by professional writers, the *Portable Lower East Side* sought out writing that added to the understanding of the city and its inhabitants, writing that was actually involved in what it represented, whether it be sex, drugs or crime. To accomplish this, the *Portable Lower East Side* included work by those who are more than just writers: that is, cop killers, geographers, porno stars, musicians, political dissidents, AIDS activists, transvestites and junkies. If this is 'outsider' writing, then it is 'outsider' writing from an insider's perspective" (Hollander, "Introduction," in *Low Rent,* xi, xv).

55. See Rubin, "Thinking Sex."

56. Foucault, "On Other Spaces," 24.

57. Betsky, *Queer Space*, 194–95.

58. Lefebvre, *The Production of Space*, trans. Nicholson-Smith, 53.

59. Ibid., 310.

60. Ibid., 166–67.

61. The introduction to this compendium explains that "In the 1990s the ghettobusting of queer nationalism and the rapid globalization of real estate markets have transformed queer space, pushing it beyond the limits of the ghetto and inspiring new linkages within and among communities. . . . This anthology takes part in a broader effort to define a new 'spatial politics' rooted in specific locales, desires, and communities, and the aesthetics that emerge from their confluences" (Ingram, Bouthillette, and Retter, "Lost in Space: Queer Theory and Community Activism at the Fin-de-Millénaire," in *Queers in Space*, 3–4). *Queers in Space* advances the initiative taken by *Mapping Desire*, ed. Bell and Valentine that serves as an "introduction to ways in which the spaces of sex and the sexes of space are being mapped out across the contemporary social and cultural terrain" (*Mapping Desire*, 1).

62. Désert, "Queer Space," 20–22.

63. Ibid., 21. See also Munt, "The Lesbian *Flâneur*."

64. For more traditional, empirical (demographic and geographical) demarcations of queer space, see, e.g., Castells and Murphy, "Cultural Identity and Urban Structure"; Lauria and Knopp, "Toward an Analysis of the Role of Gay Communities in the Urban Renaissance"; Bell, "Insignificant Others"; Adler and Brenner, "Gender and Space"; Valentine, "(Hetero)sexing Space"; and many of the articles collected in *Mapping Desires*, ed. Bell and Valentine.

65. "*The Rise and Fall of Gay Culture* traces the circuitous route of assimilation, following the long trail of debris jettisoned by a decaying civilization as it levels the features of the various tribes it comprises in order to create out of a radically pluralistic society a single monolithic culture" (Harris, *The Rise and Fall of Gay Culture*, 5).

66. Benjamin, *The Origin of German Tragic Drama*, trans. Osborne, 34–35.

67. Eagleton, "The Marxist Rabbi," 328. "A constellatory epistemology sets its face against the Cartesian or Kantian moment of subjectivity, less concerned to 'possess' the phenomenon than to liberate it into its own sensuous being and preserve its disparate elements in all their irreducible heterogeneity. The Kantian division of empirical and intelligible is thus transcended; and this is the only

98. Benjamin, cited in Buck-Morss, *The Dialectics of Seeing*, 214.

99. Benjamin, cited in Glück, "Allegory," 117.

100. Ibid.

101. Glück, *Jack the Modernist*, 55.

102. Ibid., 32–33.

103. Gilloch, *Myth and Metropolis*, 137–38.

104. Bredbeck, "New Queer Narrative."

105. Glück, Scott, Mary Burger, and Camille Roy are principal architects of the New Narrative's (new) Web site whose address is: http://www.sfsu.edu/~newlit/narrativity. Glück's article "Long Note on New Narrative" in the first issue traces the emergence of New Narrative as an experiment and movement in contemporary North American writing. Eileen Myles has recently contributed to the site.

106. Glück, "Long Note on New Narrative," 3. Glück explains that, while he and the others who started the New Narrative movement "(say, Bruce Boone, Camille Roy, Kevin Killian, Dodie Bellamy, Mike Amnasan, . . . and, to include the dead, Steve Abbott and Sam D'Allesandro)" were "fellow travellers" of Language Poetry and its "progressive formalism," he could not abandon representation, referentiality, and narrative altogether. "I experienced the poetry of disjunction as a luxurious idealism in which the speaking subject rejects the confines of representation and disappears in the largest freedom, that of language itself. My attraction to this freedom and to the professionalism with which it was purveyed made for a kind of class struggle within myself. Whole areas of my experience, especially gay experience, were not admitted to this utopia, partly because the mainstream reflected a resoundingly coherent image of myself back on me—an image so unjust that it amounted to a tyranny I could not turn my back on. . . . How to be a theory-based writer?—one question. How to represent my experience as a gay man?—another question just as pressing" (ibid., 2–3).

107. Ibid., 2.

108. "Meanwhile, gay identity was also in its heroic period—it had not settled into just another nationalism and it was new enough to know its own constructedness" (ibid., 2).

109. Ibid., 3, 4.

110. Ibid., 4, 6.

111. Under the rubric of "New Queer Narrative," Bredbeck includes writing by Bruce Boone, Robert Glück, Kathy Acker, Dennis Cooper, Michael Amnasan, Dodie Belamy, Sarah Schulman, Bo Huston, Gary Indiana, Kevin Killian, the

Canadian collective Dumb Bitch Deserves To Die, Dorothy Allison, and David Wojnarowicz (Bredbeck, "New Queer Narrative," 477–78). He also refers to "[Dennis] Cooper's important 1992 anthology [that] groups fifty-nine writers under the designation 'New Queer Writers,'" and describes their work as "a chunk of narrative energy from the margins of lesbian and gay male culture. Ultra-literary at one extreme and post-literate at the other, this collection taps into the vast, diverse, and growing anti-assimilationist queer movement" (498, n. 6). Finally, he suggests Amy Scholder and Ira Silverberg's *High Risk* anthology (1991) as a "good introduction to the field for readers unfamiliar with new queer narrative" (498, n. 6).

112. Ibid., 479.

113. Ibid., 478, 496.

114. Ibid., 478.

115. Schulman, *Stage Struck*, 42. Schulman's novel *After Delores* (1988), Bredbeck explains, "filters the conventions of hard-boiled detective fiction through an aesthetic of 'dyke noir' in order to tell of a nameless lesbian's obsessive desire for a lost lover, and in the process empties narrative of any promise of alternative narrativity. The narrator succinctly summarizes her obsessive quest as the deliverance of destruction rather than the instantiation of order" ("New Queer Narrative," 488). He foregrounds "pure critique" but totally neglects what the description on the back cover of the first Plume printing of the novel makes clear: "This hilarious, unpredictable, sexy novel is a fascinating journey into the storefronts, underground clubs, and back alleys of New York's Lower East Side lesbian subculture."

116. Ibid., 491.

117. "I remember reading Archie Comics when I was a kid and being bored because they dealt with a world that had no correlation with my own. I remember having curiosity about sex and wondering why there was no sex in the world of Archie—the world of Riverdale. I remember taking a razor and cutting apart some Archie comics and gluing pieces of their bodies in different places so that Jughead's nose on page five made a wild-looking penis when glued on Reggie's pants on page seven. After hours of cutting and pasting I had a comic that reflected a whole range of human experience that was usually invisible to me" (Wojnarowicz, *Close to the Knives*, 157). Elsewhere, Wojnarowicz recalls how a friend "cut up prose poems using fragments of newspaper headlines and subheadlines and pieces of type from advertisements" as a form of "fucking with the

validation implied in the media" (185). He describes his own collage technique of placing many photographs together or printing them one inside the other "in order to construct a free-floating sentence" as the invention of a syntax for documenting an "alternate history" (144).

118. Ibid., 157.

119. Solnit, *Wanderlust*, 192. According to Solnit, *Close to the Knives* views late-twentieth-century New York in constellation with eighteenth-century London. "Wojnarowicz's 1980's New York had come full circle to resemble [John] Gay's early eighteenth-century London. It had the scourges of AIDS, of the vast new population of homeless people, and of the drug-damaged staggering around like something out of William Hogarth's Gin Lane, and it was notoriously violent, so that the well-to-do feared its streets as they once had London's" (192–93).

120. Ibid., 192.

121. Wojnarowicz, *Close to the Knives*, 276.

122. Glück, "Long Note on New Narrative," 4.

123. Benjamin, "Surrealism," 215.

124. Ibid., 216–17.

125. In his introduction to *Foundlings*, Nealon overtly rejects a "liberationist narrative of the development of U.S. queer politics and culture" (8). His rejection is not, however, based on a critique of historical narrative, nor even capitalism's historicism. He endorses a "different narrative, one that traces a movement from isolated, urban queer subcultures to a subculture networked across urban centers, then to a 'national' queer culture linked by lesbian and gay print media and by shared habits of commodity consumption, and then—most recently—to a globalized queer culture facilitated by tourism, migration, and Internet communication" (9). Yet, while this "different narrative" locates queer culture realistically in commodity space, it concedes the loss of all critical perspective to "the vantage of a global queer culture [that] allows a way of reading . . . the deeply unfinished business between desire and history whose terminus, if it has one, may not lie within 'queer culture' at all" (9).

126. "Nowhere do these two—metaphor and image—collide so drastically and so irreconcilably as in politics. For to organize pessimism means nothing other than to expel moral metaphor from politics and to discover in the space of political action the one hundred percent image space. . . . If it is the double task of the revolutionary intelligentsia to overthrow the intellectual predominance of the bourgeoisie and to make contact with the proletarian masses, the intelligentsia

has failed almost entirely in the second part of the task because it can no longer be performed contemplatively. . . . In reality, it is far less a matter of making the artist of bourgeois origin a master of 'proletarian art' than of deploying him, even at the expense of his artistic activity, at important points in this image space" (Benjamin, "Surrealism," 217).

127. Ibid.

1. Love at Last Sight

1. Aragon, *Paris Peasant*, trans. Taylor, 66.

2. Not all readers of the gay bathhouse view it with mystique, although bathhouse historians are inclined to do so. Bruce Boone summarizes the commercial institution and development of gay urban culture, in general, as essentially contradictory: "If bars, baths and other institutions brought gays together, that much was certainly to the good, a stage of socialization that contrasts strongly with the largely isolated or individual experience of gay men in the pre-war period. But these same institutions also exploited gay men both financially and sexually. And most important of all, gay men characteristically interiorized the commodity relation thus given as the defining meaning of sexuality itself. Thus promiscuity, self-rejection, and reification of the sexual experience as a series of 'numbers' or 'tricks'—expressions whose referent is clearly the language of prostitution—often brought the commodity relation to the center of gay self-experience" ("Gay Language as Political Praxis," 79–80).

3. Defending contemporary queer culture against the rhetoric of death cultivated by "neo-conservative gay assimilationists," Toronto-based gay playwright Sky Gilbert protests that gay baths are still very much alive even in New York (Gilbert, "A Dark Victory for Queer Culture"). However, he can recall only one New York bathhouse, the East Side Club, when in their heyday there were dozens in Manhattan alone.

4. Bérubé, "The History of Gay Bathhouses." Hereafter cited in the text with page numbers. Bérubé explains that he "wrote this declaration in one week in 1984 and submitted it (in slightly different form) on November 5 of that year to the California Superior Court" and that he submitted an adapted version a year later to the New York Supreme Court "during the New York City government's campaign to close St. Marks Baths in Manhattan. (The two declarations have been combined here as one document)" (187). The declaration was picked up by the community and published "almost in its entirety as a cover story in

Coming Up!, a San Francisco lesbian and gay newspaper which is now the *San Francisco Bay Times* (December 1984) and was summarized in a long article in the *San Francisco Examiner* . . . (November 15, 1984)" (187–88).

5. Chauncey, "The Social World of the Baths," in *Gay New York*, 206–26, quote from 207. Hereafter cited in the text with page numbers.

6. "Casual prostitution sometimes occurred, particularly at the mixed baths at Coney Island, where a youth might ask for carfare home, but the organization and layout of exclusively gay baths discouraged professional hustlers. The admission fee alone proved a disincentive. . . . Moreover, it was difficult to enforce a financial agreement in a bath. . . . Such practical obstacles might have been surmounted, however, but for the even greater impediment to the hustler's success posed by the sexual culture of the baths. Most men who visited the baths were more interested in sex with other gay men than with hustlers or 'trade'" (ibid., 220).

7. See Lefebvre, *The Production of Space*, trans. Nicholson-Smith, and Lefebvre, *Writing on Cities*, trans. and ed. Kofman and Lebas. *The Production of Space* is hereafter cited in the text with page numbers.

8. "*(Social) space is a (social) product*" (ibid., 26). "Every society . . . produces space, its own space" (31). "The *ideologically* dominant tendency divides space up into parts and parcels in accordance with the social division of labour. . . . Thus, instead of . . . concentrating our attention on the production of space and the social relationships inherent to it—relationships which introduce specific contradictions into production, so echoing the contradiction between the private ownership of the means of production and the social character of the productive forces—we fall into the trap of treating space as space 'in itself,' as space as such. We come to think in terms of spatiality, and so to fetishize space" (89–90).

9. "Urban space gathers crowds, products in the markets, acts and symbols. It concentrates all these, and accumulates them" (ibid., 101).

10. "The departure point for this history of space is not to be found in geographical descriptions of natural space, but rather in the study of natural rhythms, and of the modification of those rhythms and their inscription in space by means of human actions, especially work-related actions. It begins, then, with the spatio-temporal rhythms of nature as transformed by social practice" (ibid., 117).

11. "Once brought back into conjunction with a (spatial and signifying) *social practice*, the concept of space can take on its full meaning. Space thus rejoins material production: the production of goods, things, objects of exchange . . . of accumulated knowledge . . . [and of] the signifying process" (ibid., 137–38).

12. Referring to lists made in police raids on the Lafayette Baths in 1916 and 1929, Chauncey notes that among patrons in the first raid were "four house servants, two clerks, two drivers, a watchman, a detective, a tailor, a milliner, a jeweller, a weaver, a teacher, a bartender, a cook." On both occasions, "all the men were white, but they were of disparate ethnic backgrounds, with native-born Protestants the single largest group but a third of the patrons foreign-born, and both foreign- and native-born Jews, Italians, Irish, and Scandinavians moderately represented" (ibid., 217).

13. Ross, *The Emergence of Social Space*, 33. "The rise of the bourgeoisie throughout the nineteenth-century was inscribed on the city of Paris in the form of Baron Haussmann's architectural and social reorganization, which gradually removed workers from the center of the city to its northeastern peripheries, Belleville and Menilmontant. . . . The workers' redescent into the center of Paris followed in part from the political significance of the city center within a tradition of popular insurgency, and in part from the desire to reclaim the public space from which they had been expelled, to reoccupy the streets that once were theirs" (41).

14. Ibid., 5, 33.

15. Chauncey, *Gay New York*, 219.

16. Tattelman, "The Meaning at the Wall," 400. Hereafter cited in the text with page numbers.

17. Tattelman cites B. Peters, "The Sexual Revolution Mailman Delivered," *OUT* 7/8.

18. For example, Chauncey dwells in detail on the luxury with which entrepreneurial gay bathhouses accommodated the gay civic body. Speaking of the Ariston Baths he writes: "On its staff were masseurs, a manicurist, and a chiropodist, and its facilities included a café where cigars and cool drinks were sold, a parlor with chairs and cots, a swimming pool, and a small gymnasium with dumbbells and other equipment, as well as a steam room and sauna, four cooling rooms with cots where men could rest after taking a steam bath, showers, and numerous dressing rooms with cots. . . . Men felt free to approach other men in the common rooms and hallways and to invite them back to their private dressing rooms. . . . But the homosexual character of the baths was made clearest by the amount of sexual activity that took place publicly in the dormitory and cooling rooms. The most active room was the southeast cooling room. In this long and narrow room, seven cots stood against one wall and only a two-foot-wide passageway separated them from the opposite wall. Men crowded into the room

looking for partners. . . . Although there were no lights in the room, it was partially illuminated by the light of the gaslights in the next-door parlor, which streamed in through an open door. Voyeurism and exhibitionism were an important part of the sexual excitement in the resulting steam and shadow" (*Gay New York*, 212).

19. Bérubé, "The History of Gay Bathhouses," 191. "With the beginning of the gay liberation movement in the 1970s, these [modern gay] bathhouses underwent dramatic changes. Today there are approximately 200 gay bathhouses in the United States, from Great Falls, Montana, and Toledo, Ohio, to New York City, Los Angeles, and San Francisco" (ibid.). Tattelman adds that in 1973 the Club Baths had nearly a half-million members, making it the largest national gay organizational space ("The Meaning at the Wall," 399).

20. "Several bathhouses began to feature weekly 'Movie Nights,' where they showed Hollywood films, especially gay cult classics such as *Some Like It Hot* and *The Women.* At the same time, Hollywood produced two major films situated in the gay bathhouses: *The Ritz*—modeled after New York's Continental Baths—and *Saturday Night at the Baths*" (Bérubé, "The History of Gay Bathhouses," 202).

21. "In the 1960s, '70s, and '80s, several San Francisco bathhouses, including Dave's, the Barracks, Liberty Baths, and the Bulldog Baths, encouraged gay artists who were their employees or patrons to decorate the walls with erotic murals. For some artists, these provided the first opportunity to create and display their art for an exclusively gay audience" (ibid., 201).

22. "In the late '70s, with new technology that allowed the projection of video tapes onto large screens, bathhouses began installing video rooms where patrons could masturbate alone or with each other while watching sex videos" (ibid.).

23. Betsky, *Queer Space.* Hereafter cited in the text with page numbers.

24. "[Gay] baths kept alive the delights of the Roman baths. . . . The gridded tiles that surrounded these [steam] rooms, the semidarkness, and the emptiness of expanses of water parodied the squares of middle-class gathering" (ibid., 162–63).

25. Betsky echoes Walter Benjamin's emphatic citation of *The Illustrated Guide to Paris* where the Paris arcades are likened to "inner boulevards" and "a city, a world in miniature" (AP 31 [A1, 1]).

26. Betsky, *Queer Space*, 15. The fascist/fetish aesthetic of the gay bathhouse has been observed by Dennis Altman and others. See Altman, *The Homosexualization of America*, 80. Tattelman cites Leo Bersani's scathing reflections on how gay baths' culture was "'ruthlessly naked, hierarchized, and competitive,' bringing

racist and phobic social relations from outside the baths [while] . . . women, whether lesbian or not, were also kept out of the baths," allowing for only a limited, "certain kind of self-discovery" ("The Meaning at the Wall," 402). Defying the ban against women, Rita Mae Brown toured the gay bathhouse and was equally unimpressed: "Since class peels off with clothing you might think a democracy of nakedness and need would develop. But here in the cubes [cubicles] a new hierarchy took place among these lawyers, artists, grocery clerks, stockbrokers, movement activists, professors, and cab drivers. Rank now came through size of penis, condition of body, and age. The pretty young thing reigns, a sexual prima donna. Experience, intellect, talent, compassion means nothing. . . . Here the great American principle of competition and performance keep those on the make hungry, frightened, and slightly savage" ("Queen for a Day," 73–74). In the same vein, see also Tom Savage's savage ode to "The St. Mark's Baths," 18.

27. "Separate from these open rooms were the little cubicles or lockers where you could put your belongings and then stay. You would be naked, but protected in a miniature of your private house. There you could create more private (sexual) relations, occasionally inviting a few others to join you. These little bedrooms became the most irreducible abstraction of home within this miniature city of desire" (Betsky, *Queer Space*, 164).

28. As explained in the "Introduction" to *Queer Constellations*, gay social historians have made very clear that gay social space is an appropriative production of space in capitalist space. To quote John D'Emilio: "There was, quite simply, no 'social space' in the colonial system of production that allowed men and women to be gay. Survival was structured around participation in a nuclear family. . . . By the second half of the nineteenth century, this situation was noticeably changing as the capitalist system of free labor took hold. Only when *individuals* began to make their living through wage labor, instead of as parts of an interdependent family unit, was it possible for homosexual desire to coalesce into a personal identity. . . . [Homosexual] patterns of living could evolve because capitalism allowed individuals to survive beyond the means of the family" ("Capitalism and Gay Identity," 470–71).

29. "Directly opposite the tailor and the hairdresser's, a showcase belonging to the Restaurant Arrigoni, in which a colored picture of a memorable banquet holds the place of honor amid a display of long-necked, straw-corseted Italian wine-bottles, is all that separates this corridor from the pale biscuit-colored Baths establishment" (Aragon, *Paris Peasant*, 63).

never, or rarely, any kissing—no cloying, adult impurity in the lubricious innocence of what we did" (ibid., 141).

61. Glück, *Jack the Modernist*, 9. Hereafter cited in the text with page numbers.

62. Benjamin, *Das Passagen-Werk*, 2:1010, cited and translated in Sigfried Weigel, *Body- and Space-Image*, 20.

63. Delany, *Motion of Light in Water*, 267. Hereafter cited in the text with page numbers.

64. "The greater the shock factor in particular impressions, the more vigilant consciousness has to be in screening stimuli; the more efficiently it does so, the less these impressions enter long experience [*Erfahrung*] and the more they correspond to the concept of isolated experience [*Erlebnis*]" (Benjamin, "On Some Motifs in Baudelaire," 319).

65. "Historical materialism wishes to hold fast that image of the past which unexpectedly appears to the historical subject in a moment of danger. . . . The only historian capable of fanning the spark of hope in the past is the one who is firmly convinced that *even the dead* will not be safe from the enemy if he is victorious. And this enemy has never ceased to be victorious" (Benjamin, "On the Concept of History," 391).

66. Indiana, *Rent Boy*, 117. Hereafter cited in the text with page numbers.

67. As of 2003, the Mount Morris bathhouse still thrives. Only today, the lobby is "filled with brochures warning of the dangers of casual sex and AIDS." As Alan Feuer reports, "Twenty years ago, at the height of the AIDS epidemic, the gay bathhouse scene was nearly run out of town when state officials enacted a raft of laws banning many homosexual gathering places." The Mount Morris bathhouse "has been operating continuously since 1893," and its survival is attributed to its being "*far from the city's gay meccas*," as well as to "remaining a place to meet new people and enjoy a steam, but with the reality of the city health code's prohibition on open sex" ("Mount Morris Journal," 20, my emphasis).

68. Danny circumnavigates New York's decadent, 1990s gay mecca, bypassing the bathhouses but hustling the larger commercial scene, including "Show Palace" and "Rounds" on the East Side, "Tunnel Bar" and "Sugar Reef" in the East Village, "Gaiety," "Trix," "Cats" in Times Square, "Sound Factory" and the "Chelsea Gym" in Chelsea, "La Esqualita" and "Hombre" in Hell's Kitchen, and the Port Authority urinals.

69. Fitch, *The Assassination of New York*, 236.

70. Ibid., 235.

71. Walter Benjamin, *Zentralpark*, *Gesammelte Schriften*, 1:681, cited and translated in Buck-Morss, *The Dialectics of Seeing*, 189.

2. The City of Collective Memory

1. Halbwachs, *Collective Memory*, trans. Ditter and Ditter, 76.

2. "Were the relationship between streets, homes, and groups inhabiting them wholly accidental and of short duration, then men might tear down their homes, district, and city, only to rebuild another on the same site according to a different set of plans. But even if stones are movable, relationships established between stones and men are not so easily altered. When a group has lived a long time in a place adapted to its habits, its thoughts as well as its movements are in turn ordered by the succession of images from these external objects. Now suppose these homes and streets are demolished or their appearance and layout are altered. The stones and other materials will not object, but the groups will. This resistance, if not in the stones themselves, at least arises out of their long-standing relationships with these groups. . . . The force of local tradition comes forth from this physical object, which serves as its image" (ibid., 133–34).

3. "Any inhabitant for whom the old walls, rundown homes, and obscure passageways create a little universe, who has many remembrances fastened to these images now obliterated forever, feels a whole part of himself dying with these things and regrets that they could not last at least for his lifetime. Such individual sorrow and malaise is without effect, for it does not effect the collectivity. . . . It [the collectivity] resists with all the force of its traditions. . . . It endeavors to hold firm or reshape itself in a district or on a street that is no longer ready-made for it but was once its own (ibid., 134).

4. Ibid., 134–35.

5. See *Queers in Space*, ed. Ingram, Bouthillette, and Retter; *Mapping Desire*, ed. Bell and Valentine; *Queer Sites*, ed. Higgs; Weston, "Get Thee to a Big City."

6. This is not to say that gay men lack the capital to invest in urban restoration. See Lauria and Knopp, "Toward an Analysis of the Role of Gay Communities in the Urban Renaissance." But what image of the city do they seek to restore and how does it figure collective memory?

7. Christine Boyer adapts Halbwachs's term "collective memory" for the title of her book *The City of Collective Memory*, one of the references of this chapter. I borrow Boyer's title in turn.

8. Delany, *Motion of Light in Water*, 268–71.

9. Ibid., 267. See my discussion of this passage in Chapter 1 above.

10. Halbwachs argues that history begins where collective memory ends and should be regarded with suspicion as an artificial reconstruction to which too much legitimacy is ascribed (*Collective Memory*, 57–59).

11. Benjamin, "A Berlin Chronicle," 612–13. Hereafter cited in text and notes as "BC," with page numbers.

12. "Critical historiography" is the term that Graeme Gilloch uses to describe Benjamin's Berlin chronicles: "The Berlin texts ['A Berlin Chronicle'; 'A Berlin Childhood Around 1900'] were theoretical and methodological experiments for the 'Arcades Project,' models of historical analysis and writing which sought to explore the relationships between metropolitan environment, individual memory and collective history. How does the city transform memory? How does memory give form to the urban complex? Could the narration of an individual past critically illuminate the history of an epoch? These complex questions underpin Benjamin's Berlin writings. His 'autobiographical' fragments are thus exercises in critical historiography rather than wistful nostalgia" (*Myth and Metropolis*, 60).

13. Benjamin explains: "'In this endeavour those biographical features, which appear more readily in the continuity than in the depths of experience, retreat. With them go the physiognomies—those of my family and of my friends. Instead, I have sought to capture the images which the experience of the big city left in a child of the middle class'" (cited in ibid., 58).

14. Gilloch clarifies that "[Benjamin's] purpose is not to describe the urban complex through the eyes of a child, but to dereify it through his or her special, incisive, yet 'mistaken' knowledge. . . . His childhood recollections seek to dereify and redeem the objects and spaces of the city that have become frozen and forgotten in childhood" (ibid., 65).

15. "Noisy, matter-of-fact Berlin, the city of work and the metropolis of business, nevertheless has more—not less—than some other cities of those places and moments when it bears witness to the dead, shows itself full of dead; and the obscure awareness of these moments, these places, perhaps more than anything else, confers on childhood memories a quality that makes them at once evanescent and as alluringly tormenting as half-forgotten dreams" ("BC," 613).

16. Benjamin's friend, the young poet Fritz Heinle, and Heinle's fiancée, Rika Seligson, killed themselves in response to the outbreak of World War I. Their deaths had a profound impact on Benjamin.

17. "Benjamin's reflections on the city of his childhood are underlain by the

figure of Heinle, who becomes a metaphor for Benjamin's own youthful dreams of cultural renaissance, for the optimism and naïveté of a generation that was to exterminate itself on the battlefields of France and Belgium" (Gilloch, *Myth and Metropolis*, 57).

18. "We were now walking on flagstones, which were slippery with fish water or swill and where you could easily lose your footing on carrots or lettuce leaves. Behind wire partitions, each bearing a number, were ensconced the ponderous ladies, priestesses of Venal Ceres, purveyors of all the fruits of the field and tree and of all edible birds, fishes, and mammals, procuresses, untouchable wool-clad colossi exchanging vibrant signs from booth to booth with a flash of their large mother-of-pearl buttons or a slap on their booming black aprons or their money-filled pouches. Didn't the earth bubble and seethe below the hems of their skirts, and wasn't this truly fertile ground?" ("BC," 613).

19. Benjamin acknowledges the limit of his urban imaginary, recalling how his childhood "was confined to this affluent neighborhood without knowledge of any other. The poor? For rich children of his generation, they lived at the back of beyond. . . . Only those for whom poverty or vice turns the city into a landscape in which they stray from dark till sunrise know it in a way denied to me. I always found quarters, even though sometimes tardy and also unknown ones that I did not revisit and where I was not alone" ("BC," 600, 612).

20. "To make my way independently to the synagogue was out of the question, since I had no idea where it was. This bewilderment, forgetfulness, and embarrassment were doubtless chiefly due to my dislike of the impending service, in its familial no less than its divine aspect. While I was wandering thus, I was suddenly and simultaneously overcome . . . by . . . an immense pleasure that filled me with blasphemous indifference toward the service, but exalted the street in which I stood, as if it had already intimated to me the services of procurement it was later to render to my awakened drive" ("BC," 630).

21. From Ibiza he first moved to Nice, "where he wrote his will and contemplated suicide. The crisis passed, however, and he spent the rest of the summer in Italy. It was there he reworked the 'Chronicle' . . . for publication as a book to be entitled 'A Berlin Childhood Around 1900'" (Gilloch, *Myth and Metropolis*, 57).

22. "Not to find one's way in a city may well be uninteresting and banal. It requires ignorance—nothing more. But to lose oneself in a city—as one loses oneself in a forest—this calls for quite a different schooling" ("BC," 598).

23. "The city, as it disclosed itself to me in the footsteps of a hermetic tradition

. . . was a maze not only of paths but also of tunnels. I cannot think of the underworld of the Métro and the North-South line opening their hundreds of shafts all over the city, without recalling my endless *flâneries*" ("BC," 598).

24. On "porosity," see Benjamin, "Naples." For further (Benjamin-inflected) discussion of "spacing out" as a technique of anthropological adaptation, see Taussig, *Mimesis and Alterity*.

25. "Language [i.e., the vocabulary of place names] has unmistakably made plain that memory is not an instrument for exploring the past but its theatre. It is the medium of past experience" ("BC," 611).

26. Bartlett, *Who Was That Man?* xx; emphasis in original. Hereafter cited in the text with page numbers.

27. Myles, *Chelsea Girls*, 267. Hereafter cited in the text with page numbers.

28. Scott, *Main Brides*. Hereafter cited in the text with page numbers.

29. Breton, *Nadja*, trans. Howard, 11.

30. *Le Petit Robert* defines *hanter* (to haunt) as follows: "Fréquenter (un lieu) d'une manière habituelle, familière" [To frequent (a place) in a habitual and familiar way]; "(en parlant des fantômes, des esprits) Frequenter (un lieu). On dit qu'un revenant hante cette ruine 'une maison hantée par des lémures'" [(speaking of ghosts, spirits) To frequent (a place). One says that a ghost haunts this ruin [as] "a house haunted by lemurs"] ([Paris: Dictionnaires Le Robert, 1996], 1070).

31. On prosopopoeia and melancholia in "A Berlin Chronicle," see Felman, "Benjamin's Silence." "All of Benjamin's evolving subjects," she observes, "are implicitly determined by the conceptual implications of the underlying autobiographical prosopopoeia, of the mute address to the dead friend" (218).

32. "Today, however, when I recall its [the district's] old-fashioned apartment houses, its many trees dust-covered in summer, the cumbersome iron-and-stone constructions of the municipal railway cutting through it, the sparse streetcars spaced at great intervals, the sluggish water of the Landwehr Canal that marked the district off from the proletarian neighborhood of Moabit, the splendid but wholly unfrequented cluster of trees in the Schlosspark Bellevue, and the unspeakably crude hunting groups flanking its approach at the star-shaped intersection of roads—today this point in space where we happened to open our Meeting House is for me the consummate pictorial expression of the point in history occupied by the last true elite of bourgeois Berlin. . . . In spite—or perhaps because—of this, there is no doubt that the city of Berlin was never again to impinge so forcefully on my existence as it did in that epoch when we believed

we could leave it untouched, only improving its schools, only breaking the inhumanity of their inmates' parents, only making a place in it for the words of Hölderlin or George. It was a final, heroic attempt to change the attitudes of people without changing their circumstances" ("BC," 605).

33. "*Coming to London meant moving into a life that already existed—I started to talk to other people for the first time, to go to places that already had a style, a history . . . to connect my life to other lives, even buildings and streets, that had an existence prior to mine*" (Bartlett, *Who Was That Man?* xx; emphasis in original).

34. Bartlett "celebrates" his "choice of [Wilde] as father and guide to the city" (ibid., 35).

35. The Montreal Massacre involved the killing, by a lone gunman at point-blank range, of fourteen women engineering students of the Ecole Polytechnique on 6 December 1989. The gunman separated the women students from the men in his determination to assassinate the "feminists." The event was reported across the country and around the world and has seen the construction of memorials in a number of Canadian cities, including Montreal.

36. These are "images, severed from all earlier associations, that stand—like precious fragments or torsos in a collector's gallery—in the sober rooms of our later insights" ("BC," 611).

37. Benjamin, "The Storyteller," 154. "The chronicler is the history-teller" (ibid., 152). He presents his tale for critical speculation as opposed to the historian, whose "task is to *explain* in one way or another the happenings with which he deals" (152).

38. According to Hayden White, it is "the official wisdom of the modern historiographical establishment" to regard the "chronicle" as a basic kind of historical representation that, due to its failure to attain "full narrativity of the events of which it treat[s]" can only be said to attain "imperfect historicality." "The chronicle . . . often seems to wish to tell a story, aspires to narrativity, but typically fails to achieve it. More specifically, the chronicle usually is marked by a failure to achieve narrative *closure*. It starts out to tell a story but breaks off *in media res*, in the chronicler's own present; it leaves things unresolved or, rather, leaves them unresolved in a story-like way" ("The Value of Narrativity," 5).

39. "If I chance today to pass through the streets of the neighborhood [the Tiergarten district where the Meeting House was located], I set foot in them with the same uneasiness that one feels when entering an attic unvisited for years. Valuable things may be lying around, but nobody remembers where. And

in truth this dead district with its tall apartment houses is today the junkroom of the West End bourgeoisie" ("BC," 606).

40. "Children are particularly fond of haunting any site where things are being visibly worked on. They are irresistibly drawn by the detritus generated by building, gardening, housework, tailoring, or carpentry. In waste products they recognize the face that the world turns directly and solely to them. In using these things, they do not so much imitate the works of adults as bring together, in the artifact produced in play, materials of widely differing kinds in a new, intuitive relationship" (Benjamin, "One Way Street," 449–50).

41. In his notes toward a method of historical construction, Benjamin writes: "I shall purloin no valuables, appropriate no ingenious formulations. But the rags, the refuse—these I will not inventory, but allow, in the only way possible, to come into their own: by making use of them" (AP 460 [N1a, 8]).

42. "Such moments of sudden illumination are at the same time moments when we separated from ourselves, and while our waking, habitual, everyday self is involved actively or passively in what is happening, our deeper self rests in another place and is touched by the shock" ("BC," 633).

43. Benjamin, "On Some Motifs in Baudelaire," 318.

44. "Method of this project: literary montage. I needn't *say* anything. Merely show" (AP 460 [N1a, 8]).

45. Benjamin, "On the Concept of History," 392.

46. For a recent, comprehensive mapping of nineteenth-century London as "a milieu hospitable to male same-sex desire," see Kaplan, "Who's Afraid of John Saul?" Kaplan offers what he calls a "'thick description' drawn from personal memoirs and correspondences, records of court proceedings, press accounts of notorious sex scandals, and a pornographic novel, of distinctively urban forms of life shared by men who desired sex with other men" (267). He covers three decades prior to Wilde's trial and adds references to those collected by Bartlett (who dedicates his book to John Saul).

47. Chambers, "Strolling, Touring, Cruising," 34. Chambers reads *Who Was That Man?* as indicative of a mode of counterdisciplinary narrative that he calls "loiterature." Against "disciplinary knowledge," which divides individuals into categories of identity, Bartlett's "loiterly" or "cruising" narrative collects evidence of connectedness "in which both self and other, being mutually defining, exist only as members of a community. . . . The story, in other words, is not only that personal identity—in this case, for gay men—is indistinguishable from belonging

to a community but also that the community extends into the past. . . . The reason that it is important to establish this historical connection, as the book does, is that in producing Wilde *individually* as a homosexual the trial functions—in typically disciplinary fashion (i.e. as a kind of examination)—precisely to obscure his membership in a community, and hence to deny the existence of a specifically gay identity as a communitarian phenomenon" (34–35).

48. Benjamin, "Paris, the Capital of the Nineteenth Century," 9. Hereafter cited in the text as "Paris," with page numbers.

49. See Benjamin, "Eduard Fuchs, Collector and Historian."

50. "He owned drawings by Burne-Jones and by Whistler, by Monticelli and Simeon Solomon, china, a library of rare editions, signed copies of the works of Hugo and Whitman, Swinburne and Mallarmé, Morris and Verlaine" (Bartlett, *Who Was That Man?* 173).

51. "Dorian Gray and Oscar Wilde furnished and decorated their houses at a time when most men in London lived in shared rooms crowded with their families" (ibid., 180).

52. Bartlett refers his chapter "Possessions" to Benjamin's "'Work of Art in the Age of Mechanical Reproduction' (section iv, 1936, in *Illuminations*)," which he says, "ends with the following astonishing admonition, which has animated all of my reading of Wilde ever since I realized I couldn't justify my fascination with his texts by saying he was a 'good writer.'" He then goes on to cite: "'But the instant the criterion of authenticity ceases to be applicable to artistic production, the total function of art is reversed. Instead of being based on ritual, it begins to be based on another practice—politics'" (Bartlett, *Who Was That Man?* 251). The author's astonishment over this passage does not, however, translate into a political analysis of the art of collecting and its role in the production of gay culture.

53. A passage from her poem "Hot Night" evokes a similar scene: Hot night, wet night / you've seen me before. / when the streets are / drenched and shimmering / with themself, the / mangy souls that wan- / der & fascinate its / puddles" (Myles, *Not Me*, 51).

54. Though certain institutions do just that, for example, The Lesbian and Gay Community Services Centre on West 13th, the Herstory Archives in Brooklyn, and the New York Organization of Lesbian and Gay Architects and Designers.

55. Myles, *Not Me*, 51.

56. Lehman, *The Last Avant-Garde*, 254, 259. See the chapter "James Schuyler: Things As They Are."

57. Schuyler, *Collected Poems*, 366. Lehman writes: "The 1970s were particularly difficult for Schuyler. He lived in nursing homes and fleabag hotels and burned down an apartment when he fell asleep with a lit cigarette in his hand. Schuyler knew some stability only after he moved into the Chelsea Hotel in New York City in 1979. He lived at the Chelsea for the rest of his life, and a plaque in front of the hotel's entrance informs guests and visitors of Schuyler's place among the writers—like Arthur Miller and Dylan Thomas—who made this their New York headquarters. The Chelsea, a hotel with a history, was notoriously the place where Sid Vicious of the Sex Pistols killed his girlfriend" (*The Last Avant-Garde*, 263).

58. Standing in the clearing of his old apartment, Eileen is moved by the aura of dereliction. "Just out of a hospital, almost killed himself. Jimmy Schuyler was my new job. Slowly I moved his possessions to the Chelsea from an 8th Avenue flophouse where on the final day among the dry cleaned clothes still in plastic bags, charred bits of poetry on papers, art prints books—I masturbated because it was a filthy interesting place" (Myles, *Chelsea Girls*, 274).

59. The title of Myles's book and chapter may allude to Andy Warhol's experimental film *Chelsea Girls* about free love in Manhattan in the 1960s. The collective character of her memory is foregrounded by the book's cover photo of a painting by Nicole Eisemann. The painting figures Amazons, reminiscent of Greek friezes, featuring women entangled in what could be a war or an orgy.

60. In "An American Poem," Myles poses as a renegade "Kennedy," recalling in mock-confession how: "I thought / Well I'll be a poet. / What could be more / foolish and obscure. / I became a lesbian. / Every woman in my / family looks like / a dyke but it's really / stepping off the flag / when you become one" (Myles, *Not Me*, 14). In 1991, she ran for president of the United States, campaigning for better representation for citizens without money, property, or medical insurance. For details of her platform, see Eileen Myles, Collected Papers, Lesbian Herstory Archives in Brooklyn.

61. The work of transforming "traumatic memory" into "narrative memory" entails painstaking processes of association. See Van der Kolk and Van der Hart, "The Intrusive Past"; and Cvetkovich, "Sexual Trauma/Queer Memory."

62. "Did you have your license on you, Toots? Sure Dad. The silence grew. . . . She pulled it out of her little black billfold. . . . He walked slowly over to the fireplace, read it and dipped it into the flames for a moment until it lit up. He held it, looked at Toots. It flared and he dropped it on the flagstone and ground it

with the toe of his black shoe. Then he grabbed Tootsie by the back of her jacket, shook her for a moment. She looked incredibly frail. He shoved her with all his might across the room. Piss for brains, he bellowed. It was so cruel" (Myles, *Chelsea Girls*, 102–03).

63. Robert Siegle describes the East Village of the late 1980s as a scene of "demystifying" grittiness: "Perhaps the most potent demystifiers of the illusions in which most of us live are the gritty streets from which the tactility of East Village writing takes its cue. Buildings burned out by junkies so that they can sell off the copper piping, boarded-up dead stores with their graffiti-laced steel shutters, postnuclear vacant lots, jumpy-eyed adolescent males and twelve-year-old girls with Mona Lisa smiles, scruffy winos and children exploding out of school into side-walk tag-team mayhem—all this still exists on the Lower East Side, where yet to conquer is the gentrification of lace-curtain ice-cream shops, antique stores with Aztec Jaguars, Italian boutiques' akimbo mannequins, damask tablecloth dining salons, and designer shower-curtain shops. Writers, painters, musicians, performance artists, and the otherwise unclassifiably creative still live in this quarter of alphabet avenues and single-digit streets in refuge from the suburbanization carried into Manhattan by the bridge and the tunnel set" (*Suburban Ambush*, 1).

64. For an insightful, narratological analysis of "focus" in *Main Brides*, see Henderson, "Femme(s) Focale(s)."

65. Michael Taussig's discussion of Roger Caillois's studies on "mimesis" (studies that Benjamin, he infers, may well have influenced) helps explain Lydia's disposition to space. "Caillois suggests that mimesis is a matter of 'being tempted by space,' a drama in which the self is but a self-diminishing point amid others, losing its boundedness. Caillois tries to describe this drama in its most extreme form where the mimicking self, tempted by space, spaces out: . . . 'The individual breaks the boundary of his skin and occupies the other side of his senses. He tries to look at himself from any point whatever in space. He feels himself becoming space'" (Taussig, *Mimesis and Alterity*, 34). Tempted by the space of the city, Lydia dramatizes this "mimetic excess."

66. I refer to the dream image in "One Way Street" entitled "Underground Works" where the dreamer unearths "a Mexican shrine from the time of preanimism," in "the marketplace at Weimar" where "excavations were in progress" (Benjamin, "One Way Street," 455).

67. "In his *Vague de rêves* [Wave of dreams], Louis Aragon describes how the

mania for dreaming spread over Paris. . . . This all in order to blaze a way into the heart of things abolished or superseded, to decipher the contours of the banal as rebus, . . . or to be able to answer the question, 'Where is the Bride?'" (Benjamin, "Dream Kitsch," 4).

68. Sally Munt suggests that "the lesbian flâneur" who cruises the sub/urban sprawl of shopping malls catering to, and populated by, crowds of families must rally memory and desire from literary history. "As I become a victim to, rather than a perpetrator of, the gaze, my fantasies of lesbian mobility/eroticism return to haunt me.[But] as I pursue myself through novels, the figure of the flâneur has imaginatively refigured the mobility of my desire. These fictional voyages offer me a dream-like spectacle which returns as a memory I have in fact never lived. Strolling has never been so easy, as a new spatial zone, the lesbian city, opens to me" ("The Lesbian *Flâneur*," 115). Scott's flâneur desires lesbian contact but, like Benjamin's flâneur, remains impotent, enveloped in an aura of autoerotic fantasy. Her spectral brides, lovers of the city and projections (specularizations) of Lydia's lesbian desire, present further examples of what Terry Castle calls "the apparitional lesbian," a figure of lesbian (im)possibility, traces of which Castle finds throughout literary history (*The Apparitional Lesbian*).

69. Lydia's fantasy of women's space "recalls" those ritual spaces designated to the women of Greek antiquity. "The Adonia celebrated women's sexual desire; sweetly fragrant, drunken and bawdy, this aromatic festival set free female powers to speak about their desires in an odd and normally unused space of the house, the roof" (Sennett, *Flesh and Stone*, 75).

70. See Walkowitz, *City of Dreadful Night*.

71. Benjamin, "On the Concept of History," 392.

72. Ibid.

3. Queer Passages in *Gai Paris*

1. Benjamin constructed two constellations of the flâneur: "M—The Flâneur," AP 416–55; and "The Flâneur" [Part II of "The Paris of the Second Empire in Baudelaire"]. The latter is drawn from the former and presented in the semblance of an essay. Rebecca Solnit sums up Benjamin's importance to the history of walking: "Benjamin is one of the great scholars of cities and the art of walking, and Paris drew him into its recesses as it had drawn so many before, coming to overshadow all the other subjects of his writing during the last decade before his death in 1940. . . . It was he who named Paris 'the capital of the nineteenth

century' and he who made the flâneur a topic for academics at the end of the twentieth" (*Wanderlust*, 198).

2. Benjamin, "Paris Diary," 351.

3. "In that little harbor bar, the hashish then began to exert its canonical magic with a primitive sharpness that I had scarcely felt until then. For it made me into a physiognomist, or at least a contemplator of physiognomies, and I underwent something unique in my experience: I positively fixed my gaze on the faces that I had around me. . . . It was, above all, men's faces that had begun to interest me. Now began the game, which I played for quite a while, of recognizing someone I knew in every face" (Benjamin, "Hashish in Marseilles," 675).

4. Benjamin, "A Berlin Chronicle," 614.

5. Benjamin, "The Return of the *Flâneur*," 262.

6. Ibid., 262. "If we recollect that not only people and animals but also spirits and above all images can inhabit a place, then we have a tangible idea of what concerns the *flâneur* and of what he looks for. Namely, images, wherever they lodge" (264).

7. Szondi, "Walter Benjamin's 'City Portraits,'" 143.

8. Ibid., my emphasis.

9. Buck-Morss, "The *Flâneur*, the Sandwichman and the Whore," 131–32.

10. Scott, *My Paris*. Hereafter cited in the text, with page numbers. Dalkey Archive has published a recent U.S. edition (2003) of this work.

11. White, *The Flâneur*. Hereafter cited in the text, with page numbers.

12. Klein, "Wander, Lust," 173.

13. The situation of women in French government was in turmoil during this time. Under Mitterand, Edith Cresson became France's first woman premier. After a poor showing by Socialists in local elections, she resigned and was replaced by Bérégovoy in 1992. Following a conservative victory in the 1993 legislative elections, Mitterand appointed Balladur, a Gaullist, as premier. After defeating Lionel Jospin in the next presidential election, Jacques Chirac appointed another Gaullist, Alain Juppé as premier. Juppé set out to feminize ("*féminiser*") the government, naming twelve women ("*les Juppettes*") to his cabinet in 1995. But in November 1995, he revoked thirteen persons from his Cabinet, including eight women.

14. *Le Sexe de l'Art* exhibition ran at the Centre Pompidou from November 1995 to February 1996.

15. The narrator of *My Paris* refers, obsessively, to murdered women wanderers,

the subject of the author's last book, *Main Brides*. Wandering Paris alone, she is preoccupied with violence against women in big cities. When her book is rejected for publication, her fears are reinforced by feelings of persecution. Rebecca Solnit's history of walking outlines the prohibitions and dangers that women have endured walking the city through the ages: "Women have routinely been punished and intimidated for attempting that most simple of freedoms, taking a walk, because their walking and indeed their very beings have been construed as inevitably, continually sexual in those societies concerned with controlling women's sexuality" (*Wanderlust*, 233). For further discussion, see Solnit's chapter "Walking after Midnight: Women, Sex, and Public Space" (232–46).

16. In a curious twist of the conventional "Note on Author" that follows most books (and indeed does follow the text of White's *Flâneur*), a note from "Narrator on Author" prefaces the text of *My Paris*. It outlines an allegory (of the author of experimental writing): "she kept an old postcard of a white 'Saltimbanque' stuck on the fridge. Titled 'Man in experiment, white–clad and sunlit, passing in front of a black screen on a curved white sidewalk.' Giving a strange feeling of running in reverse. While trying to grasp some point in the future" (n.p.).

17. Charles Baudelaire, "*Les Foules*" ["The Crowds"], cited and translated in White, *The Flâneur*, 36–37.

18. "In 1839 it was considered elegant to take a tortoise out walking. This gives us an idea of the tempo of flânerie in the arcades" (AP 422 [M3, 8]).

19. Benjamin cites Edmond Jaloux, "Le Dernier Flâneur," *Le Temps*, 22 May 1936.

20. "Basic to flânerie, among other things, is the idea that the fruits of idleness are more precious than the fruits of labor" (AP 453 [M20a, 1]).

21. Characteristically, the flâneur performs the paradox of *productive loitering*. "The flâneur, as is well known, makes 'studies.' . . . 'Most men of genius were great flâneurs—but industrious, productive flâneurs. . . . Often it is when the artist and the poet seem least occupied with their work that they are most profoundly absorbed in it'" (ibid., citing Pierre Larousse, "Flâneur," *Grand Dictionnaire universel*, vol. 8 [Paris, 1827], 436). Scott's flâneur also creates while she strolls, only she does so much less industriously and much more slowly, using most of her energy to fight traffic and manage anxiety.

22. Priscilla Parkhurst Ferguson writes that "The privatization of *flânerie*, the withdrawal into the interior and into the self, finds perhaps its greatest expression, but also its caricature, with Proust. The famous cork-lined room insulates

him from the city that nevertheless supplies so much material for his work" ("The *Flâneur*," 38).

23. Ferguson argues that it was precisely the *interiorization* of the flâneur that brought about his downfall. "With time, *flânerie* loses its city location. The *flâneur*'s defining mobility—he is, after all, an indefatigable walker—becomes immobility. And in an even more drastic dislocation, *flânerie* moves indoors. . . . With the shift to the interior the *flâneur* is on his way from a public to a private personage" (ibid., 32). During the Restoration, the flâneur strolled the arcades at a lobster's pace with eccentric *bonhomie*. During the Second Empire, he dodges traffic on the boulevards with grimacing heroics. As the ethic of industriousness advances, the flâneur loses his battle to stay aloof and afloat. He detours indoors, like J.-K. Huysman's Des Esseintes, "the aristocratic ex-dandy [who] withdraws from the city entirely ('so that the waves of Paris will no longer reach him') to devote himself to the systematic exploration of sensory and intellectual experience" (37, citing Huysman). Or like Proust, who, unable to cope with the noise and pollution, retreats to his cork-lined bedroom to conjure ambling reminiscences (38). The withdrawal of the flâneur from direct city contact allegedly signals the defeat of the public artist (35).

24. Scott's protagonist daydreams that she is Balzac's hero*ine*, the *girl* of "The Girl with the Golden Eyes." But the daydream is short-lived, and in any case ironic, for the girl with the golden eyes is not a romantic heroine. She allegorizes Parisian avarice during the city's "golden era" of utopian capitalism. On reading Benjamin, Scott's flâneur begins to look on Paris, and Balzac, with critical distance: "[Benjamin's] Volume falling open. At allusion to favourite Balzac heroine: *Girl With Golden Eyes*. In some oriental get-up. Guarded by duenna. In absence of marquise. So girl incapable of making contact with handsome young Tom. Who stalking her in Tuileries. Before marquise finding out. And killing her. Allusion not far from anecdote about ancient Chinese puzzle. Representing hachured parts of human form. Prefiguring cubism. Which puzzle fashionable under Second Empire. Reign of terror and indifference. According to B" (19). White, on the other hand, seems to identify with Balzac's hero in earnest. He may have "Ferragus" in mind, Balzac's exemplary flâneur, who explains that "only a few devotees, people who never walk along in heedless inattention, sip and savour their Paris and are so familiar with its physiognomy that they know its every wart, every spot or blotch on its face. For all others, Paris is still the same monstrous miracle, an astounding assemblage of movements, machines and ideas,

51. See Benjamin, Convolute "I—The Interior, the Trace," AP, 212–27.

52. Scott's montage bears comparison with Benjamin's 1935 constellation of "Paris, the Capital of the Nineteenth Century." Juxtaposing six pairs of images ("Fourier or the Arcades"; "Daguerre or the Dioramas"; "Grandeville or the World Exhibitions"; "Louis Philippe or the Interior"; "Baudelaire or the Streets of Paris"; "Haussmann or the Barricades"), each pair featuring a new collective space matched to a "star" architect/artist of the period, Benjamin breaks up the traditional chronicle of progress into a montage of phases of city development. His assemblage of images reveals a dialectical passage of history that "begins" with Fourier's vision of the arcades as *phalansteries* and "ends" with the Commune's barricades raised against Haussmann's boulevards. For an instructive analysis of this exposé, see Higonnet, Higonnet, and Higonnet, "Façades: Walter Benjamin's Paris."

53. *The Shorter Oxford English Dictionary on Historical Principles* (London: Oxford University Press, 1973), 361.

54. References to the war in Bosnia occur with the frequency of a refrain. See *My Paris*, entries 12, 19, 24, 31, 38, 45, 57, 62, 78, 88, 113, 115, 119.

55. See Benjamin, "On Some Motifs in Baudelaire," 324.

56. Benjamin, "On the Concept of History," 392.

57. Ibid.

58. Buci-Glucksmann, *Baroque Reason*, trans. Camiller, 111. For further discussion "on this feminization of the divine," Buci-Glucksman directs us to Gershom Scholem, *The Kabbalah and Its Symbolism* (London: Routledge and Kegan Paul, 1965), 105ff.

59. Benjamin, "The Flâneur," 32.

60. "Prostitution opens the possibility of a mythical communion with the masses. The masses came into being at the same time as mass production. Prostitution seems to offer the possibility of enduring a life in which the most immediate objects of our use have turned more and more into mass commodities. In big-city prostitution, the woman herself becomes the mass-produced article" (Benjamin, "Central Park," 171). Susan Buck-Morss remarks that this "redemptive image of the whore" is one "which feminists find disturbing: 'the image of value to everyone and which is tired out by no one'; she becomes the 'unquenchable fountain' of the sweet milk of 'the giving mother.' This is quite far from the militant image of women of the June insurrection of 1848 [that, elsewhere, he presents], rebelling against capitalism *and* patriarchy (in distorted form, to be sure)

by 'cutting out the genitals of several prisoners" (citing Benjamin, "The *Flâneur*, the Sandwichman and the Whore," 123–24).

61. Benjamin, "Modernity," 56.

62. Ibid, my emphasis. "Incidentally," Benjamin notes, "[Baudelaire] was by no means the first to bring the lesbian into art. Balzac had already done this in his *Fille aux yeux d'or*, and so had Gautier in *Mademoiselle de Maupin* and Delatouche in *Fragoletta*. Baudelaire also encountered her in the work of Delacroix; in a critique of Delacroix's paintings he speaks, somewhat elliptically, of the 'modern woman in her heroic manifestation, in the sense of infernal or divine'" (ibid).

63. Benjamin, "Central Park," 167.

64. Benjamin, "Modernity," 56.

65. Ibid., 56–57.

66. Ibid., 58.

67. Buci-Glucksmann, *Baroque Reason*, 88.

4. The Lesbian Bohème

1. Gluck, "Theorizing the Cultural Roots of the Bohemian Artist."

2. In a recent study of Lower East Side socioeconomic and cultural development, Christopher Mele reports: "The musical *Rent* plays eight times a week to a packed Nederlander Theater in New York City's Broadway district. For a few hours, the staple Broadway patrons—white-upper-middle-class residents of the tonier suburbs of Long Island and Westchester County—follow the lyrical narrative of urban struggles with AIDS, heroin addiction, homelessness, squatting, forced evictions, real estate gouging, and the dilemma of 'making art' or 'selling out.' . . . This updated version of Puccini's *La Bohème* is set not in Paris but in the East Village, thirty blocks south of the theater and considerably further from the experiences of many of those in attendance. The success of the musical has prompted the opening of a 'Rent' clothing boutique at Bloomingdale's, the upscale department store on the Upper East Side. There customers may familiarize themselves with an 'East Village look' and an accompanying attitude by consuming high-priced sartorial reproductions of secondhand clothing. MTV, the music television network, offered a one-year lease on an East Village apartment as part of a promotion for a film about a white male tenement dweller's love/hate relationship with his cockroach-infested walk-up. . . . On the Internet, curiosity in the East Village has prompted the appearance of a cyber soap opera that bears the neighborhood's name. . . . Symbols, images, and rhetoric

typify local social life as 'peculiar' or 'off beat' but always aesthetically pleasing and penetrable to the inquisitive (and acquisitive) middle and upper classes" (*Selling the Lower East Side*, 1–2).

3. Schulman, *Stage Struck*. Hereafter cited in the text, with page numbers.

4. "Subcultures, whose identity, social practices, and rituals intentionally embraced and espoused cultural difference, ranging from the bohemians in the 1920s, the beats in the 1950s, the punks in the 1970s, to the queer subcultures in the 1980s, found the East Village reputation propitious to the expression of alternative lifestyles. These groups expressed their opposition to bourgeois society by rejecting familiar and comfortable surroundings and taking up residence among the 'undesirables' in the urban 'abyss.' . . . The Lower East Side emerged as a preferred *site* for subcultures and avant-garde movements in New York City primarily because the struggles between insiders (ethnic and racial working class) and outsiders (white, middle and upper classes) became a *source* of inspiration and expression of a critique of capitalist culture and, in particular, of a bourgeois lifestyle. . . . Yet the very presence of these *middle-class* cultural dissidents provided a glimmer of hope to desperate landowners who sought to develop a new identity for the Lower East Side that was decidedly neither working-class nor ethnic. . . . Capitalists found in subcultures innovations that they themselves could not produce. . . . Corporate and the subcultural realms grew increasingly intertwined. . . . Despite the continued subjective desires among members of subcultures to take up the causes of their poorest neighbors, the appropriation of cultural differences as commodities has threatened historical alliances of the avant-garde with working-class residents" (Mele, *Selling the Lower East Side*, 26–30). [Note: the names "Lower East Side" and "East Village" designate overlapping areas. See n. 41 below.]

5. "Representations that imaginatively venerate the ethnic, racial, sexual, and cultural diversity of place but intentionally understate the material dimensions of structural inequality have become increasingly prominent in forms of urban development in New York and similar Western cities. In the East Village, real estate developers have translated the symbolic value of cultural difference into economic value, attracting middle-class renters, diners, and shoppers who find allure in this edgier version of 'bohemian mix,' flush with modern living spaces and other amenities. . . . Local cultural practices and social interactions provide the symbolic matériel for the representation of the neighborhood as attractive and alluring. In recently opened restaurants, boutiques, and apartment houses,

gestures toward inclusion of 'local color' are purely token as these spaces (and their intended patrons) remain detached from the impoverished social and economic conditions that continue to plague many area residents" (ibid., 3–4).

6. Mele presents his study of urban development as a "*historical narrative* of struggles over space on the Lower East Side since 1870 [that] suggests how we might more successfully read and interpret the diverse ways in which the symbolic realm of reputations and characterizations of place are implicated in the material production and consumption of urban space" (ibid., 5, my emphasis).

7. "What seems absent in contemporary theories of bohemia is the cultural middle ground that could connect the social and the aesthetic dimensions of the bohemians and thus reestablish the historical specificity and concreteness of the figure" (Gluck, "Theorizing the Cultural Roots of the Bohemian Artist," 352).

8. As this passage indicates, the category "lesbian bohemian" does not cover all of Schulman's characters. Clearly, not all East Village lesbians are bohemians (in fiction as in fact). I would argue, however, that those lesbian characters who are also artists and bohemians form a primary, collective type in the "trilogy" of novels that are the focus of this investigation. This is an inherently diverse type, comprising a constituency of "false" as well as "real" bohemians. The latter are uncompromising with respect to "selling out." Low renters, they align themselves with lesbians who are not artists, but are poor, and with other Villagers who are not lesbians, including ethnic poor and working-class neighbors, homeless people, and gay men who are artists and/or down and out.

9. Sarah Schulman, in a letter to me dated 16 November 2001.

10. Mele, *Selling the Lower East Side*, 3.

11. In her excellent essay, Mary Gluck argues that social theorists perpetuate an image of the bohemian artist that has "oscillated between visions of the bohemian as a creator of transcendental art and as a characteristic product of capitalist modernity" ("Theorizing the Cultural Roots of the Bohemian Artist," 352). Walter Benjamin and Pierre Bourdieu are among the theorists that she commends and criticizes. Benjamin, she explains, "has claimed that the true significance of the bohemian lay within the tensions of capitalism, which radicalized the modern artist but also transformed him into a cultural commodity bought and sold in the marketplace" (352). Bourdieu, "too, has stressed the role of the capitalist marketplace in the emergence of bohemia, but he also has argued that the bohemian found a modus vivendi with capitalism by creating an independent intellectual field and becoming a pioneer of aesthetic autonomy or l'art pour l'art in

the modern world" (352). Noting how these theories both radicalize and reify the bohemian artist, Gluck aims to resolve contradictions that derive from overlooking the cultural history and formation of bohemia. While I applaud her tracing bohemia's roots to "a radical artistic subculture that emerged in the late-1820s and early-1830s and defined itself in opposition to bourgeois modernity . . . within the generic conventions of specific cultural forms" (352–53), I would maintain with Benjamin that bohemia's material contradictions are inherent to its emergence as destabilizing subculture.

12. Benjamin, "On the Concept of History," 396.

13. Schulman, *Girls, Visions, and Everything*; *People in Trouble*; *Rat Bohemia*. Hereafter cited in the text, with page numbers.

14. Benjamin, "The *Bohème*," 17. Hereafter cited in the text, with page numbers.

15. Benjamin, "Central Park."

16. Karl Marx, cited by Danae Clarke in the epigram to her essay, "Commodity Lesbianism," 186.

17. Benjamin cites Pierre Martino, *Le Roman réaliste sous le Second Empire* (Paris, 1913).

18. Wilson confirms that "Bohemia is a cultural *Myth* about art in modernity, a myth that seeks to reconcile Art to industrial capitalism, to create for it a role in consumer society. The bohemian is above all an idea, the personification of a myth. . . . He was not simply a creative individual; he created and performed an identity which rapidly became a stereotype. . . . Components of the myth are transgression, excess, sexual outrage, eccentric behaviour, outrageous appearance, nostalgia and poverty" (*Bohemians*, 3).

19. "An essential precondition for the emergence of the bohemian was the expansion of urban society. In the vast new cities of modernity increased social mobility and the development of new callings and ways of life resulted in the appearance of new figures and identities that were less fixed, more fluid and changeable. The bohemian was one such figure, and for him the metropolis was a kind of counter-utopia. . . . The bohemians transformed the city into their own promised land" (ibid., 28).

20. "Paradoxically the bohemian myth was embedded in and reliant on the popular, the 'legend' disseminated through mass entertainment. Created initially in journalism, on the stage and in salon painting, it was later amplified in fiction, biography, popular music, film, television and even cyberspace" (ibid., 6).

21. Benjamin, "The Flâneur," 18–19. Hereafter cited in the text with page

numbers. "In 1841 there were seventy-six new physiologies. After that year the genre declined, and it disappeared altogether with the reign of the Citizen King Louis Philippe. . . . Nowhere did these physiologies break through the most limited horizon" (18).

22. "They constituted, so to speak, the blinkers of the 'narrow-minded city animal' that Marx wrote about. A description of the proletarian in Foucaud's *Physiologie de l'industrie française* [1844] shows what a thoroughly limited vision these physiologies offered when the need arose: 'Quiet enjoyment is almost exhausting for a workingman. The house in which he lives may be surrounded by greenery under a cloudless sky; it may be fragrant with flowers and enlivened by the chirping of birds. But if a worker is idle, he will remain inaccessible to the charms of solitude. On the other hand, if a loud noise or a whistle from a distant factory happens to hit his ear, if he so much as hears the monotonous clattering of the machines in a factory, his face immediately brightens. He no longer senses the choice fragrance of flowers. The smoke from the tall factory chimney, the booming blows on the anvil, make him tremble with joy. He remembers the happy days of his labors, which were guided by the spirit of the inventor.' The entrepreneur who read this description may have gone to bed more relaxed than usual" (ibid., 20).

23. Ibid. "But their method could not get them very far. People knew one another as debtors and creditors, salesmen and customers, employers and employees, and above all as competitors. In the long run, it seemed quite unlikely that they could be made to believe their associates were harmless oddballs. So these writings soon . . . went back to the physiognomists of the eighteenth century, although they had little to do with the more solid endeavors of those earlier authors. In Lavater and Gall there was, in addition to speculative and visionary impulses, genuine empiricism. The physiologies eroded the reputation of this empiricism without adding anything of their own. They assured people that everyone could—unencumbered by any factual knowledge—make out the profession, character, background, and lifestyle of passers-by (ibid.).

24. Easton, *Artists and Writers in Paris*, 125.

25. "It was early in 1849, when he was living in abject poverty in the sixth-floor attic at No. 78, Rue Mazarine . . . that Murger received a visit from . . . Théodore Barrière . . . who proposed that Murger and he should collaborate in a stage version of the stories that had been appearing in the *Corsaire*. . . . The play's resounding success . . . made his name. . . . *La Vie de Bohème* succeeded in

making the artist's way of life a subject of increased curiosity. This could be a nuisance. The Café Momus, for instance, began to attract sightseers; and serious artists and writers like Courbet, Baudelaire, and Gérard de Nerval, who had been patronizing Louvet's establishment for a number of years, found themselves suddenly the centre of vulgar interest. . . . *La Vie de Bohème* created a demand for fiction and *reportage* with a similar background, and, in 1851, Michel Lévy published a first collection of Murger's *Corsaire* stories under the title of *Scènes de la Bohème* (later to become *Scènes de la vie de Bohème*), followed by a second collection within the year, *Scènes de la vie de jeunesse*" (ibid., 124–26).

26. Stansell, *American Moderns*, 17. Hereafter cited in the text with page numbers.

27. "Greenwich Village was an old neighborhood in Lower Manhattan. In 1910, Greenwich Village meant the area demarcated by Washington Square and Fifth Avenue to the east, Tenth Street to the north, Houston Street to the south, and the Hudson River to the west. Its old brick row houses and winding streets, remnants of New York's original street plan, distinguished part of the district from the rest of downtown, nestled as it was within a regular grid of hulking buildings and tenements" (ibid., 41).

28. "To be a part of bohemia was to elevate oneself and one's ambitions—to enhance one's identity—beyond the mundane lot of the illustrators, journalists, actors and actresses, art students, fiction writers, and playwrights who were its clientele. It was to enter in an arresting plot. It was also to locate oneself advantageously in a market eager for cultural products bearing bohemia's imprint" (ibid., 18).

29. "The idea of the Village as an appealing arty neighborhood—indeed, the name 'the Village' itself—came from middle-class people who moved in after 1900. Working-class residents of the tenements that dominated the less charming spots called the neighborhood 'the Ward' or the 'Lower West Side.' Indeed, a social scientist who interviewed plebeian Villagers in a 1935 survey argued that bohemian Greenwich Village was what we would call a commercial fiction, 'very largely manufactured and imposed from without,' not least by the realtors and landlords who reaped profits from the newly discovered attractions of rundown houses. . . . Although labor questions would become prominent in the bohemians' concerns . . . they did not see their own neighborhood, packed with working-class residents, as a community of labor but rather as one of leisured sociability. . . . There was virtually no recognition of the Irish, who were a considerable presence, or of the black laborers who remained after an Italian influx pushed

the residents of 'Little Africa' on Houston Street (dating from the 1830s) up into the Tenderloin" (ibid., 41–43).

30. The Lower East Side is known for its sordid history of overcrowded and impoverished tenements as much as for its revolutionary bohème. The plight of tenement dwellers was brought to public attention by Jacob Riis's disturbing and influential book, *How the Other Half Lives*. What Riis (police reporter turned social reformer) saw "was the cankered fruit of decades of callous exploitation and neglect by rapacious landlords in connivance with venal and vapid politicians. For nearly a century the lower East Side area was developed by builders who herded the incoming immigrants—Irish, followed by Germans, Jewish and Italian—into dark, airless, and unsanitary tenements. . . . The area teemed with the offal of human wretchedness. Thieves, pimps, prostitutes, gangsters, beggars and criminals—all kinds of rascality—along with drunks, tramps, and ne'er do-wells crowded the saloons and lodging-houses of the neighborhood" (vi). The subjects of Riis's photodocumentary are ethnographic "types," including "Jewtown," "Chinatown," "The Italian in New York," "Waifs of the City's Slums," "The Street Arab," "The Working Girls of New York," "The Wrecks and the Waste." Pictured in inhuman conditions, they are the dismal negative of the physiologies' *bonhomie*. His chapter on "The Bohemians—Tenement-house Cigar-making" portray another kind of bohemian, refugees from the state of Bohemia, who were among the Lower East Side's most exploited and oppressed.

31. Wilson, citing Hutchins Hapgood, *Bohemians*, 109. Stansell also cites Hapgood, asserting that bohemian feminism was more influential than modernist misogynies of Pound, Lewis, Marinetti, and T. S. Eliot (*American Moderns*, 225–26).

32. "Writing about the New Woman contributed a variety of figures beyond the Victorian dichotomy of the 'true' woman and the woman of ill-repute: the Bohemian Girl was one neologism, the Gibson Girl and the Bachelor Girl were others. These images were reiterated and recycled so continuously in light fiction and social commentary that they took on independent weight and plausibility, announcing a widened spectrum of respectable femininity" (ibid., 29).

33. "[Goldman] must have been so easily recognizable as a type that any passerby could direct her to her proper niche in the ecology of the Lower East Side. She found Sachs' café, where fellow spirits gathered; there she met other New Women. . . . Bohemia became a showcase for her newfound fame. She would have already seen how performers in the Yiddish theater, poets, musicians, and

political notables used the café scene to show themselves off to gawkers and make themselves available to reporters and critics. Goldman extended the practice. She settled in at Justus Schwab's saloon, a meeting place for neighborhood radicals and uptown bohemians. She printed Schwab's address on her cards and correspondence and used the place to talk to reporters and receive admirers. She mixed with new friends there, consorting not only with leading French and German anarchists, socialists who had escaped Bismarck's Germany, and graying veterans of the Paris Commune, but also with American-born artists and critics as well" (ibid., 36–38).

34. Barnes reported on cultural events around town to several New York newspapers (*Brooklyn Daily Eagle, New York Morning Telegraph Sunday Magazine, New York Sun Magazine, New York Tribune, New York Press*) 1913–1919. Writing within the tradition of the physiognomies, she produced a series of short narrative sketches of emergent "city types." She also grafted a series of drawings (called "Types") for the *Brooklyn Daily Eagle* that appeared weekly from April to November of 1913, all of which are cast in the mold of *bonhomie*. See, for example, "Greenwich Village as It Is," "How the Villagers Amuse Themselves," "Becoming Intimate with the Bohemians," in Barnes, *New York*, ed. Barry, and "The Terrible Peacock," "Paprika Johnson," "Monsieur Ampee," in Barnes, *Smoke and Other Early Stories*. In sharp contrast, the types that populate Barnes's *The Book of Repulsive Women* are grotesque and perverse (see, e.g., "From Fifth Avenue Up," "From Third Avenue On," and as "Seen From the L").

35. For an analysis of *Nightwood*'s queer characters in light of Benjamin's essay on "Surrealism," see my article on "Obscene Modernism."

36. "In social discourse, only the hardiest, most intrepid defenders of female paid work rose to defend women's prerogative to remain single and virtually no one dared defend publicly the benefits of bohemia for women. Rather, writers often updated an old Victorian morality tale about unsuspecting girls seduced and abandoned in big cities, admonishing young women that their foolish infatuation with art could lead to dead ends and disappointments and, worse, disqualify them forever from marriage" (Stansell, *American Moderns*, 31).

37. "Women's push into journalism strengthened an alliance with bohemian urbanity that, by the late teens, was so strong that the reporter Djuna Barnes could swagger around as a more-or-less open lesbian-about-town in her job as a roving New York journalist, writing hermetic, involuted essays on Village life" (ibid., 153).

38. See Edwards, "'Why Go Abroad?'"

39. See Barnes's sketch of the Bohemian boy-girl in "Becoming Intimate with the Bohemians" (*New York*, 235–37). Barnes animates her physiognomy with a negativity that cannot easily be consumed. On the one hand, her Bohemian girl is "one of the best sports I know"; on the other, "she has all the maladies in the almanac, and she doesn't care. She was born laughing, and she will die that way—a boy's laugh, a laugh that springs up from the gutter like the flower."

40. "There was a muted gay life in Greenwich Village for both men and women, although little is known about it except for manifestations in a few bars and tearooms. . . . Homosexuality, if elliptically allowed, did not signify in the new sexuality" (Stansell, *American Moderns*, 250, 258). See also Faderman, "Lesbians in Bohemia," in *Odd Girls and Twilight Lovers*, 81–88. Joseph Boone traces the emergence of queer bohemian types in modernism—namely, in Bruce Nugent's "Smoke, Lilies, and Jade," Charles Henri Ford and Parker Tyler's *The Young and Evil*, Blair Niles's *Strange Brother*, and Djuna Barnes's *Nightwood*. See "Queer Sites in Modernism."

41. The place-names "Lower East Side" and "East Village" vary in usage depending on the historical and political perspectives of the speaker. Mele explains: "The area between Fourteenth and Houston Streets and Avenue A and the East River . . . is referred to as part of the Lower East Side, Loisaida, Alphabet City, and part of the East Village. . . . The first name, Lower East Side, referred to New York's old working-class residential and industrial area that expanded northward in the nineteenth century as a tenement district. . . . For many, the contemporary use of Lower East Side to describe the area north of Houston Street emphasizes a commitment to maintaining the district as a working-class neighborhood. . . . The name East Village . . . appeared with the earlier hippie movement and signified the opposite to the stodgy, middle-class West Village. . . . In the 1970s and 1980s, East Village was synonymous with downtown underground culture" (*Selling the Lower East Side*, x–xii).

42. Schulman, "When We Were Very Young," in *My American History*, 125.

43. Conventional *bonhomie* and liberal optimism triumph over poverty. The opera ends with Mimi's miraculous recovery from near death, whereupon the chorus breaks into song on a theme of carpe diem. Bohemia thus resurrects itself for the next episode of generational recycling.

44. In Act I, Scene 23, Larson has his company chant in unison "La Vie Bohème / La Vie Bohème / La Vie Bohème / La Vie Bohème" before a solo dedication to hackneyed ideals.

45. "The [first] bohemians," Elizabeth Wilson contends, "established the concept of what, a hundred years later, would be called a subculture. It is [the] collective aspect of bohemianism that distinguishes the bohemian from the mere eccentric" ("The Death of Bohemia?" 53). Pierre Bourdieu refers to bohemia as "a genuine society" whose artistic, alternative lifestyle, makes it "a society within society": "With the assemblage of a very numerous population of young people aspiring to live by art, and separated from all other social categories by the art of living they are in the course of inventing, a genuine society within society makes its appearances. . . . The bohemian lifestyle, which has no doubt made an important contribution (with fantasy, puns, jokes, songs, drink and love in all forms) to the invention of the artistic lifestyle, was elaborated as much against the dutiful existence of official painters and sculptors as against the routines of bourgeois life" (*Rules of Art*, 55–56).

46. "It is no accident that the earliest appearance of the bohemian as a cultural figure was in the context of a theatrical scandal that transgressed social and cultural norms and shocked all of Paris. The 'Battle of *Hernani*' . . . represents the first time the bohemian appeared as a public figure in French cultural life. . . . The battle took place on the opening night of Victor Hugo's *Hernani*, scheduled to be performed at the Théâtre Française on 28 February 1830. . . . The real outrage of the evening hinged not on the innovation of Hugo's play but on his youthful followers, who gathered to support the romantic dramatist against his classicist foes. The innovation had to do with the author's decision to forgo the well-established custom of hiring professional clappers to ensure the success of his play and to rely on his own unpaid supporters among the students and artists of the Latin Quarter. . . . Hugo's calculation . . . was not mistaken. . . . The real significance of the mock-heroic battle was, it turns out, not the triumph of romanticism over classicism, which was a foregone conclusion by 1830, but the transformation of the long-standing aesthetic conflict into a more modern cultural antagonism, that of the artist versus bourgeois, bohemian versus philistine. The Battle of *Hernani* witnessed the emergence of radical artists as a recognizable, collective presence in public life. It represented the first enactment of bohemian identity in modern culture" (Gluck, "Theorizing the Cultural Roots of the Bohemian Artist," 354–55).

47. Benjamin cites Adolphe d'Ennery and Grangé, *Les Bohémiens de Paris* <A play in five acts and eight tableaux> (L'Ambigu-Comique, 27 September 1843; series entitled *Magasin théatral*).

48. Benjamin cites Martino, *Le Roman réaliste sous le Second Empire.*

49. It is well known that one of the tools of Louis Napoléon's presidential period was the Society of the Tenth of December whose cadres, according to Marx, were supplied by "the whole indeterminate, disintegrated, fluctuating mass which the French call *la bohème.*" As emperor Napoleon continued to develop his conspiratorial customs. Surprising proclamations and mystery-mongering, sudden sallies, and impenetrable irony were part of the *raison d'état* of the Second Empire. (Benjamin, "The *Bohème,*" 3–4.)

50. Bourdieu, *Rules of Art,* 58. Schulman states the frustration of producing locally well-attended work while receiving no social support: "It was a difficult but fascinating conundrum, for while we got no reviews, no grants, no workshops, no staged readings, and no dramaturgy and had to produce our own shows, we had the one thing that institutional playwrights lacked, a passionate audience. It has always amazed me how much the audiences loved and appreciated precommodification gay and lesbian work. It is actually shocking to go to a dominant-culture theater and see the dominant-culture playwright's audiences, who are supremely disengaged from the work. However, as satisfying as it has been to have audiences that consistently love and need the play, the discrepancy between the urgency of that relationship and the complete lack of social support or acknowledgement is personally hard to take. The more the marginalized audience loves it, the clearer it becomes for the playwright to what extent she is being professionally punished for the lesbian content of her work. And ultimately this base in the community and lack of university connections has been an overwhelming factor in our continued isolation from structures of support" (*Stage Struck,* 69–70).

51. Benjamin cites Martino, *Le Roman réaliste sous le Second Empire.*

52. Bourdieu, *Rules of Art,* 56–57.

53. "Adding to its ambiguity, bohemia does not stop changing in the course of time, as it grows numerically and as its prestige (or mirages) attracts destitute young people, often of provincial and working-class origin, who around 1848 dominate the 'second bohemia.' In contrast to the romantic dandy of the 'golden bohemia' of rue de Doyenné, the bohemia of Mürger, Champfleury or Duranty constitutes a veritable intellectual reserve army, directly subject to the laws of the market and often obliged to live off a second skill (sometimes with no direct relation to literature) in order to live an art that cannot make a living. In fact, two bohemias coexist in practice, but with different social weights at different times" (ibid., 57).

54. Ibid.

55. Holly Hughes is an East Village playwright and performance artist. She began working at the W.O.W. Café in 1982 and has published two collection of plays, including the locally acclaimed *Clit Notes.*

56. "The man was known as 'the world's greatest actor' and if there was such a person it probably was him, plus he had a mythology to prove it. He did shows. He didn't care about reviews. He didn't care about grants. He barely cared if he had an audience. When you got a chance to see him in action, there might be five other people in the theatre because of his refusal to advertise, but one of them might be Susan Sontag or Meredith Monk. . . . Jeff Weiss won an Obie, an off Broadway version of an Oscar, but he gave it back, and then he won it again, and gave that one back too. He was asked to sit on the board of a powerful grant-giving organization, but he refused" (Schulman, *Girls, Visions and Everything,* 101).

57. Schulman reports that Weiss and his partner carlos ricardo martinez later moved to the Acting Academy, "a storefront underneath their apartments on East Tenth Street . . . in the middle of the violent gentrification of the East Village [where it] served as a real people's theater of outrage against the destruction of the neighborhood. Songs like 'Dear Mister Mayor' from *Teddy* were on-stage manifestations of the increasingly public protests. His [martinez's] hand-painted signs on walls and dumpsters were visible daily reminders of opposition to the occupation of the neighborhood by mounted police, the influx of cocaine culture through the art galleries, and the removal of Latinos from the neighborhood (*Stage Struck,* 58–59).

58. "Once Isabel and Lila went to an off-Broadway theatre to see what shows were like when you paid twenty-five dollars for a ticket. The piece was by a playwright from Missouri, with actors from Chicago and an audience from New Jersey. All were pretending that they were dramatically interpreting the reality of New York Street life. The actors strutted around, jiving like bad imitations of Eddie Murphy imitating a Black teenager imitating what he saw Eddie Murphy do on TV the night before. The lesbian characters kissed each other and hit each other. The gay male characters made jokes about the size of each other's penises. The Black characters ran around with afro-picks in their pockets and occasionally stopped combing their hair long enough to play three-card monte while saying 'motha-fucka' a lot and grabbing their own crotches. All of this provided an appropriately colorful background for the white heterosexual characters to

expose their deeply complex emotional lives. . . . 'That's called fake social realism,' Isabel said, and a new category was born" (Schulman, *Girls, Visions and Everything*, 18).

59. "AVANT-GARDE-ARAMA" is a showcase that is still performed today (2004). The P.S.122 Web page of August 2000 describes "a 2-day, multi-media mini festival with a host of 6 to 7 performers from all branches of the performing arts: performance, dance, theatre, installation, film and music. AGA exists to give seasoned and emerging performers alike access to P.S. 122 and its audience. AGA is one of the oldest performance series in New York." P.S.122 is a nonprofit arts center serving the New York City dance and performance community that claims to be "fully dedicated to finding, developing, and bringing to the public eye artistic creations from a diversity of cultures, points of view, ages and sexual orientations" with special commitment to "the cultural life of the Lower East Side, an area with a diverse population of cultures."

60. Futuransky is torn between her love for a particular woman and her larger love for the city; the former promises intimacy but not without diminishing her world out on the streets. Rebecca Solnit observes that "as the novel progresses, her world becomes more intimate rather than more open: she falls in love and the possibility of a free life in public space recedes" (*Wanderlust*, 246). It is unclear whether Futuransky heeds the warning of Isabel Schwartz and drops the affair in favor of freedom or embraces her woman and abandons the city for a recess of intimacy and security.

61. Benjamin cites Marcel Jouhandeau, *Images de Paris* (Paris 1934).

62. As documented by Walkowitz, *City of Dreadful Night*, and Parsons, *Streetwalking the Metropolis*. Parsons argues, however, that the flâneur narratives of women's literary modernism created a new practice of "streetwalking the metropolis" that helped liberate women from the appearances and persecutions of prostitution.

63. The New York–based lesbian graphics project "Dyke Action Machine!" ("DAM!") produces and distributes posters that address the invisibility of lesbians in advertising and other media. For a review of DAM!'s strategy and history, see Moyer "Do You Love the Dyke in Your Face?" See also DAM!'s Web site: http://www.dykeactionmachine.com.

64. The omission of lesbian artists from the public sphere wins them severe economic hardship. See Schulman's poignant chapter on "Selling AIDS and Other Consequences of the Commodification of Homosexuality" (*Stage Struck*, 99–143).

65. Rechy's fictional documentary of hustling and cruising the urban American underworld made the *Time*'s national bestseller list *before* the book's official publication date. As the author boasts, "what followed matched the headline. The book climbed quickly to the No.1 spot on bestseller lists in New York, California. Nationally on all lists it reached third place. . . . The book went into a second, third, fourth, sixth, seventh printing and remained on the bestseller lists for almost seven months" ("Introduction" to *City of Night*, 1984 edition). Could lesbian tales of promiscuity ever be so bestselling?

66. Pat Califia helps explain this discrepancy: "Gay men comprise the only sexual minority to have established its own enclave in the modern city. . . . The lesbian community is still at an earlier point in its development, although it could be argued that neighborhoods like Park Slope in Brooklyn and Valencia Street in San Francisco are nascent 'lesbian ghettos.' The fact that male sexuality is recognized to be a valid, strong, organizing principle in men's lives contributes to the ability of gay men to structure their own ghettos. So does their greater amount of money, freedom to travel, and ability to live away from their parents—conditions enjoyed by all men relative to women" ("City of Desire," 208).

67. Ford and Tyler, *The Young and the Evil.* See Boone's discussion of this queer hobohemia in "Queer Sites in Modernism," 257–60.

68. See n. 79 below.

69. "A direct action group using grassroots activism to fight for lesbian survival and visibility," the Lesbian Avengers was founded by Schulman and friends in June 1993 (*The Lesbian Avenger Handbook*, 5). See also "Part Two—The Lesbian Avengers" in *My American History*, 279–319. By summer 1994, the group had launched thirty-five chapters across the continent, from Vancouver to Tampa, Santa Barbara to Northampton, Winnipeg, Manitoba, to London, England. By 1995, it had dissolved. "The Lesbian Avengers" might be regarded as another "chapter" in Schulman's bohemian fiction, an activist text that was written and staged between the writing and publication of *People in Trouble* and *Rat Bohemia.*

70. Benjamin cites Gabriel Guillemot, *Le Bohème* in the series entitled *Physiognomies parisiennes* (Paris, 1869).

71. Wilson, "The Death of Bohemia?" 58–59.

72. Kathy Acker's protagonists also raise subversive dissent in the character of abject resistance. We see this throughout her writing, from "New York City in 1979" to *Pussy, King of the Pirates* (1996), though Acker's "realism" is heavily mediated by pastiche, citation, and plagiarism. Like Schulman's rat bohemians, Acker's

pirates figure a constituency of failure-victims—*filthy* girls, who are the only real survivors of capitalism's global holocaust and thoroughly unfit for social, political, cultural, or sexual recuperation.

73. Since the publication of *Girls, Visions and Everything*, the community garden at the corner of Avenue B and East Sixth, just south of Tompkins Square Park and proximal to Loisaida (the Hispanic sector of the East Village) has been taken over by the city's "Operation Greenthumb."

74. Christopher Mele describes the Beats' East Side scene: "Like the bohemian movement that flourished in the 1920s, the postwar New York avant-garde—the beatniks or beats—was centered in Greenwich Village. As the movement matured, the Lower East Side setting emerged as an alternative or, for some, a corrective to the more popular west side beat scene. . . . The beats comprised an eclectic mix of white, Latino, and black urban dwellers as well as the first generation of frustrated young, middle-class refugees from the idyllic suburbs. The beat style of dress, the idiomatic expressions, the proclivity toward drugs and casual sex, and the expressive genre of literature and music were signifiers of an antibourgeois lifestyle played out in the Village's coffee shops, jazz clubs, and taprooms" (*Selling the Lower East Side*, 141–42).

75. In her letter to me dated 18 November 2001, Schulman qualifies: "turning the junkie's lot into a garden is resistance to poverty. And, of course, the beginning of the gardens movement ['Operation Greenthumb'] which later became very political. But turning the farmhouse into a club was an act of gentrification, because 8BC was for the white art arrivals in the middle of a Puerto Rican neighborhood [Loisaida]." Jeff Weiss, she adds, performed at 8BC for only one week.

76. "Loisaida . . . refers to the Puerto Rican enclave east of Avenue A formed in the late 1950s and early 1960s. The area's present minority residents (Puerto Ricans, Dominicans, other Latinos, and Blacks) refer to their neighborhood as Loisaida, as do many housing activists and community organizers and other low- and moderate-income residents who weathered the ravages of abandonment in the 1970s and redevelopment in the 1980s. Loisaida is synonymous with community action, hope, and resistance" (Mele, *Selling the Lower East Side*, xi). Beat hangouts were concentrated between Third Avenue and Avenue A east of Tompkins Square Park and between East Fourth and East Eighth Streets (141).

77. Benjamin, "The Author as Producer," 779.

78. "There is no better trigger for thinking than laughter. In particular,

convulsion of the diaphragm usually provides better opportunities for thought than convulsion of the soul. Epic Theater is lavish only in occasions for laughter" (ibid., 779).

79. What has come to be known as the 1988 Tompkins Square Park riot began as an antigentrification protest by squatters and resident activists before the excessive use of police force provoked angry reaction. For a poignant eyewitness report of this event, see Smith, "Tompkins Square Park." For a sociological analysis of circumstances leading up to and following the riot, see Mele, *Selling the Lower East Side*, 262–71.

80. Schulman's view of gentrification as a bourgeois conspiracy finds support in Martha Rosler's analysis: "The fall and rise of cities are consequences not only of financial and productive cycles and state fiscal crises but also of deliberate social policy. . . . The term 'gentrification' describes the conversion of decaying industrial or working-class neighborhoods into residential zones for the professional-managerial class. Gentrification requires, perforce, a process of disinvestment before reinvestment takes place. Under whatever rubric, the process involves not only the withdrawal of monetary support on the part of the private sector, including both landlords and banks (in an illicit policy called 'redlining'), but also the withdrawal of city services such as fire protection, hospital services, schools, and road maintenance. When the recapitalization of gentrification occurs, many of the original residents have already been forced out or are forced to live under grotesque conditions. Many inner-city residents not displaced by the abandonment and disinvestment are finally cast out of their neighborhoods by this process of gentrification. Some of those displaced double or triple up with friends and relatives in already cramped apartments, and others simply find themselves on the streets" ("Fragments of a Metropolitan Viewpoint," 25–26).

81. Schulman models her vanguard on the militant group ACT UP! (AIDS Coalition to Unleash Power).

82. Kate's agent informs her that "the city, in preparations for upcoming mayoral elections, is about to make a token gesture to the arts. They have promised real-estate developers millions in tax rebates if they provide funding for public artwork on their properties. There are a number of projects under way to convert former public buildings, long in disrepair, into refurbished private space, relocating the public facilities onto barges. The mayor's office will be promoting and publicizing the efforts in a bus card campaign called 'Privacy Is Golden.' . . . Frankly, it is your only available financial option and the work would be seen

by people on the streets going to work, et cetera. It would not be shut up in some exclusive, out-of-the-way gallery" (Schulman, *People in Trouble*, 99).

83. Christine Boyer examines New York, with other global or first tier cities, "that experienced explosive real estate growth in the 1980s," and explains how commercial architecture, in collaboration with realtors and entrepreneurs, reconstructs the historic city into a mammoth advertising pastiche. The South Street Seaport is a case in point: "South Street Seaport's story is typical of waterfront restructuring projects where the dynamics of buying and selling not only determined its origin but controlled its future as well. An elaborate and detailed series of real estate transactions has been set into play in order to gain instrumental control over the saving of history and the production of place. . . . From its earliest conception the Seaport was intended to be a twentieth-century outdoor museum stressing involvement, not contemplation, and acting on behalf of people, not simply preserving artifacts. But this contemporary museum has consuming at its very core, for the money used to preserve its historic structures and maintain the ambience of its street of ships comes from its share of the revenues that this street of shops can produce. Consequently the Seaport is in reality an outdoor advertisement that narrates a story about trade and commodities stretching far beyond the ordinary shopping mall. This mode of advertising blurs the distinction between the atmospheric stage set and the commodities being sold, for its well-constructed historic tableau not only enhances the products displayed but locks the spectator into a consuming mode" (*City of Collective Memory*, 426, 438).

84. Schulman's description of this exclusive men's health club recalls the "Downtown Athletic Club," built in 1931 and featured as one of the extravagant follies of entrepreneurial delirium in Rem Koolhaas's *Delirious New York*, 152–59.

85. "The melodrama satisfied the newly awakened taste for public excitement and passionate spectacle that originally had been nourished by revolutionary events. But it also provided a language and ideology that could explain the meaning of these events and make transparent to ordinary citizens the hidden workings of the modern world. . . . It demonstrated the cosmic struggle between the forces of good and evil. . . . The tyrant, who embodied absolute corruption and pure evil, was 'placed in the melodrama to try the patience and virtue of his victims.' . . . For young bohemians concerned with the emancipation of passion, imagination, and artistic liberty, the appeal of the melodramatic tradition is not surprising" (Gluck, "Theorizing the Cultural Roots of the Bohemian Artist," 360–61).

86. In a letter to me, dated 18 November 2001, Schulman indicates that she wrote *People in Trouble* in the tradition of Socialist Realism, "which has a very high kitsch and camp quotient." She also mentions that the novel was "very influenced by Zola's novel *Germinal.*"

87. The title also derives from a work (*People in Trouble* [1976]) by Wilhelm Reich, the socialist sex radical whose several works are among Kate's books (Schulman, *People in Trouble,* 50).

88. "Kate developed a high profile as a result of Horne's death and could be read about in an essay by Gary Indiana in the *Village Voice* and one by Barbara Kruger in *Art Forum.* In fact, Kate began working extensively in burning installations and quickly got commissions from a number of Northern European countries to come start fires there" (ibid., 225).

89. Schulman's attack on government echoes that of David Wojnarowicz, who denounced seven high ranking officials of the Bush/Koch administration as directly responsible for turning the AIDS crises into genocide. They are *Alfonso D'Amato* for being "more interested in lining his rich real estate friends' pockets than saving people's lives [and] voting for the Helms amendments denying AIDS education"; *Stephen Joseph* for "shut[ting] down bathhouses in n.y.c. rather than treating them as possible places where education about AIDS and safer-sex possibilities could take place [and for promoting] new ideology (and the attendant specter of funding cuts) [that] required new epidemiology"; Mayor *Edward Koch* for leaving "8,000–10,000 P.W.A.'s (People With AIDS) homeless in the streets [and a] projected 33,000 . . . by 1993 [and for] letting landlords warehouse apartments and letting city-owned buildings remain bricked up while he spends taxpayers' money for rat-infested welfare rooms to the tune of $1500 a month per room for those homeless who manage to get help through city agencies" (*Close to the Knives,* 124–30).

90. "Rita Mae Weems" alludes, ironically, to American best-selling author and outrageously out lesbian Rita Mae Brown, and to African-American documentary photographer Carrie Mae Weems. Weems uses narrative as counterpoint to her images, focusing on marginal culture in an attempt to make it more visible.

91. Ann Powers observes that "The mind-set of contemporary bohemia is rooted in the critique of the family. . . . Right now, no arena is so troubled as that old stereotype of home. 'Are you my family?' people ask each other everywhere, and their answers often astonish and dismay them. To establish new standards, we need to examine the informal arrangements and uncelebrated ties people

have cultivated outside the norm" (*Weird Like Us*, 45). Powers contends that the most effective alternative is the "gay family," the idea of which derives from the coupling of two radical elements: "the lesbian-feminist movement, which demanded a fundamental change in women's domestic role [and] . . . the flourishing of San Francisco's Castro district, the first openly gay American neighborhood" (46).

92. Vivian Gornick argues that Schulman fails to see the "genuine inclination" of bohemians to take ideas "seriously" and reject "admission to middle-class life" ("Outside Looking In," 9). She criticizes, in particular, the voice that "laments" rejection by family as a desire for readmission to middle-class life that flies in the face of real bohemianism. However, as I read it, this "lament," voiced most loudly by David, is but one of a host of antithetical voices. To exclude it would be a travesty of "truth." Heard in a constellation, not chorus, of voices, it is a chord of discordant dissent.

93. The term "conscientious abjection" signifies a prevailing strategy of expression in neo-avant-garde art. See Foster, *The Return of the Real*, 156.

94. Wilson, "The Death of Bohemia?" 59.

95. Ibid.

96. Schulman's death's head alludes to a painting by Diego Rivera (Schulman, in a letter to me dated 18 November 2001).

97. See Benjamin, *The Origin of German Tragic Drama*, trans. Osborne, 117; also my discussion in the "Introduction" ("Some Motifs in Queer Constellations"—"Allegory").

Conclusion

1. Benjamin, citing Théophile Gauthier, cited in Max Nordau, *Aus dem wahren Milliardenlande: Pariser Studien und Bilder* (Leipzig, 1878), ("Belleville"), AP 91 [C4a, 3]. The full citation begins: "'In a book by Théophile Gauthier, *Caprices et zizags*, I find a curious page. 'A great danger threatens us,' it says. 'The modern Babylon. . . .'"

2. Benjamin, "Surrealism," 210.

3. Benjamin, "On the Concept of History," 396.

4. Schulman, *Rat Bohemia*, 53–54. Hereafter cited in the text with page numbers.

5. Tony Kushner, from the cover of Schulman, *Rat Bohemia*.

6. See, for example, Geis and Kruger, eds., *Approaching the Millennium.*

Numerous essays in this collection refer to the play's adaptation of Benjamin's angel of history and/or other theses and themes of Benjamin's, including Savran, "Ambivalence, Utopia, and a Queer Sort of Materialism"; Cadden, "Strange Angel"; Solomon, "Wrestling with *Angels*"; Kruger, "Identity and Conversion in *Angels in America*"; Garner, "*Angels in America*: The Millennium and Postmodern Memory"; Harries, "Flying the Angel of History"; Reinelt, "Notes on *Angels in America* as American Epic Theatre"; Borreca, "'Dramaturging' the Dialectic."

7. Borreca, "'Dramaturging' the Dialectic," 249.

8. Ibid. "Kushner's vision," Borreca concludes, "is more teleological than apocalyptic" (250). Accordingly, the epilogue is where Kushner's play most digresses from Benjamin's view of history: "In this moment the play refuses Benjamin's visionary leap beyond historical dialectics, choosing, instead, the uncertainty of the historical future that is in the process of being shaped by those dialectics. The moment is the culmination of the play's teleological vision of history and society: it implicitly calls for the spectator to make his or her own choice for more life while remaining unaware of the contradictory sociohistorical forces that the play has dramatized. The moment affirms this choice as one by which the destructive course of history might be altered, the impasse between ideal and reality transcended, and society redeemed—*all from within*" (259).

9. Geis and Kruger, paraphrasing Savran in the editor's "Introduction," in *Approaching the Millennium*, 4. Savran, the editors note, highlights "the expansionist and communitarian movement of Mormonism" as a basis for the play's theory of history and utopia.

10. Ibid.

11. The "Angela Lesbia" of the coda to Gail Scott's *My Paris* and Schulman's "rat bohemian" present alternative allegories of history: do they not resemble the messianic and nihilistic character of Benjamin's eschatology? The former rises from the ruins of Sarajevo through the mists of love, heralding a women's front against perpetual war. A projection of cultural memory, she recalls the Vésuviennes of past insurrection. Her auspicious appearance at the end of the millennium militates awareness of the work of an era left undone. At the same millennial moment, the rat bohemian descends to the slums with the rats and the homeless, where rebellion survives in defeat. The bohème down the line bears grave witness to the accumulating wreckage of civilization. These are figures of waking in the wake of metropolitan culture. They portray the dual apprehension of a "Messianic arrest of happening" (Benjamin, "On the Concept of History,"

396)—an apprehension that sees, on the one hand, the unfinished work of revolutionary history and, on the other, the devastating future of that history's deferral.

12. I allude, for example, to BBC Channel 4's series "Metrosexuality." A recent queer development in mainstream entertainment, "Metrosexuality" features sexual drama of everyday life in London's Notting Hill, where "every sexual, racial, social and even 'physical' type" converge in once space. Billed as "the future of gay television," the series deploys highly distractive high-tech montage to showcase "fast and furious, hectic and hilarious" plot twists (http://www.wolfevideo.com).

13. Lehman, "A Poet's View," B6.

14. Fitch, *The Assassination of New York*, 100.

Bibliography

Abbas, Ackbar. "Walter Benjamin's Collector: The Fate of Modern Experience." In *Modernity and the Text: Revisions of German Modernism*, ed. Andreas Huyssen and David Battrick, 216–39. New York: Columbia University Press, 1989.

———. "On Fascination: Walter Benjamin's Images." *New German Critique* 48 (fall 1989): 87–107.

Abelove, Henry, Michèle Aina Barale, and David M. Halperin, eds. *The Lesbian and Gay Studies Reader.* New York: Routledge, 1993.

Acker, Kathy. *Pussy, King of the Pirates.* New York: Grove Press, 1996.

———. "New York City in 1979." In *Hannibal Lecter, My Father,* 36–50. New York: Semiotext(e), 1991.

Adler, Sy, and Johanna Brennan. "Gender and Space: Lesbians and Gay Men in the City." *International Journal of Urban and Regional Research* 16 (1992): 24–34.

Adnan, Etel. *Paris, When It's Naked.* Sausalito: Post-Apollo Press, 1993.

Agrest, Diana, Patricia Conway, and Leslie Kanesweisman, eds. *The Sex of Architecture.* New York: Harry N. Abrams, 1996.

Altman, Dennis. *The Homosexualization of America.* 1982. Reprint, Boston: Beacon Press, 1983.

Aragon, Louis. *Paris Peasant.* Trans. Simon Watson Taylor. London: Picador, 1971.

Baedeker Paris. 3rd ed. New York: Macmillan Travel, 1995.

Balzac, Honoré de. *History of the Thirteen* ("Ferragus"; "The Duchesses of Langeais"; "The Girl with the Golden Eyes"). Trans. Herbert J. Hunt. Harmondsworth: Penguin, 1974.

Barber, Stephen. *Edmund White: The Burning World.* New York: St. Martin's Press, 1999.

Barnes, Djuna. *Smoke and Other Early Stories.* Los Angeles: Sun & Moon Press, 1993.

———. *New York.* Ed. Alyce Barry. Los Angeles: Sun & Moon Press, 1989.

———. *Nightwood.* New York: New Directions Press, 1937.

———. *The Book of Repulsive Women.* 1915. Reprint, Los Angeles: Sun & Moon Press, 1994.

Barta, Peter I. *Bely, Joyce, and Döblin: Peripatetics in the City Novel.* Miami: University of Florida Press, 1996.

Bartlett, Neil. *Who Was That Man? A Present for Mr. Oscar Wilde.* London: Serpent's Tale, 1988.

Baudelaire, Charles. *Les Fleurs du mal.* Trans. Richard Howard. London: Picador, 1982.

———. *Paris Spleen.* Trans. Louise Varése. New York: New Directions Press, 1970.

———. *The Painter of Modern Life and Other Essays.* Trans. and ed. Jonathan Mayne. New York: Phaidon, 1964.

Bell, David J. "Insignificant Others: Lesbian and Gay Geographics." *Area* 23 (1991): 323–29.

Bell, David, and Gill Valentine, eds. *Mapping Desire: Geographies of Sexuality.* London: Routledge, 1995.

Benjamin, Walter. *Selected Writings.* Vol. 4, *1938–1940.* Trans. Edmund Jephcott et al. Ed. Howard Eiland and Michael W. Jennings. Cambridge: Harvard University Press, 2003.

———. *Selected Writings.* Vol. 3, *1935–1938.* Trans. Edmund Jephcott, Howard Eiland, et al. Ed. Howard Eiland and Michael W. Jennings. Cambridge: Harvard University Press, 2002.

———. *Selected Writings.* Vol. 2, *1927–1934.* Trans. Rodney Livingstone et al. Ed. Michael W. Jennings, Howard Eiland, and Gary Smith. Cambridge: Harvard University Press, 1999.

———. *Selected Writings.* Vol. 1, *1913–1926.* Trans. Edmund Jephcott et al. Ed. Marcus Bullock and Michael W. Jennings. Cambridge: Harvard University Press, 1996.

———. "On Love and Related Matters (A European Problem)" (1996). SW1: 229–30.

———. *The Arcades Project* (1982).Trans. Howard Eiland and Kevin McLaughlin. Cambridge: Harvard University Press, 1999. Prepared on the basis of the

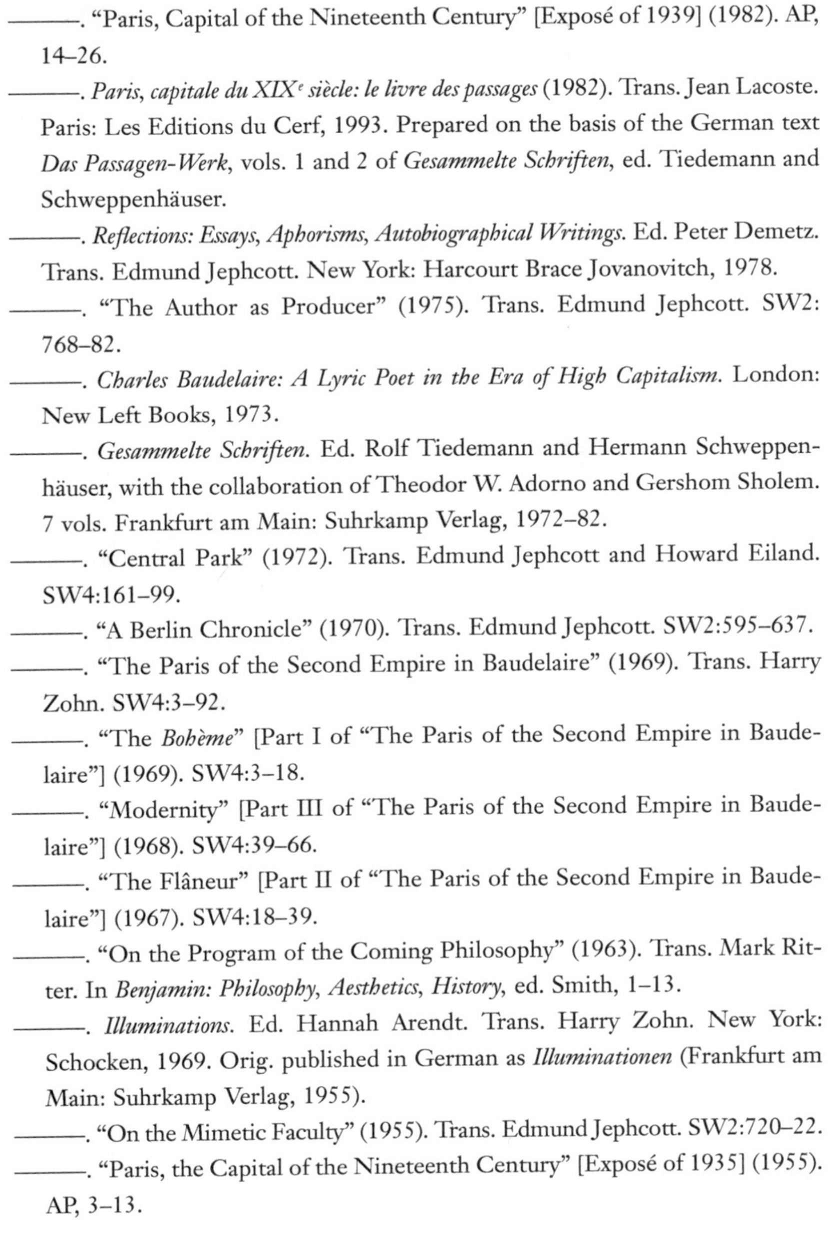

German text *Das Passagen-Werk*, vols. 1 and 2 of *Gesammelte Schriften*, ed. Tiedemann and Schweppenhäuser.

———. "Paris, Capital of the Nineteenth Century" [Exposé of 1939] (1982). AP, 14–26.

———. *Paris, capitale du XIX*^{e} *siècle: le livre des passages* (1982). Trans. Jean Lacoste. Paris: Les Editions du Cerf, 1993. Prepared on the basis of the German text *Das Passagen-Werk*, vols. 1 and 2 of *Gesammelte Schriften*, ed. Tiedemann and Schweppenhäuser.

———. *Reflections: Essays, Aphorisms, Autobiographical Writings*. Ed. Peter Demetz. Trans. Edmund Jephcott. New York: Harcourt Brace Jovanovitch, 1978.

———. "The Author as Producer" (1975). Trans. Edmund Jephcott. SW2: 768–82.

———. *Charles Baudelaire: A Lyric Poet in the Era of High Capitalism*. London: New Left Books, 1973.

———. *Gesammelte Schriften*. Ed. Rolf Tiedemann and Hermann Schweppenhäuser, with the collaboration of Theodor W. Adorno and Gershom Sholem. 7 vols. Frankfurt am Main: Suhrkamp Verlag, 1972–82.

———. "Central Park" (1972). Trans. Edmund Jephcott and Howard Eiland. SW4:161–99.

———. "A Berlin Chronicle" (1970). Trans. Edmund Jephcott. SW2:595–637.

———. "The Paris of the Second Empire in Baudelaire" (1969). Trans. Harry Zohn. SW4:3–92.

———. "The *Bohème*" [Part I of "The Paris of the Second Empire in Baudelaire"] (1969). SW4:3–18.

———. "Modernity" [Part III of "The Paris of the Second Empire in Baudelaire"] (1968). SW4:39–66.

———. "The Flâneur" [Part II of "The Paris of the Second Empire in Baudelaire"] (1967). SW4:18–39.

———. "On the Program of the Coming Philosophy" (1963). Trans. Mark Ritter. In *Benjamin: Philosophy, Aesthetics, History*, ed. Smith, 1–13.

———. *Illuminations*. Ed. Hannah Arendt. Trans. Harry Zohn. New York: Schocken, 1969. Orig. published in German as *Illuminationen* (Frankfurt am Main: Suhrkamp Verlag, 1955).

———. "On the Mimetic Faculty" (1955). Trans. Edmund Jephcott. SW2:720–22.

———. "Paris, the Capital of the Nineteenth Century" [Exposé of 1935] (1955). AP, 3–13.

———. "On the Concept of History" (1950). Trans. Harry Zohn. SW4:389–400.

———. "On Some Motifs in Baudelaire" (1939). Trans. Harry Zohn. SW4:313–55.

———. "Eduard Fuchs, Collector and Historian" (1937). Trans. Howard Eiland and Michael W. Jennings, on the basis of a prior translation by Knut Tarnowski. SW3:260–302.

———. "The Storyteller: Observations on the Works of Nikolai Leskov" (1936). Trans. Harry Zohn. SW3:143–66.

———. "The Work of Art in the Age of Mechanical Reproduction" (1936). Trans. Harry Zohn. In *Illuminations*, 253–64.

———. "Hashish in Marseilles" (1932). Trans. Edmund Jephcott. SW2:673–79.

———. "Paris Diary" (1930). Trans. Rodney Livingstone. SW2:337–54.

———. "The Return of the *Flâneur*" (1929). Trans. Rodney Livingstone. SW2: 262–67.

———. "Surrealism" (1929). Trans. Edmund Jephcott. SW2:207–21.

———. "One Way Street" (1928). Trans. Edmund Jephcott. SW1:444–88.

———. "Dream Kitsch" (1927). Trans. Howard Eiland. SW2:3–5.

———. "Naples" (1925). Trans. Edmund Jephcott. SW1:414–21.

———. *The Origin of German Tragic Drama* (1925). Trans. John Osborne. London: Verso, 1985. Prepared on the basis of the German text *Ursprung des deutschen Trauerspiels* in *Gesammelten Schriften*, vol. 1, ed. Tiedemann and Schweppenhäuser.

Bergson, Henry. *Matter and Memory*. Trans. N. M. Paul and W. S. Palmer. New York: Zone, 1994.

Berman, Marshall. *All That Is Solid Melts into Air: The Experience of Modernity*. 1982. Reprint, Harmondsworth: Penguin, 1988.

Bérubé, Allan. "The History of Gay Bathhouses." In *Policing Public Sex*, ed. Dangerous Bedfellows, 187–221.

Betsky, Aaron. *Queer Space: Architecture and Same-Sex Desire*. New York: William Morrow, 1997.

Blanchard, Marc Eli. *In Search of the City: Engels, Baudelaire, Rimbaud*. Saratoga, CA: Anma Libri, 1985.

Bolton, Ralph, John Vincke, and Rudolf Mak. "Gay Baths Revisited: An Empirical Analysis." *GLQ: A Journal of Lesbian and Gay Studies* 1, no. 3 (1994): 255–73.

Bondi, Liz. "Gender and Geography: Crossing Boundaries." *Progress in Human Geography* 17 (1993): 241–46.

Bondi, L., and M. Domosh. "Other Figures in Other Places: On Feminism, Postmodernism, and Geography." *Environment and Planning D: Society and Space* 10 (1992): 199–213.

Boone, Bruce. "Gay Language as Political Praxis: The Poetry of Frank O'Hara." *Social Text* 1, no. 1 (1979): 59–92.

Boone, Joseph. "Queer Sites in Modernism: Harlem/The Left Bank/Greenwich Village in the 1920s and 1930s." In *Libidinal Currents: Sexuality and the Shaping of Modernity*, 204–87. Chicago: University of Chicago Press, 1998.

Borreca, Art. "'Dramaturging' the Dialectic: Brecht, Benjamin, and Declan Donnellan's Production of *Angels in America*." In *Approaching the Millennium*, ed. Geis and Kruger, 245–70.

Bourdieu, Pierre. *Rules of Art: Genesis and Structure of the Literary Field.* Trans. Susan Emanuel. Stanford: Stanford University Press, 1996.

Boyer, M. Christine. *The City of Collective Memory: Its Historical Imagery and Architectural Entertainments.* Cambridge: MIT Press, 1996.

Bravmann, Scott. *Queer Fictions of the Past: History, Culture and Difference.* Cambridge: Cambridge University Press, 1997.

Bredbeck, Gregory W. "The New Queer Narrative: Intervention and Critique." *Textual Practice* 9, no. 3 (1995): 477–502.

Breton, André. *Nadja.* Trans. Richard Howard. New York: Grove Weidenfeld, 1960.

Brown, Rita Mae. "Queen for a Day: Stranger in Paradise." In *Lavender Culture*, ed. Karla Jay and Allen Young, 69–76. New York: Jove, 1978.

Browning, Frank. *Queer Geography: Journeys Towards a Sexual Self.* New York: Crown, 1996.

Buci-Glucksmann, Christine. *Baroque Reason: The Aesthetics of Modernity.* Trans. Patrick Camiller. London: Sage, 1994.

Buck-Morss, Susan. *The Dialectics of Seeing: Walter Benjamin and the Arcades Project.* Cambridge: MIT Press, 1989.

———. "The *Flâneur*, the Sandwichman and the Whore: The Politics of Loitering." *New German Critique* 39 (fall 1986): 99–140.

———. "Benjamin's Passagen-Werk: Redeeming Mass Culture for the Revolution." *New German Critique* 29 (spring/summer 1983): 211–40.

Burgin, Victor. "The City in Pieces." *New Formations* 20 (1993): 33–45.

Cadden, Michael. "Strange Angel: The Pinklisting of Roy Cohn." In *Approaching the Millennium*, ed. Geis and Kruger, 78–89.

Califia, Pat. “The City of Desire: Its Anatomy and Destiny.” In *Public Sex: The Culture of Radical Sex*, 205–13. San Francisco: Cleis Press, 1994.

Castells, Manuel, and Karen Murphy. “Cultural Identity and Urban Structure: The Spatial Organization of San Francisco’s Urban Gay Community.” In *Urban Policy Under Capitalism*, ed. Norman I. Fainstein and Susan S. Fainstein, 237–59. Beverly Hills, CA: Sage, 1983.

Castle, Terry. *The Apparitional Lesbian: Female Homosexuality and Modern Culture.* New York: Columbia University Press, 1993.

———. “Phantasmagoria: Spectral Technology and the Metaphorics of Modern Reverie.” *Critical Inquiry* 15, no. 1 (1988): 27–61.

Chambers, Ross. *Loiterature.* Lincoln: University of Nebraska Press, 1999.

———. “Strolling, Touring, Cruising: Counterdisciplinary Narrative and the Loiterature of Travel.” In *Understanding Narrative*, ed. J. Phelan and P. J. Rabinowitz, 17–42. Columbus: Ohio State University Press, 1994.

———. “Poaching and Pastiche: Reproducing the Gay Subculture.” *Canadian Review of Comparative Literature/Revue Canadienne de la littérature comparée* 21, nos. 1–2 (1994): 169–92.

———. “Messing About: Gayness and Loiterature in Alan Hollinghurst’s *The Swimming-Pool Library*.” In *Textuality and Sexuality: Reading Theories and Practices*, ed. Judith Still and Michael Worton, 207–17. New York: Manchester University Press, 1993.

Chauncey, George. *Gay New York: Gender, Urban Culture, and the Making of the Gay Male World, 1890–1940.* New York: Basic, 1994.

Chevalier, Louis. *The Assassination of Paris.* Chicago: University of Chicago Press, 1994.

Chisholm, Dianne. “A Queer Return to Walter Benjamin.” *The Journal of Urban History* 29, no. 1 (2002): 25–38.

———. “The Traffic in Free Love and Other Crises: Space, Pace, Sex and Shock in the City of Late Modernity.” *Parallax* 5, no. 3 (1999): 69–89.

———. “Obscene Modernism: *Eros Noir* and the Profane Illumination of Djuna Barnes.” *American Literature* 69, no. 1 (1997): 167–206.

———. “Outlaw Documentary: David Wojnarowicz’s Queer Cinematics, Kinerotics, Autothanatographics.” *Canadian Review of Comparative Literature/Revue Canadienne de la littérature comparée* 21, no. 1 (1994): 81–102.

Choquette, Leslie. “Homosexuals in the City: Representations of Lesbian and Gay Space in Nineteenth-Century Paris.” *Journal of Homosexuality* 41, nos. 3–4 (2001): 149–67.

Clarke, Danae. "Commodity Lesbianism." In *The Lesbian and Gay Studies Reader*, ed. Abelove, Barale, and Halperin, 186–201.

Cobb, Richard C. "The Assassination of Paris" [Review of Norma Evenson, *Paris: A Century of Change, 1878–1978* (New Haven, CT: Yale University Press, 1980)]. *New York Review of Books* 27, no. 1 (7 February 1980).

Cohen, Margaret. *Profane Illumination: Walter Benjamin and the Paris of Surrealist Revolution.* Berkeley: University of California Press, 1993.

Crisp, Quentin. *Resident Alien: The New York Diaries.* London: Harper Collins, 1996.

Cvetkovich, Ann. "Sexual Trauma/Queer Memory: Incest, Lesbianism and Therapeutic Culture." *GLQ : A Journal of Lesbian and Gay Studies* 2, no. 4 (1995): 351–78.

Damon, Maria. "Dirty Jokes and Angels: Jack Spicer and Robert Duncan Writing the Gay Community." In *The Dark End of the Street: Margins in American Vanguard Poetry*, 142–201. Minneapolis: University of Minnesota Press, 1993.

Dangerous Bedfellows, eds. *Policing Public Sex: Queer Politics and the Future of AIDS Activism.* Boston: South End Press, 1996.

Daoust, Jean-Paul. *111, Wooster Street.* Montreal: VLB Éditeur, 1996.

De Certeau, Michel. *The Practice of Everyday Life.* Berkeley: University of California Press, 1984.

Delany, Samuel R. *Times Square Red, Times Square Blue.* New York: New York University Press, 1999.

———. *The Motion of Light in Water: Sex and Science Fiction Writing in the East Village: 1960–1965.* 1988. Reprint, Minneapolis: University of Minnesota Press, 2004.

D'Emilio, John. "Capitalism and Gay Identity." In *The Lesbian and Gay Studies Reader*, ed. Abelove, Barale, and Halperin, 467–76.

———. *Sexual Politics, Sexual Communities: The Making of a Homosexual Minority in the United States, 1940–1970.* Chicago: University of Chicago Press, 1983.

Denizet-Lewis, Benoit. "Double Lives on the Down Low." *New York Magazine*, 3 August 2003, 28–33, 48, 52–53.

Désert, Jean-Ulrick. "Queer Space." In *Queers in Space*, ed. Ingram, Bouthillette, and Retter, 17–26.

Desnos, Robert. *Liberty or Love.* Trans. Terry Hale. London: Atlas, 1993.

Duteurtre, Benoît. *Gaieté Parisienne.* Paris: Éditions Gallimard, 1996.

Eagleton, Terry. "The Marxist Rabbi." In *The Ideology of the Aesthetic*, 316–40. Oxford: Blackwell, 1990.

———. *Walter Benjamin, or Towards a Revolutionary Criticism.* London: Verso, 1981.

Easton, Malcolm. *Artists and Writers in Paris: The Bohemian Idea, 1803–1867.* New York: St. Martin's Press, 1964.

Edwards, Justin. "'Why Go Abroad?' Djuna Barnes and the Urban Travel Narrative." *Journal of Urban History* 29, no. 1 (2002): 6–24.

Faderman, Lillian. *Odd Girls and Twilight Loves: A History of Lesbian Life in Twentieth-Century America.* 1991. Reprint, New York: Penguin, 1992.

Felman, Shoshana. "Benjamin's Silence." *Critical Inquiry* 25, no. 2 (199): 201–34.

Ferguson, Priscilla Parkhurst. "The *Flâneur*: On and Off the Streets of Paris." In *The Flâneur*, ed. Tester, 22–42.

Feuer, Alan. "Mount Morris Journal: In Harlem, a Bathhouse and the Lifestyle It Represents Are Open Secrets." *New York Times*, 19 January 2003, 20.

Fitch, Robert. *The Assassination of New York.* New York: Verso, 1993.

Ford, Charles Henri, and Parker Tyler. *The Young and the Evil.* 1933. Reprint, New York: Richard Kasak, 1996.

Foster, Hal. *The Return of the Real: The Avant-Garde and the Turn of the Century.* Cambridge: MIT Press, 1996.

Foucault, Michel. "On Other Spaces." *diacritics* 16 (1986): 22–27.

———. "Questions on Geography" (1976). In *Power/Knowledge*, ed. Colin Gordon, trans. C. Gordon, L. Marshall, J. Pepham, and K. Soper, 63–77. New York: Pantheon, 1980.

Frisby, David. "The *Flâneur* in Social Theory." In *The Flâneur*, ed. Tester, 81–110.

Fritscher, Jack. *Some Dance to Remember.* Stamford, CT: Knights Press, 1990.

Gage, Carolyn. "Gentrified" [Review of Schulman, *Stage Struck*]. *Lambda Book Report* 7, no. 5 (1998): 17.

Garner, Stanton B., Jr. "*Angels in America*: The Millennium and Postmodern Memory." In *Approaching the Millennium*, ed. Geis and Kruger, 173–84.

Geis, Deborah R., and Steven F. Kruger. *Approaching the Millennium: Essays on Angels in America.* Ann Arbor: University of Michigan Press, 1997.

Geist, Johann Friederich. *Arcades: The History of a Building Type.* Cambridge: MIT Press, 1983.

Gilbert, Sky. "A Dark Victory for Queer Culture." *Toronto Globe and Mail*, 16 August 1997, D9.

Gilfoyle, Timothy J. "From Soubrette Row to Show World: The Contested Sexualities of Times Square, 1880–1995." In *Policing Public Sex*, ed. Dangerous Bedfellows, 263–94.

Gilloch, Graeme. *Myth and Metropolis: Walter Benjamin and the City.* Cambridge: Polity Press, 1996.

Ginsberg, Allen. *Howl and Other Poems.* San Francisco: City Lights, 1956.

Glassco, John. *Memoirs of Montparnasse.* 1970. 2d ed, Toronto: Oxford University Press, 1995.

Gluck, Mary. "Theorizing the Cultural Roots of the Bohemian Artist." *Modernism/Modernity* 7, no. 3 (2000): 351–78.

Glück, Robert. "Long Note on New Narrative." http://www.sfsu.edu/~newlit/narrativity/issue_one/gluck.html, spring 2000, 1–8.

———. *Jack the Modernist.* New York: Serpent's Tale, 1985.

———. "Allegory." *Ironwood* 23 (1984): 112–18.

Gold, Herbert. "Travels in the East Village/Loizaida." In *Bohemia: Where Art, Angst, Love, and Strong Coffee Meet,* 228–41. New York: Simon & Schuster, 1993.

Gornick, Vivian. "Outside Looking In" [Review of Schulman, *Rat Bohemia*]. *Women's Review of Books* 13, no. 5 (5 February 1996): 9.

Graña, César. *Bohemian Versus Bourgeois: French Society and the French Man of Letters in the Nineteenth Century.* New York: Basic Books, 1964.

Green, Jesse. "Where the Boys Went: Why the Gay Mecca Moved Uptown." *New York Magazine,* 19 October 1997, 68–72.

Grosz, Elizabeth. "Bodies-Cities." In *Sexuality and Space,* ed. Beatriz Colomina, 241–53. New York: Princeton Architectural Press, 1992.

A Guide to Lesbian and Gay New York: Historical Landmarks. New York: Organization of Lesbian and Gay Architects and Designers, 1994.

Halbwachs, Maurice. *The Collective Memory.* Trans. Francis J. Ditter and Vida Yazdi Ditter. New York: Harper and Row, 1980.

Harries, Martin. "Flying the Angel of History." In *Approaching the Millennium,* ed. Geis and Kruger, 185–98.

Harris, Daniel. *The Rise and Fall of Gay Culture.* New York: Hyperion, 1997.

Hartlen, Neil. "'Choreographie affriolante': Sexuality and Urban Space in Jean-Paul Daoust's *111, Wooster Street.*" *Quebec Studies* 26 (fall 1998): 62–78.

Harvey, David. *Consciousness and the Urban Experience: Studies in the History and Theory of Capitalist Urbanization.* Baltimore: Johns Hopkins University Press, 1985.

Hays, Matthew. "Bad Boys Boost Montréal Tourism." *Toronto Globe and Mail,* 28 February 1997, A16–17.

Henderson, Jennifer. "Femme(s) Focale(s): Gail Scott's *Main Brides* and the Post-Identity Narrative." *Studies in Canadian Literature* 20, no. 1 (1995): 93–144.

Herland, Karen. *People, Potholes and City Politics*. Montreal: Black Rose, 1992.

Hertz, Betti-Sue, Ed Eisenberg, and Lisa Maya Knauer of the REPOhistory Collective. "Queer Spaces in New York City: Places of Struggle/Places of Strength." In *Queers in Space*, ed. Ingram, Bouthillette, and Retter, 357–70.

Higgs, David, ed. *Queer Sites: Gay Urban History since 1600*. London: Routledge, 1999.

Higonnet, Anne, Margaret Higonnet, and Patrice Higonnet. "Façades: Walter Benjamin's Paris." *Critical Inquiry* 10, no. 3 (1984): 391–419.

Hillel, Edward. *The Main: Portrait of a Neighbourhood*. Toronto: Key Porter, 1987.

Hollander, Kurt, ed. *Low Rent: A Decade of Prose and Photographs from The Portable Lower East Side*. New York: Grove Press, 1994.

Hollinghurst, Alan. *The Swimming Pool Library*. London: Penguin, 1988.

Hughes, Holly. *Clit Notes: A Sapphic Sampler*. New York: Grove Press, 1996.

Indiana, Gary. *Rent Boy*. New York: Serpent's Tale, 1994.

Ingram, Gordon Brent, Anne-Marie Bouthillette, and Yolanda Retter, eds. *Queers in Space: Communities, Public Spaces, Sites of Resistance*. Seattle: Bay Press, 1996.

Ivornel, Philippe. "Paris, Capital of the Popular Front or the Posthumous Life of the 19th Century." *New German Critique* 39 (fall 1986): 61–84.

Jackson, Earl, Jr. *Strategies of Deviance: Studies in Gay Male Representation*. Bloomington: Indiana University Press, 1995.

Jacobs, Jane. *The Death and Life of the Great American Cities*. New York: Random House, 1961.

Jennings, Michael. *Dialectical Images: Walter Benjamin's Theory of Literary Criticism*. Ithaca: Cornell University Press, 1987.

Kaiser, Charles. *The Gay Metropolis: The Landmark History of Gay Life in America since World War II*. New York: Harcourt, 1997.

Kaplan, Morris B. "Who's Afraid of John Saul? Urban Culture and the Politics of Desire in Late Victorian London." *GLQ: A Journal of Lesbian and Gay Studies* 5, no. 3 (1999): 267–314.

Klein, Richard. "Wander, Lust." *Village Voice Literary Supplement*, March 2001, 173.

Knopp, Lawrence. "Sexuality and Urban Space: A Framework for Analysis." In *Mapping Desire*, ed. Bell and Valentine, 149–61.

Koepnick, Lutz P. "Fascist Aesthetics Revisited." *Modernism/Modernity* 6, no. 1 (1999): 51–74.

Koolhaas, Rem. *Delirious New York: A Retroactive Manifesto for Manhattan.* New York: Monacelli Press, 1995.

Kracauer, Siegfried. *The Mass Ornament: Weimar Essays.* Trans. Thomas Y. Levin. Cambridge: Harvard University Press, 1995.

Kronenberger, Louis. "A Taste of Money: On 'Upper Bohemia,' or the Writer in America Today." *Encounter* 22, no. 5 (1964): 14–21.

Kruger, Steven F. "Identity and Conversion in *Angels in America.*" In *Approaching the Millennium,* ed. Geis and Kruger, 151–69.

Kushner, Tony. *Angels in America: A Gay Fantasia on National Themes.* Part One: *Millennium Approaches.* New York: Theater Communications Group, 1992.

Laermer, Richard. *The Gay and Lesbian Handbook to New York City.* New York: Plume, 1994.

Larson, Jonathan. *Rent.* New York: William Morrow, 1997.

Lauria, M., and L. Knopp. "Toward an Analysis of the Role of Gay Communities in the Urban Renaissance." *Urban Geography* 6 (1985): 152–69.

Lefebvre, Henri. *Writing on Cities.* Trans. and ed. Eleonore Kofman and Elizabeth Lebas. Oxford: Blackwell, 1996.

———. *The Production of Space.* Trans. Donald Nicholson-Smith. Oxford: Blackwell, 1991.

———. "Space: Social Product and Use Value." In *Critical Sociology,* ed. J. W. Freiberg, 285–95. New York: Irvington, 1979.

LeGates, Richard T., and Frederic Stout, eds. *The City Reader.* New York: Routledge, 1996.

Lehan, Richard. *The City in Literature: An Intellectual and Cultural History.* Los Angeles: University of California Press, 1998.

Lehman, David. "A Poet's View: Finding Solace in Books for an Escape into the City." *New York Times,* 9 December 2001, B6.

———. *The Last Avant-Garde: The Making of the New York School of Poets.* New York: Anchor, 1999.

Levin, James. *The Gay Novel in America.* New York: Orlando, 1991.

Little, J., L. Peake, and P. Richardson. *Women in Cities: Gender and the Urban Environment.* London: Macmillan Education, 1988.

Lockard, D. "The Lesbian Community: An Anthropological Approach." *Journal of Homosexuality* 11, nos. 3–4 (1986): 83–95.

Lynch, Kevin. *The Image of the City*. Cambridge: MIT Press, 1960.

Martin, Robert K. *The Homosexual Tradition in American Poetry*. 1979. Reprint, Iowa City: University of Iowa Press, 1998.

Massey, Doreen. *Space, Place and Gender*. Cambridge: Polity Press, 1994.

———. "Flexible Sexism." *Environment and Planning D: Society and Space* 9 (1991): 31–57.

McCool, Grant. "Kings of the Urban Jungle: New Yorkers Declare War Against the Rats Taking Over Their Streets and Homes." *Toronto Globe and Mail*, 12 May 2001, A10.

McCourt, James. *Queer Street: The Rise and Fall of an American Culture, 1945–1987*. New York: W.W. Norton, 2003.

McDowell, Linda. "Space, Place and Gender Relations: Part I. Feminist Empiricism and the Geography of Social Relations." *Progress in Human Geography* 17 (1993): 157–79.

McLaughlin, Kevin, and Philip Rosen, eds. *Benjamin Now: Critical Encounters with "The Arcades Project."* Special Issue of *boundary 2* 30, no. 1 (2003).

Mele, Christopher. *Selling the Lower East Side: Culture, Real Estate, and Resistance in New York City*. Minneapolis: University of Minnesota Press, 2000.

Missac, Pierre. *Walter Benjamin's Passages*. Trans. Shierry Weber Nicholsen. Cambridge: MIT Press, 1995.

Moncan, Patrice de. *Les Passages Couverts de Paris*. Paris: Éditions Mécène, 1995.

Moyer, Carrie. "Do You Love the Dyke in Your Face?" In *Queers in Space*, ed. Ingram, Bouthillette, and Retter, 436–46.

Mueller, Cookie. *Walking through Clear Water in a Pool Painted Black*. New York: Semiotext(e), 1990.

Mumford, Lewis. *The History of the City: Its Origins, Its Transformations, and Its Prospects*. New York: Harcourt, 1961.

Muñoz, José Esteban. "Ghosts of Public Sex: Utopian Longings, Queer Memories." In *Policing Public Sex*, ed. Dangerous Bedfellows, 355–94.

Munt, Sally. "The Lesbian *Flâneur*." In *Mapping Desire*, ed. Bell and Valentine, 114–25.

———. "'*Somewhere Over the Rainbow . . .*': Postmodernism and the Fiction of Sarah Schulman." In *New Lesbian Criticism: Literary and Cultural Readings*, ed. Sally Munt, 31–50. New York: Columbia University Press, 1992.

Mürger, Henri. *The Bohemians of the Latin Quarter* [Based on the text of *Scènes de la vie de Bohème*]. Paris, London, New York: Société Des Beaux-Arts, 1912.

Myles, Eileen. *Chelsea Girls*. Santa Rosa, CA: Black Sparrow Press, 1994.

———. *Not Me*. New York: Semiotext(e), 1991.

Myles, Eileen, and Liz Kotz, eds. *The New Fuck You: Adventures in Lesbian Reading*. New York: Semiotext(e), 1995.

Nealon, Christopher. *Foundlings: Lesbian and Gay Historical Emotion before Stonewall*. Durham, NC: Duke University Press, 2001.

Nepveu, Pierre, and Gilles Marcotte, eds. *Montréal Imaginaire: Ville et littérature*. Montreal: Editions Fides, 1992.

Nord, Deborah Epstein. "The Urban Peripatetic: Spectator, Streetwalker, Woman Writer." *Nineteenth-Century Literature* 46, no. 3 (1991): 351–75.

Owens, Craig. "The Allegorical Impulse: Toward a Theory of Postmodernism." In *Art after Modernism: Rethinking Representation*, ed. Bruce Wallis, 203–36. New York: The New Museum of Contemporary Art, 1984.

Paris: Guide Bleus. Paris: Hachette, 1995.

Parsons, Deborah L. *Streetwalking the Metropolis: Women, the City, and Modernity*. Oxford: Oxford University Press, 2000.

Patke, Rajeev S. "Benjamin's *Arcades Project* and the Postcolonial City." *diacritics* 30, no. 4 (2000): 3–14.

Pearl, Betty. *Betty & Pansy's Severe Queer Review of New York*. San Francisco: Bedpan Productions, 1994.

Pellegrini, Ann. "Market Forces" [Review of Schulman, *Stage Struck*]. *Women's Review of Books* 16, no. 2 (1998): 16–17.

Pepper, Choral. *Walks in Oscar Wilde's London*. Salt Lake City: Peregrine Smith Books, 1992.

Persky, Stan. *Then We Take Berlin*. Toronto: Alfred A. Knopf, 1995.

Pidduck, Julianne. "Montreal's Nouveau-Queer Communities: Uneasy Alliances, Trendy Activism, and Marginality in the Balance." *Semiotext(e): canadas* 6, no. 2 (1994): 246–55.

Pike, Burton. *The Image of the City in Modern Literature*. Princeton, NJ: Princeton University Press, 1981.

Pile, Steven. *The Body and the City: Psychoanalysis, Space and Subjectivity*. New York: Routledge, 1966.

"Le Plateau: Hors Ghetto." *HOMOsapiens* 20, no. 2 (1995): 11.

Pollock, Griselda. "Modernity and the Spaces of Femininity." In *Vision and Difference: Femininity, Feminism and Histories of Art*, 50–90. London: Routledge, 1988.

The Portable Lower East Side. Ed. Kurt Hollander. Vols. 1–10. New York, 1984–94.

Powers, Ann. *Weird Like Us: My Bohemian America*. 2000. Reprint, New York: Da Capo, 2001.

Pratt, G., and S. Hanson. "Gender, Class, and Space." *Environment and Planning D: Society and Space* 6 (1988): 15–35.

Probyn, Elspeth. "Lesbians in Space: Gender, Sex and the Structure of the Missing." *Gender, Place and Culture* 2, no. 1 (1995): 77–84.

Rebein, Robert. *Hicks, Tribes and Dirty Realists: American Fiction After Postmodernism*. Lexington: University of Kentucky Press, 2001.

Rechy, John. *Sexual Outlaw: A Documentary*. New York: Grove Weidenfeld, 1977.

———. *City of Night*. 1963. Reprint, New York: Grove Weidenfeld, 1984.

Reinelt, Janelle. "Notes on *Angels in America* as American Epic Theatre." In *Approaching the Millennium*, ed. Geis and Kruger, 234–44.

Riis, Jacob. *How the Other Half Lives*. 1890. Reprint, New York: St. Martin's Press, 1996.

Rose, Gillian. "The Struggle for Political Democracy: Emancipation, Gender, Geography." *Environment and Planning D: Society and Space* 8 (1990): 395–408.

Rosen, Philip. "Introduction." In *Benjamin Now*, ed. McLaughlin and Rosen, 1–15.

Rosler, Martha. "Fragments of a Metropolitan Point of View." In *If You Lived Here*, ed. Wallis, 15–44.

Ross, Kristin. *The Emergence of Social Space: Rimbaud and the Paris Commune*. Minneapolis: University of Minnesota Press, 1988.

Rotella, Carlo. *October Cities: The Redevelopment of Urban Literature*. Los Angeles: University of California Press, 1998.

Rothenberg, Tamar. "'And She Told Two Friends': Lesbians Creating Urban Social Space." In *Mapping Desire*, ed. Bell and Valentine, 165–81.

Rubin, Gayle. "Thinking Sex: Notes for a Radical Theory of the Politics of Sexuality." In *The Lesbian and Gay Studies Reader*, ed. Abelove, Barale, and Halperin, 3–44.

Savage, Michael. "Walter Benjamin's Urban Thought: A Critical Analysis." *Environment and Planning D: Society and Space* 1 (1984): 3–22.

Savage, Tom. "The St. Mark's Baths." *Portable Lower East Side* 1, no. 2 (1984): 18.

Savran, David. "Ambivalence, Utopia, and a Queer Sort of Materialism: How *Angels in America* Reconstructs the Nation." In *Approaching the Millennium*, ed. Geis and Kruger, 13–39.

Schor, Naomi, and Elizabeth Weed, eds. *The City.* Special issue of *differences* 5, no. 3 (1993).

Schulman, Sarah. *Stage Struck: Theater, AIDS, and the Marketing of Gay America.* Durham, NC: Duke University Press, 1999.

———. *Rat Bohemia.* New York: Dutton, 1995.

———. *My American History: Lesbian and Gay Life During the Reagan/Bush Years.* New York: Routledge, 1994.

———. *The Lesbian Avenger Handbook: A Handy Guide to Homemade Revolution.* New York: The Lesbian Avengers, 1993.

———. *People in Trouble.* 1990. Reprint, New York: Plume, 1991.

———. *Girls, Visions and Everything.* Seattle: Seal Press, 1986.

Schuyler, James. *Collected Poems.* New York: Farrar, Straus, and Giroux, 1993.

Schwartzwald, Robert. "Passages/Home: Paris as Crossroads." *L'esprit créateur* 61, no. 3 (2002): 172–90.

Scott, Gail. *My Paris.* Toronto: Mercury Press, 1999.

———. *Main Brides: Against Ochre Pediment and Aztec Sky.* Toronto: Coach House Press, 1993.

Sennett, Richard. *Flesh and Stone: The Body and the City in Western Civilization.* New York: Norton, 1994.

Servinis, Ellen. "Urban Space and Barstool *flânerie* in Gail Scott's *Main Brides.*" *Studies in Canadian Literature* 23, no. 1 (1998): 250–63.

Shields, Rob. "Fancy Footwork: Walter Benjamin's Notes on *flânerie.*" In *The Flâneur,* ed. Tester, 61–80.

Sibalis, Michael D. "Paris." In *Queer Sites,* ed. Higgs, 10–37.

Sibley, David. *Geographies of Exclusion: Society and Difference in the West.* New York: Routledge, 1995.

Siegel, Jerrold. *Bohemian Paris: Culture, Politics, and the Boundaries of Bourgeois Life, 1830–1930.* New York: Viking, 1986.

Siegle, Robert. *Suburban Ambush: Downtown Writing and the Fiction of Insurgency.* Baltimore: Johns Hopkins University Press, 1989.

Simmel, Georg. "The Metropolis and Mental Life." In *On Individuality and Social Forms: Selected Writings,* ed. Donald N. Levine, 324–39. Chicago: University of Chicago Press, 1971.

Smith, Gary, ed. *Benjamin: Philosophy, Aesthetics, History.* Chicago: University of Chicago Press, 1989.

Smith, Joan W. "Experience." In *Feminists Theorize the Political,* ed. Judith Butler and Joan W. Scott, 22–40. Routledge: New York, 1992.

Smith, Neil. "Tompkins Square Park: Riots, Rents and Redskins." *Portable Lower East Side* 6, no. 1 (1989): 1–36.

Solnit, Rebecca. *Wanderlust: A History of Walking*. New York: Penguin, 2001.

Solnit, Rebecca, and Susan Schwartzenberg. *Hollow City: The Siege of San Francisco and the Crisis of Urbanism*. New York: Verso, 2000.

Solomon, Alisa. "Wrestling with *Angels*: A Jewish Fantasia." In *Approaching the Millennium*, ed. Geis and Kruger, 118–33.

Spencer, Lloyd. "Introduction to 'Central Park.'" *New German Critique* 34 (winter 1985): 28–31.

———. "Allegory in the World of the Commodity: The Importance of 'Central Park.'" *New German Critique* 34 (winter 1985): 59–77.

Spiegelman, Art. *MAUS: A Survivor's Tale*. Vols 1 and 2. New York: Pantheon, 1991.

Stansell, Christine. *American Moderns: Bohemian New York and the Creation of a New Century*. New York: Metropolitan, 2000.

Steinberg, Michael P. *Walter Benjamin and the Demands of History*. Ithaca: Cornell University Press, 1996.

Stout, Janis P. *Sodoms in Eden: The City in American Fiction Before 1860*. Westport, CT: Greenwood Press, 1976.

Sue, Eugène. *Les Mystères de Paris*. 1841. Reprint, Paris: Editions du Milieu du Monde, 1941.

Szondi, Peter. "Walter Benjamin's 'City Portraits.'" In *On Textual Understanding and Other Essays*, trans. Harvey Mendelsohn, 133–44. Minneapolis: University of Minnesota Press, 1986.

Tattelman, Ira. "The Meaning at the Wall: Tracing the Gay Bathhouse." In *Queers in Space*, ed. Ingram, Bouthillette, and Retter, 391–406.

Taussig, Michael. *Mimesis and Alterity: A Particular History of the Senses*. New York: Routledge, 1993.

Tea, Michelle. *Valencia*. Seattle: Seal Press, 2000.

Tester, Keith, ed. *The Flâneur*. London: Routledge, 1994.

Tiedemann, Rolf. "Historical Materialism or Political Messianism? An Interpretation of the Theses 'On the Concept of History.'" In *Benjamin: Philosophy, Aesthetics, History*, ed. Smith, 175–209.

Tillman, Lynne. *No Lease on Life*. New York: Harcourt, Brace, 1998.

Toth, Jennifer. *The Mole People: Life in the Tunnels beneath New York City*. Chicago: Chicago Review Press, 1995.

Trumbach, Randolph. "London." In *Queer Sites*, ed. Higgs, 89–111.

Valentine, Gill. "(Hetero)Sexing Space: Lesbian Perceptions and Experiences of Everyday Spaces." *Environment and Planning D: Society and Space* 11 (1993): 395–412.

———. "The Geography of Women's Fear." *Area* 21 (1989): 385–90.

Van der Kolk, Bessel A., and Onno Van der Hart. "The Intrusive Past: The Flexibility of Memory and the Engraving of Trauma." *American Imago* 48 (1991): 425–54.

Vidal, Gore. "Paris, Proust's Whorehouse, Gide, Bowles, and Isherwood." In *Palimpsest: A Memoir*. Harmondsworth: Penguin, 1995.

Vidler, Anthony. "Bodies in Space/Subjects in the City: Psychopathologies of Modern Urbanism." *differences* 5, no. 3 (1993): 31–51.

Virilio, Paul. "The Overexposed City." *Zone*, 1986, 14–39.

Walkowitz, Judith. *City of Dreadful Night: Narratives of Sexual Danger in Late-Victorian London*. London: Virago, 1992.

Wallis, Brian, ed. *If You Lived Here: The City in Art, Theory, and Social Activism* [A Project by Martha Rosler/Dia Art Foundation]. Seattle: Bay Press, 1991.

Ward, Geoff. "Lyric Poets in the Era of Late Capitalism." In *Statutes of Liberty: The New York School Poets*, 2d ed, 135–76. New York: Palgrave, 2001.

Warner, Michael, ed. *Fear of a Queer Planet: Queer Politics and Social Theory*. Minneapolis: University of Minnesota Press, 1993.

Watson, Sophie, and Katherine Gibson. *Postmodern Cities and Spaces*. Oxford: Blackwell, 1995.

Watson, Steven. *Strange Bedfellows: The First American Avant-Garde*. New York: Abbeville Press, 1991.

Weber, Samuel. "'Streets, Squares, Theaters': A City on the Move—Walter Benjamin's Paris." In *Benjamin Now*, ed. McLaughlin and Rosen, 17–30.

Weber, Shierry M. "Walter Benjamin: Commodity Fetishism, the Modern and the Experience of History." In *The Unknown Dimension: European Marxism Since Lenin*, ed. Dick Howard and Karl E. Klare, 249–75. New York: Basic, 1972.

Weeks, Jeffrey. *Coming Out: Homosexual Politics in Britain from the Nineteenth Century to the Present*. 1977. Reprint, London: Quartet, 1990.

Weigel, Siegfried. *Body- and Space-Image: Re-Reading Walter Benjamin*. New York: Verso, 1997.

Weightman, Barbara A. "Commentary: Towards a Geography of the Gay Community." *Journal of Cultural Geography* 1, no. 2 (1981): 106–12.

Weston, Kath. "Get Thee to a Big City: Sexual Imaginary and the Great Gay Migration." *GLQ: A Journal of Lesbian and Gay Studies* 2, no. 3 (1995): 253–78.

Westwood, Sallie, and John Williams, eds. *Imagining Cities: Scripts, Signs, Memory.* New York: Routledge, 1997.

White, Edmund. *The Flâneur: A Stroll through the Paradoxes of Paris.* London: Bloomsbury, 2001.

———. *Marcel Proust.* New York: Viking, 1999.

———. *Genet.* New York: Knopf, 1993.

———. *States of Desire: Travels in Gay America.* New York: Dutton, 1980.

White, Edmund, with Hubert Sorin. *Our Paris: Sketches from Memory.* New York: Alfred A. Knopf, 1995.

White, Hayden. "The Value of Narrativity in the Representation of Reality." In *On Narrative,* ed. W. J. T. Mitchell, 1–24. Chicago: University of Chicago Press, 1981.

Whitman, Walt. *Leaves of Grass.* New York: Modern Library, 1993.

Wilson, Elizabeth. *Bohemians: The Glamorous Outcasts.* New Brunswick, NJ: Rutgers University Press, 2000.

———. "The Death of Bohemia?" In *Ambient Fears: Random Access 2,* ed. Pavel Büchler and Nikos Papastergiadis, 46–60. London: Rivers Oram Press, 1996.

———. "The Invisible *Flâneur.*" *New Left Review* 191 (1992): 90–110.

———. *The Sphinx in the City.* London: Virago, 1991.

Winchester, H. P. M., and P. E. White. "The Location of Marginalized Groups in the Inner City." *Environment and Planning D: Society and Space* 6 (1988): 37–54.

Wirth-Nesher, Hana. *City Codes: Reading the Modern Urban Novel.* New York: Cambridge University Press, 1996.

Wisman, Heinz, ed. *Walter Benjamin et Paris.* Paris: Cerf, 1986.

Wojnarowicz, David. *Close to the Knives: A Memoir of Disintegration.* New York: Grove Press, 1989.

Wolf, Deborah. *The Lesbian Community.* Berkeley: University of California Press, 1979.

Wolfe, Maxine. "Invisible Women in Invisible Places: The Production of Social Space in Lesbian Bars." In *Queers in Space,* ed. Ingram, Bouthillette, and Retter, 301–24.

Wolff, Janet. "The Invisible *flâneuse*: Women and the Literature of Modernity." In *Feminine Sentences: Essays on Women and Culture,* 34–50. Berkeley: University of California Press, 1990.

Woods, Tim. "'Looking for Signs in the Air': Urban Space and the Postmodern." In *In the Country of Small Things. Beyond the Red Notebook: Essays on Paul Auster*, ed. Dennis Barone, 107–28. Philadelphia: University of Pennsylvania Press, 1995.

Wright, Les. "San Francisco." In *Queer Sites*, ed. Higgs, 164–89.

Index